21世纪英语专业系列教材

总主编 胡壮麟

基础英语写作

（第二版）

主编：陈法春

编者：刘建喜　傅　铮　刘红英　孙　维

北京大学出版社

PEKING UNIVERSITY PRESS

图书在版编目(CIP)数据

基础英语写作/陈法春主编.—2版.—北京：北京大学出版社，2012.7
（21世纪英语专业系列教材）

ISNB 978-7-301-20853-3

Ⅰ.基… Ⅱ.陈… Ⅲ.英语–写作–高等学校–教材 Ⅳ.H315

中国版本图书馆CIP数据核字（2012）第132653号

书　　　　名：基础英语写作（第二版）
著作责任者：陈法春　主编
责 任 编 辑：黄瑞明
标 准 书 号：ISBN 978-7-301-20853-3/H·3089
出 版 发 行：北京大学出版社
地　　　　址：北京市海淀区成府路205号　　100871
网　　　　址：http://www.pup.cn
电　　　　话：邮购部 62752051　　　　发行部 62750672
　　　　　　　编辑部 62754382　　　　出版部 62754962
电 子 邮 箱：zbing@pup.pku.edu.cn
印　刷　者：三河市博文印刷有限公司
经　销　者：新华书店
　　　　　　　787毫米×1092毫米　16开本　　18.25印张　　400千字
　　　　　　　2007年8月第1版
　　　　　　　2012年7月第2版　2022年8月第9次印刷
定　　　　价：36.00元

《21世纪英语专业系列教材》
编写委员会

（以姓氏笔画排序）

王立非	王守仁	王克非
王俊菊	文秋芳	石 坚
申 丹	朱 刚	仲伟合
刘世生	刘意青	殷企平
孙有中	李 力	李正栓
张旭春	张庆宗	张绍杰
杨俊峰	陈法春	金 莉
封一函	胡壮麟	查明建
袁洪庚	桂诗春	黄国文
梅德明	董洪川	蒋洪新
程幼强	程朝翔	虞建华

总　序

　　北京大学出版社自2005年以来已出版"语言与应用语言学知识系列读本"多种,为了配合第十一个五年计划,现又策划陆续出版"21世纪英语专业系列教材"。这个重大举措势必受到英语专业广大教师和学生的欢迎。

　　作为英语教师,最让人揪心的莫过于听人说英语不是一个专业,只是一个工具。说这些话的领导和教师的用心是好的,为英语专业的毕业生将来找工作着想,因此要为英语专业的学生多多开设诸如新闻、法律、国际、经济、旅游等其他专业的课程。但事与愿违,英语专业的教师们很快发现,学生投入英语学习的时间少了,掌握英语专业课程知识甚微,即使对四个技能的掌握并不比大学英语学生高明多少,而那个所谓的第二专业在有关专家的眼中只是学到些皮毛而已。

　　英语专业的路在何方?有没有其他路可走?这是需要我们英语专业教师思索的问题。中央领导关于创新是一个民族的灵魂和要培养创新人才等的指示精神,让我们在层层迷雾中找到了航向。显然,培养学生具有自主学习能力和能进行创造性思维是我们更为重要的战略目标,使英语专业的人才更能适应21世纪的需要,迎接21世纪的挑战。

　　如今,北京大学出版社外语编辑部的领导和编辑同志们,也从教材出版的视角探索英语专业的教材问题,从而为贯彻英语专业教学大纲做些有益的工作,为教师们开设大纲中所规定的必修、选修课程提供各种教材。他们把英语专业教材的出版看作是第十一个五年计划期间组织出版"十一五"国家重点出版规划项目——《面向新世纪的立体化网络化英语学科建设丛书》的重要组成部分。这套系列教材要体现新世纪英语教学的自主化、协作化、模块化和超文本化,结合外语教材的具体情况,既要解决语言、教学内容、教学方法和教育技术的时代化,也要坚持弘扬以爱国主义为核心的民族精神。因此,今天北京大学出版社在大力提倡专业英语教学改革的基础上,编辑出版各种语言、文学、文化课程的教材,以培养具有创新性思维、具有实际工作能力的学生,充分体现了时代精神。

　　北京大学出版社的远见卓识,也反映了英语专业广大师生盼望已久的心愿。由北京大学等全国几十所院校具体组织力量,积极编写相关教材。这就是说,这套教材是由一些高等院校有水平、有经验的第一线教师们制定编写大纲,反复讨论,特别是考虑到在不同层次、不同背景学校之间取得平衡,避免了先前的教材或偏难或偏易的弊病。与此同时,一批知名专家教授参与策划和教材审定工作,保证了教材质量。

　　当然,这套系列教材出版只是初步实现了出版社和编者们的预期目标。为了获得更大效果,希望使用本系列教材的教师和同学不吝指教,及时将意见反馈给我们,使教材更加完善。

　　航道已经开通,我们有决心乘风破浪,奋勇前进!

胡壮麟

北京大学蓝旗营

2007年2月

第二版前言

英语写作课重在实践,讲写作知识易,提高学生写作能力难。一步步启发学生思路,一遍遍引导学生用恰当的形式表达思想,在此过程中让学生感到受益,不仅语言知识技能、文化知识逐步得到提高,而且逻辑思维能力、语言表达艺术和综合素质不断提升,心智日趋成熟,从而激发追求创作出更高质量作品的强烈愿望和信心,才是基础阶段英语写作课的首要任务。

教材注定是呆板的,而学生永远是鲜活的,鲜有一本教材适用于所有课堂教学,包括同一所学校不同年级乃至同一年级不同班级的教学。所以,写作课教师不应依赖教材,而应充分发挥主观能动性,精心设计教学,与时俱进地提供语言输入材料,因材施教,以高度的事业心和对学生的满腔热忱,认真和学生商讨不断改进习作质量的途径。《基础英语写作》教程2007年出版以来,我们在课堂教学中一方面以大量的学生习作作为课堂讨论和修改素材,一方面不断更新语言输入内容。现以我们课堂教学中使用效果较好的一些活动和材料为基础,对教材进行更新,主要体现在以下四个方面:一是替换了约半数的例文和素材,注重例文的可读性和时效性;二是每个章节都增加了中国文化元素,以期提高学生用目标语表达和传播中华文化的能力;三是在保持原有体例基本不变的前提下,删除了反映写作过程的专门章节,而将学生写作过程反映在每一种写作方法中,通过教师对学生习作的点评和学生相应的修改,引导学生领悟提高写作质量之道;四是在书信章节,把便条列为私人信件的一种,合并了两种应用文写作的常用表达方式,更新了样品信件。

学生英语写作水平的提高不是一本教材能够实现的。教师要在"深知学生的底细"的基础上,引导"本不想写文章"的学生达到"觉得大有可写"的境界(叶圣陶);学生要"从容地忙着,总不要失掉耐心,还要十遍、二十遍修改你的作品……有时候要可以增添,却常常要割爱删弃"(尼·布瓦洛)。教和学从来都不是孤立的,求学者自当有创作的热情,授业者则不可置身学生写作过程之外。唯如此,方可实现写作课的教学相长。愿本版教材有助于使用者。

感谢北京大学出版社外语编辑部张冰主任、黄瑞明编辑对本书再版所做出的努力和心血,欢迎读者对本书的疏漏和错误批评指正。

编者

2012 年 6 月

第一版前言

英语写作是普通高等学校英语专业基础阶段的必修课。近20年来,我国英语教学与研究界同仁充分吸收第二语言习得、英语作为第二语言和英语作为外语教学的研究成果,积极进行教学改革,取得了丰硕的成果,为本教材提供了大量具体的指导。

20世纪70年代以来,人本主义教育提倡在学习过程中以人为中心,在肯定教师的促进和指导作用的同时强调学生的参与。交际理论认为,写作过程是群体交际活动而非个人行为。Murray(1980)和Richards(1990)提出的过程写作教学模式(the process-focused approach)注重以学生为中心,倡导写作过程中学生的体验、实践、参与、合作与交流。Zamel(1982)指出,"写作课的重点应放在写作表达和创作的过程中。"与传统的成果教学法不同,过程教学法把作文教学分成三个阶段:写作前、写作中和写作后,重视通过一系列的交流、协商活动和修正机会,帮助学生在各个阶段发挥主观能动作用,激发创造力,提高作文质量。过程教学法对传统的重视语法、语言形式等教学法提出挑战,旨在把注意力从评价、评估学生的写作成品转向帮助学生更好地认识写作过程。20世纪90年代以后,后过程(post-process)理论指出写作的"公开性、解释性和环境局限性"("the writing act is public, thoroughly heremeneutic and always situated")(Kent, 1999),对文本、读者和用外语写作的社会文化背景予以关注(Matsuda, 2003)。这实际上表明,作文教学不仅要关注写作过程,还应该在更宽阔的领域内帮助学生把握写作内容和表达方式。

实践表明,学生在写作中遇到的两大障碍,一是缺乏思想,不知道该写什么;二是写完初稿后除了提高语言的准确性外,不知如何对文章进行修改、提高。Zamel(1987)发现,有经验的写作者在开始写作时脑子里并没有太多具体想法,而只是一些模糊的东西。因此,作文课教学既要在学生开始写作前帮助他们启动思维,通过讨论、辩论、重组故事、音像资料评论、头脑风暴(brainstorming)、自由写作(free writing)等方式帮助学生拓展思路,发现素材,形成观点,产生写作冲动,又要强调写作的反复性,消除不良心理因素的影响,引导学生反复思考,不断明确思路,选择更为有效的形式表达思想。如果说写作前阶段的各种活动"就像运动前的热身一样必要,可以让写作者伸展四肢,放松肌肉"(Raimes, 1996),那么,写作水平的提高也应向运动水平的提高一样允许循序渐进,容忍和理解失误,写作课教师应该像教练员一样通过多种途径帮助学生提高写作技能。

因此,教师在写作教学过程中应发挥三种作用:写作活动的组织者、写作内容的引导者、写作成果的反馈者。写作是一种复杂的认知过程,其非线性、动态性和反复性要求教师在写作过程的各道程序辅助学生。教师要合理安排课堂时间,灵活设置活动内容,有效评估课堂活动,发挥写作活动组织者的作用。

除了帮助学生形成观点、明确思路外,教师在写作课中的引导作用还表现在对英语写作知识、技巧的介绍和结合优秀范文进行的导读两个方面。后者呼应了后过程理论对文本、读者和用外语写作的社会文化背景的关注。由于我国高等学校英语专业的学生在中小学都受过中文写作训练,教师对英语写作知识和技巧的介绍应重点放在中英文的差异方面,以减少英语学习者所受的文化差异方面的限制。在这方面,阅读优秀文章可以有很大的帮助,这不仅是因为足够的可以理解的语言输入是有效语言输出的前提,而且还是因为写作教师引导的阅读有很强的针对性。教师可以把以技巧为本的教学模式与语篇分析相结合,根据不同的教学内容与对象选择具有针对性的方法,引导学生从宏观和微观层面理解阅读材料(Kintsch & van Dijk, 1978),分析范文的整体结构、作者的思维模式、语言的灵活运用、作者和作品所处的社会历史背景等问题,进而引导学生从他人文章的成败得失中领悟作文之道,把所获得的各种有效信息加工后进行语言重组和再造,同时引导学生掌握推理和逻辑思维方法,使他们具备写好文章的基础(祁寿华,2001)。

修改是写好文章的关键(Murray,1978)。区别一个写作能手与写作新手的关键之一在于作者是否愿意并有能力大幅度修改自己的原始作品(Beach, 1976)。学生在一次写作过程中对其习作进行不少于三次的修改是把写作看成不断发现和完善思想的过程的最直接体现。传统写作教学习惯于关注学生一次性写作成品,教师在批改作业时侧重语言形式,如语法、句法、词汇的使用,而常常忽视内容、篇章结构、逻辑思维等因素,对学生所处的环境关注更少,所提出的改进意见更多是评价性的,即便提出了建设性的改进意见,也很少在乎学生对意见的反应,学生则更关心分数或者评价的高低,对教师提出的修改意见往往不予以重视。这种师生间一对一的一次性单向交流作业模式是导致多数学生写作水平停滞不前的重要因素。

三次三向反馈交流模式以学生的写作过程为核心,旨在带动同学间和师生间的多次交流,达到提高写作水平的目的。Keh (1990)把过程教学法中的信息交互分为三种形式:同伴反馈(peer feedback)、会谈式反馈(conferences as feedback)和批语式反馈(comments as feedback)。经过写作前阶段,学生根据讨论或辩论记录、自由写作的底稿构思完成作文初稿,然后自行修改,判断所写文章是否有明确的主题,所选内容是否与主题相关,所述观点是否有支撑并连贯一致。在此基础上,学生可以对彼此的作文初稿进行互评、互改。研究表明,同伴反馈能为学习者提供真实的读者,让学习者得以了解他人对自己作品的不同看法,帮助学习者学会批判性地阅读自己的作品(Keh, 1990)。学生可以分组交换阅读彼此的作文,讨论、评点小组内每篇文章。教师可以参与讨论,提供会谈式反馈。该过程还可以促进学生之间运用目的语交流,增加语言实践的机会,提高学生主动学习参与度,创造出积极的学习氛围(Long & Porter, 1985)。

对于学生根据交流意见完成的作文第二稿教师要进行认真阅读并提出反馈意见。从理论上讲,比学生更强的语言能力和更加丰富的英语写作经验使教师成为学生写作结果的重要反馈者。Swain (1995)指出,教师的反馈能让学习者重新构建对目的语形成的假设,对语言结构进行重组,使学习者沿着目的语的轨道前进。需要注意的是,教师的反馈首先还是帮助学生完善构思,充实内容,寻求更佳的表达方式,而不是急于或者仅仅指出、改正学生在语言准确性方面出现的失误。当然,为了减少外语学习者所受的语言限制，教师提供的语言帮助也是必要的。这就需要教师做出适合学生外语水平的判断，把握反馈的最终目的是使学生掌握自我修改能力的原则。教师在反馈中应该多给一些鼓励和具体的修改建议。Fathman 和 Whalley（1990）的研究结果显示，教师带有具体修改建议的鼓励性批语对于学生作文内容的改进有很大帮助。对于学生作业中的语言失误，教师可以标出错误类型，鼓励学生自己改正（张雪梅、戴炜栋，2001）。同时，教师还应该因材施教，区别对待不同的学生。我们发现，对学习热情高和英语水平好的学生进行的诸如谋篇布局、思维拓展、高级词汇运用等方面的"高级关注点"（high order concerns—HOCs，Keh，1990）的修改能有效地促进师生感情，进一步提高学生的学习兴趣。教师还可以对学生作文二稿进行集中点评，分析普遍问题和常见错误，让学生了解错误的原因，开展合作学习讨论错误的修改方式。

学生根据教师的修改建议和讨论结果进一步修改作文，写出三稿。教师对作文三稿进行具体的修改并就"高级关注点"进行再次反馈。实践表明，通过三次改进，学生作文的整体水平有明显的提高。因为篇幅限制，同时考虑到不同类型学校的实际，本教材没有充分展示学生作文的修改过程，但是，不少于三次的修改过程是本教材推崇的核心理念。同时，我们认为，英语写作课的成效在很大程度上取决于学生提高英语水平的热情和意志，取决于教师对英语写作课的热爱程度和投入精力。

本教材有关常用英语写作技巧的章节包括概念导入、概念简介、范文阅读、写作建议、相关词汇、实践训练等内容。为了提高学生的综合素质，满足 TEM-4 的相关要求，本教材用一章篇幅介绍英语书信和便条的体例及写作注意事项。教材努力体现英语写作教学的研究成果，降低学生对用英语写作的畏难情绪，营造友好的学习环境，提高学生的学习兴趣。但是，因为编者水平有限，经验不足，谬误之处在所难免，敬请读者批评指正。

本教材在天津外国语学院经过多年实践，效果良好。2005年，天津外国语学院基础英语写作课被评为天津市普通高等学校 2004—2005 学年精品课程，课程组成员除本教材编者外还有刘红英、胥丽华、胡向华和美国教师 Joshua Parker。本教材在合理利用原有材料的基础上，根据最新教学实践，大幅度更新了内容。

编　者
2006年8月

Table of Contents

Unit 1   Brushing up on Sentence Skills ············· 1

Unit 2   The Paragraph ········· 19

Unit 3   The Narrative Essay ········· 40

Unit 4   The Descriptive Essay ········· 70

Unit 5   The Comparison and Contrast Essay ········· 99

Unit 6   The Process Analysis Essay ········· 128

Unit 7   The Classification Essay ········· 153

Unit 8   The Cause and Effect Essay ········· 184

Unit 9   The Definition Essay ········· 219

Unit 10   Letters and Notes ········· 254

Brushing up on Sentence Skills

Types of Sentences

A. Declarative, Interrogative, Imperative and Exclamatory Sentences

According to their **use**, sentences are declarative (making an assertion or a statement), interrogative (asking a question), imperative (issuing a command or a request) or exclamatory (expressing a strong feeling or emotion).

B. Simple, Compound, Complex, and Compound-Complex Sentences

According to their **structure,** sentences can be divided into four categories: simple, compound, complex, and compound-complex sentences.

1. Simple Sentence

A simple sentence contains one main clause without any subordinate clause. It has only one subject and one predicate-verb, but it may contain more than one object, attribute or adverb. Short simple sentences are usually emphatic and powerful; they have special clarity and provide variety when used with longer sentences.

For example

1. He is a handsome boy.
2. What has happened here?
3. It can't be true.
4. Man holds in his mortal hands the power to abolish all forms of human poverty and all forms of human life.

2. Compound Sentence

A compound sentence is made up of two or more main clauses but no subordinate clauses. That is, all the clauses express a complete thought. If the clauses are separated with a full stop, they can be independent sentences except with the coordinate conjunction, *for*. All main clauses are joined by either a semicolon or one of these seven coordinate conjunctions: *and, but, or, nor, for, so, yet*. Coordinated ideas should be compatible and roughly equal in importance, or take shape one by one in orderly sequence.

For example

1. The heavy rain started suddenly, so we had to cancel all the outdoor activities.
2. Dennis wanted to go camping, but his girlfriend wanted to go skating.
3. Mary majors in English; Tim majors in Economics.

3. Complex Sentence

A complex sentence is made up of one main clause and at least one subordinate clause with a subordinate conjunction denoting the relation between the two parts. The subordinate clause may play the part of a subject, an object, a predicative, an attribute, or an adverbial in the main clause. As a rule, the major idea is expressed in the main clause and the idea or ideas of lesser importance in the subordinate clauses.

For example

1. The government took some effective measures to purify the air, because the air pollution became serious.
2. Although the shop sold some bargains, I didn't buy what I didn't need.
3. These apple trees, which had borne lots of fruit before, were cut down for some reasons.

4. Compound-Complex Sentence

A compound-complex sentence is made up of at least two main clauses and at least one dependent clause—a combination of a compound and a complex sentence.

For example

1. **When** I returned to school after a long absence, the warm-hearted English teacher helped me with my make-up work, **but** the cold-hearted Physics teacher made me flunk.
2. **When** an examination is approaching, some students begin to study harder than before, **and** other students still keep their usual attitude toward it.
3. Helen hated overtime work, **because** the boss was mean with the overtime pay **and** it made her very tired.

Exercise

Rewrite the following by putting the short sentences into compound or complex sentences.

1. The students have made great progress with their English. They still have a long way to go.

_____

2. Napoleon was born in 1769. At that time, France had just acquired Corsica.

_____

3. The new workers lacked experience. They were eager to learn from the experienced ones.

_____

4. He came back to his hometown. He had been away for many years. He couldn't find the familiar landmarks.

_____

5. She appeared on the stage. A stormy applause broke forth.

_____

C. Loose and Periodic Sentences

★ A loose sentence puts the main idea before all less important information. In other words, it puts the more important things first to let the reader know what it is mainly about when s/he has read the first few words.

★ The reverse arrangement makes a periodic sentence: The main idea is expressed at or near the end of it, and it is not grammatically complete until the end is reached. The reader does not know what it is mainly about until he finishes reading it. Compared with a loose sentence, a periodic sentence is more effective and emphatic.

Compare

1. The scientist was offered a long-term professional contract after he won the Nobel Prize in Medicine, according to the newspaper reports.
2. According to the newspaper reports, after he won the Nobel Prize in Medicine, the scientist was offered a long-term professional contract.

The main idea of both sentences is the fact that the scientist was offered a long-term professional contract. This idea is put at the beginning of Sentence 1 and towards the end of Sentence 2, thus making Sentence 1 a loose sentence and Sentence 2 a periodic one. Besides, the first part of Sentence 1 is complete in structure, but that of Sentence 2 consists only of prepositional phrases and cannot be called a sentence without the second part. So loose sentences are easier, simpler, more natural and direct; periodic sentences are more complex, emphatic, formal, or literary. In written English, periodic sentences are favored.

Exercise

Read the following sentences and say whether each is a loose or a periodic sentence.

1. He played the piano very well because he had been trained for many years.
2. His world collapsed when he wasn't chosen for the promising football team.
3. Badly frightened by the violent explosion, the boy couldn't move or cry for help.
4. Our friends set off before us and promised that they would meet us, but when we arrived at the meeting place, they didn't show up.

3

D. Short and Long Sentences

A short sentence is usually emphatic and powerful, whereas a long sentence is capable of expressing complex ideas with precision, because it may contain many modifiers. Short sentences are suitable for the presentation of important facts and ideas, and long sentences for the explanation and illustration of views and theories, or the description with many details.

The following passage, which describes how a man saved a drowning girl, makes good use of short sentences.

> He crouched a little, spreading his hand under the water and moving them round, trying to feel for her. The dead cold pond swayed upon his chest. He moved again, a little deeper, and again, with his hands underneath, he felt all around under the water. And he touched her clothing. But it evaded his fingers. He made a desperate effort to grasp it...
>
> He laid her down on the bank. She was quite unconscious and running with water. He made the water come from her mouth, he worked to restore her. He did not have to work very long before he could feel the breathing begin again in her; she was breathing naturally. He worked a little longer. He could feel her live beneath his hands; she was coming back. He wiped her face, wrapped her in his overcoat, looked round into the dim, dark gray world, then lifted her and staggered down the bank and across the fields.

In contrast to short sentences, long sentences are particularly useful for presenting a set of complex, interlocking ideas. They are common in legal, political and theoretical writing, which depends on modification for accuracy. In fiction long sentences are sometimes used to describe a person, a thing or a scene for a particular effect. In the following sentence from *All the Pretty Horses*, American writer Cormac McCarthy relates the dream in its purest form. A dream is a continuous story and when people talk about dreams, they tend to just bubble on. Through the use of a long sentence, McCarty recreates this feeling and experience of dreaming. Moreover, the protagonist, John Grady, a displaced rancher, continuously compares himself to wild horses in his dream. The Dream is therefore his fantasy, an escape from reality. Through the long sentence, McCarthy also creates John Grady's fantasy.

> That night he dreamt of horses in a field on a high plain where the spring rains had brought up the grass and the wild flowers out of the ground and the flowers ran all blue and yellow far as the eye could see and in the dream he was among the horses running and in the dream he himself could run with the horses and they coursed the young mares and fillies over the plain where their rich bay and their rich chestnut colors shone in the sun and the young colts ran with their dams and trampled down the flowers in a haze of pollen that hung in the sun like powdered gold and they ran he and the horses out along the high

4

mesas where the ground resounded under their running hooves and they flowed and changed and ran and their manes and tails blew off them like spume and there was nothing else at all in that high world and they moved all of them in a resonance that was like a music among them and they were none of them afraid horse nor colt nor mare and they ran in that resonance which is the world itself and which cannot be spoken but only praised.

Although series of short and long sentences can both be effective in individual situations, frequent alternation in sentence length characterizes much memorable writing. Sentence variety to prose can give it life and rhythm. Too many sentences with the same structure and length can grow monotonous for readers. Varying sentence style and structure can also reduce repetition and add emphasis. After long sentences that express complex ideas or images, a short sentence can be refreshing. Look at the following example:

The violence of breaking down the door seemed to fill this room with pervading dust. A thin, acrid pall as of the tomb seemed to lie everywhere upon this room decked and furnished as for a bridal: upon the valance curtains of faded rose color, upon the rose-shaded lights, upon the dressing table, upon the delicate array of crystal and the man's toilet things backed with tarnished silver, silver so tarnished that the monogram was obscured. Among them lay a collar and tie, as if they had just been removed, which, lifted, left upon the surface a pale crescent in the dust. Upon a chair hung the suit, carefully folded; beneath it the two mute shoes and the discarded socks.

The man himself lay in the bed.

Similarly, a long sentence that follows a series of short ones can serve as a climax or summing-up that relaxes the tension or fulfills that expectation created by the series, giving the reader a sense of completion. Here is a good example:

Oh, how fascinating it was! How she enjoyed it! How she loved sitting here, watching it all! It was like a play. It was exactly like a play. Who could believe the sky at the back wasn't painted? But it wasn't till a little brown dog trotted on solemn and then slowly trotted off, like a little "theatre" dog, a little dog that had been drugged, that Miss Brill discovered what it was that made it so exciting. They were all on the stage. They weren't only the audience, not only looking on; they were acting. Even she had a part and came every Sunday. No doubt somebody would have noticed if she hadn't been there; she was part of the performance after all. How strange she'd never thought of it like that before! And yet it explained why she made such a point of starting from home at just the same time each week—so as not to be late for the performance—and it also explained she had quite queer, shy feeling at telling her English pupils how she spent her Sunday afternoons. No wonder! Miss Brill nearly laughed out loud. She was on the stage.

5

Effective Sentences

A sentence is effective when it is unified, coherent, concise, varied or emphatic.

A. Unity

Unity is the first quality of an effective sentence. A unified sentence expresses a single complete idea. It does not contain ideas that are not related, nor does it express a thought that is not complete by itself.

B. Coherence

Coherence means clear and reasonable connection between parts. A sentence is coherent when its words or parts are properly connected and their relationships unmistakably clear. An incoherent sentence includes faulty parallel constructions, pronouns with ambiguous reference, dangling or misplaced modifiers, confusing shifts in person and number, or in voice, tense, and mood.

Exercise

The following sentences are not unified or coherent. Try to revise them.

1. Bernard Shaw was one of the best-known playwright.

_____

2. I read the novel on the train, which did not interest me at all.

_____

3. Tell Peter, if he is at home, I will come to visit him.

_____

4. The children promised to be careful and that they would go home early.

_____

5. If interested in painting, a course can be taken at the evening school.

_____

C. Conciseness

A sentence should contain no unnecessary words. If the idea is fully expressed, the fewer words, the better. Wordiness only obscures the idea.

Compare

Wordy: One of my close personal friends who lives in the city of Taipei at the present time is under consideration of moving his residence to Beijing for the reason that he has been offered a promising position in that metropolis.

Concise: One of my friends in Taipei is considering moving to Beijing because he has been offered a good job there.

Wordy: With regard to the fact that our environment is polluted, members of the committee should draft and consequently enact laws that prohibit pollution in our nation.

Concise: Because our environment is polluted, the committee should pass laws prohibiting pollution.

Exercise

Revise the following sentences, making them as concise as possible without changing their meaning.

1. Although they were few in number, the early settlers who came to this country brought with them strong and devout religious faith and beliefs.

_____

2. At approximately ten o'clock last night, I found a quiet and peaceful spot in the park and perused my academic lecture.

_____

3. In view of the fact that the job market is constantly changing, the counselor urged each and every student to work out alternate plans for the future.

_____

4. Various aspects of personal behavior are studied and analyzed by the specialists in the field of psychology.

_____

5. In this modern day and age there is little to do, and nothing is difficult to do, in order to have a clean house as far as today's cleaning tasks are concerned.

_____

🌸 D. Variety

Variety is essential to good writing. Beginning with the same noun or pronoun as the subject, a series of sentences of the same structure and length would sound monotonous. Variety is achieved when short sentences are used in between long ones, simple sentences in between compound and complex ones, periodic sentences in between loose ones. An occasional question, command, or exclamation among statements may also be helpful. The following ways may help to achieve variety.
1. combining sentences with phrases
2. combining sentences by coordination or subordination
3. beginning some sentences with participles
4. beginning some sentences with prepositional phrases
5. using -*ly* openers
6. using *to* openers

Exercise

The following paragraph is monotonous in sentence structure and sounds childish. Please vary the sentences.

Dennis and Tom walk to school. Jane follows them. Coco is Dennis's dog. She is a beautiful dog. She walks at Dennis's heels. She plays in the street. Now she will try to find her friends.

_____

_____

E. Emphasis

Effective sentences emphasize their main ideas, making them forceful, and keeping related but less important ideas in the background. Emphasis is a reflection of purposes. The following ways are helpful to obtain emphasis.

1. inversion and other emphatic word orders
2. periodic sentences
3. repetition
4. parallelism
5. active voice

Exercise

Rewrite the following sentences, emphasizing the main idea in each.

1. Tom Joseph O'Neil, the famous writer, won the writing contest.

_____

2. China will not be the first to use nuclear weapons under any circumstances.

_____

3. The students were patiently helped by their teachers and good progress was made by them.

_____

4. On July 4th, 1973, a plane crash killed 88 people and was the first fatal crash for Delta Airlines.

_____

5. On weekends we watch football games in a stadium or visit the museum.

_____

Common Errors

A. Run-on Sentences

A run-on sentence wrongly runs together two or more independent clauses without a conjunction or punctuation. It confuses the reader, who will not know where one thought stops and where the next begins. We should add a conjunction and a comma to combine clauses, or separate it into two or more sentences.

For example

1. The exam was difficult most of the students failed.

   Revised: The exam was difficult, so/and most of the students failed.

Another run-on sentence runs together two clauses with only a comma, or a comma with an adverb or adverbal phrase, which is not enough to join two complete ideas as a conjunction.

For example

2. They planned to go camping for their summer vacation, they couldn't afford the activity.

   Revised: They planned to go camping for their summer vacation, but they couldn't afford the activity.

Exercise

Revise the following run-on sentences by using any method discussed.

1. The next chapter has a lot of difficult information in it, you should start studying right away.

   _____

2. The sun is high, put on some sunscreen.

   _____

3. Mr. Nelson has sent his four children to ivy-league colleges, he has sacrificed his health working day and night in the dusty bakery.

   _____

4. Throughout history money and religion were closely linked there was little distinction between government and religion.

   _____

5. Judy leads a charmed life; she never seems to have a serious accident.

   _____

✿ B. Sentence Fragments

Every sentence must have a subject and a verb and must express a complete idea. A word group that lacks a subject or a verb and that does not express a complete idea is a sentence fragment. The following are the most common types of fragments students write.

Dependent-word fragments

-ing and *to* fragments

Added-detail fragments

Missing-subject fragments

For example

1. For example, apples.

   Revised: Fruit does good to people's health, such as apples and oranges.

2. Because you didn't follow my advice.

   Revised: Because you didn't follow my advice, you failed in the competition.

3. With a smile on her face.

   Revised: With a smile on her face, she accepted my suggestion willingly.

4. To buy a new dress.

   Revised: She saved money for a long time to buy a new dress.

5. Given enough time.

   Revised: Given enough time, I can work out the plan.

Exercise

Make the following fragments into sentences.

1. To find the answer to the question. David looked in five reference books.

   _____

2. Because Samuel was sure he had heard the same strange story many months ago.

   _____

3. Many of his customers coming back three or four times over the summer.

   _____

4. Many English words are derived from the Indian languages. For example, pecan, chipmunk, gloo, moose, and raccoon.

   _____

5. Now, as always, is greatly influenced by his willful wife.

   _____

C. Faulty Parallelism

Placing two or more ideas of equal value in the same grammatical form will enable us to express these ideas clearly and emphatically. Faulty parallelism occurs when the form of the ideas being paralleled is not identical, as in the following examples.

1. I was told to report to the manager and that I should bring the documents.

   Revised: I was told to report to the manager and to bring the documents.

2. Our new house not only is more economical but also it is more comfortable than our old one.

   Revised: Our new house is not only more economical but also more comfortable than our old one.

3. When I arrived home, I unpacked my suitcases, took showers, and then I went to sleep after eating something.

   Revised: When I arrived home, I unpacked my suitcases, took showers, ate something and went to sleep.

4. He always has and always will remember the happy time.

   Revised: He has always remembered and always will remember the happy time.
5. The computers in our school are more advanced than your school.

   Revised: The computers in our school are more advanced than those in your school.

Exercise

Rewrite the following non-parallel sentences.

1. Many college students have the same goals: playing hard, doing well in classes, and find a job after graduation.

   _____

2. People often try to avoid eye contact with others, whether riding on a bus, strolling through a shopping mall, or when they are in line at a supermarket.

   _____

3. When trying to impress a prospective employer, people should pay attention to their clothing, their posture, and that they don't use too much slang.

   _____

4. The delegates spent the day arguing with one another rather than work together to find common solutions.

   _____

5. A battery powered by aluminum is simple to design, clean to run, and it is inexpensive to produce.

   _____

6. The Johnsons were cheerful and knowledgeable traveling companions, and behaved generously.

   _____

7. By the time she was two, the child was not only active but also she was well coordinated.

   _____

8. To keep horses at home, the owner must commit a significant amount of time to daily care and knowing how to identify signs of illness or injury in the horse.

   _____

9. New potatoes out of the garden, vine-ripened beefsteak tomatoes, and freestone peaches picked by hand from our tree: these are my favorite summer foods.

   _____

10. Influential factors in any nation's economic regression are bad management of natural resources, policies regarding national debt might be unwise, and worker's demands may be inflationary.

    _____

D. Misplaced Modifiers

Misplaced modifiers are words that do not describe the words the writer intends them to describe. Misplaced modifiers often confuse the meaning of a sentence. To avoid this problem, modifiers should be placed as close as possible to what they modify.

For example

1. Mother returned the can to the supermarket that was spoilt.

   Revised: Mother returned the can that was spoilt to the supermarket.

2. Her invention among the public did not cause much interest.

   Revised: Her invention did not cause much interest among the public.

Exercise

Correct the misplaced modifiers in the sentences below.

1. They just said it's going to rain on the radio.

   _____

2. Please take time to look over the brochure that is enclosed with your family.

   _____

3. He barely kicked that ball twenty yards.

   _____

4. Her husband asked her if they might consider having another baby during their friends' baby shower.

   _____

5. The fish was greatly enjoyed by the fisherman, which was tasty.

   _____

6. We returned the lawn-mower to our neighbor that was broken.

   _____

7. The guest speaker had dedicated his new book to his dog who was an archaeologist.

   _____

8. Marin watched a radiant sunset climbing a hill.

   _____

E. Dangling Modifiers

A dangling modifier is a phrase or an elliptical clause (a clause without a subject or verb or both) that is illogically separated from the word it modifies. Thus it appears disconnected from the rest of the sentence. We should locate its implied subject and then make it the stated subject of the main clause.

For example

1. While in the frying pan, I heated butter until melted.

   Revised: While in the frying pan, butter was heated until melted.

      Or: While I put butter in the frying pan, I heated it until it melted.

2. Although working very hard, his research paper was not turned in on time.

   Revised: Although he worked very hard, his research paper was not turned in on time.

      Or: Although working very hard, he couldn't turn in his research paper on time.

3. Comparing with that of many other schools, our campus is small but exquisite.

   Revised: Compared with that of many other schools, our campus is small but exquisite.

Exercise

Correct the misplaced modifiers in the sentences below.

1. Eagerly awaiting her birthday, Mary's presents were all picked up and admired by Mary many times throughout the course of the day.

   _____

2. Covered in wildflowers, George pondered the hillside's beauty.

   _____

3. The experiment was a failure, not having studied the lab manual carefully.

   _____

4. To keep the young recruits interested in getting in shape, an exercise program was set up for the summer months.

   _____

5. After reading the great new book, the movie based on it is sure to be exciting.

   _____

6. Having seen Blackpool Tower, the Eiffel Tower is more impressive.

   _____

7. With a sigh of disappointment, the expensive dress was returned to the rack.

   _____

8. While taking a test, there was a fire alarm.

   _____

9. Strolling hand in hand to the farm, the young bulls broke out of the field and headed toward us.

   _____

10. Exhausted after a long hike, a tall, cool glass of water was a welcome sight.

   _____

13

Homework

A. Rewrite each of the following sentences according to the requirements.

1. I always take my raincoat whenever I go out these days. (periodic)

   _____

2. They were on holiday. Their house was broken into. Some valuable paintings were stolen. (compound-complex)

   _____

3. The firemen fought for three hours. They finally managed to put out the fire. (complex)

   _____

4. Nobody in this world is quite perfect. We all have some faults. (compound)

   _____

5. The train is going to Shanghai. The train leaves at 21:35. (simple)

   _____

6. It began to rain, but the children went on playing outdoors. (complex)

   _____

7. In spite of the interruption, he was able to finish all his exercises before the class was over. (loose)

   _____

8. It was strange that he avoided mentioning her name. (-_ly_ opener)

   _____

B. Correct the errors in the following sentences.

1. One of her greatest joys in life is eating desserts. Such as pudding, cake and ice cream.

   _____

2. Because he had drunk too much. He had to leave the party early. His stomach was like a volcano. That was ready to erupt.

   _____

3. While sitting in the office, she realized she had lost her valuable ring. But happily found it in the women's room after work.

   _____

4. My favorite teacher, a native of Indian, and who is also our volleyball coach, is moving to another city next year.

   _____

5. After sitting for a long time in his office, the doctor finally let me into the examining room.

   _____

6. Wedging his way out of the dining hall, his discovery was a terrible hall beyond imagination.

_____

7. The spreading of educational and culture norms may affect and forming the attitudes and sensible of a nation.

_____

8. Everyone nearly knows the truth after our leader mentioned it at the conference.

_____

C. Combine the sentences and make them a compound, complex or compound-complex sentence.

1. In 1934 Walt Disney became a star. An eight-minute Mickey Mouse movie was produced.

_____

2. The worst time to be in the street in Cairo was after the midnight. The night-clubs were closing. Everybody went home.

_____

3. There was a power cut in the hospital. The surgeon had to cancel the operation. It was very dangerous to operate in dim light.

_____

4. George is an amicable person. He gets on well with everyone in the company.

_____

5. Tom wanted to come back home. The telephone in the office began to ring.

_____

6. The energy goes in every direction. Only a small part of it falls on the earth. The sun radiates the energy.

_____

7. I slid my aching bones into the hot tub water. I realized that there was no soap. I did not want to get out again.

_____

8. Bob's furniture store just went out of business. I worked there as a shop assistant. I'll have to look for another job.

_____

9. You are sent damaged goods. The store must replace the items. The store must issue a full refund.

_____

10. I'm not going to eat in the school cafeteria any more. The service is unbearable. The price is high. The food lacks variety.

_____

D. Combine each group of sentences to form a single sentence by eliminating, adding, or moving words.

1. Helena is an interesting girl. She is a freshman in college. She is a practicing minister. She majors in literature.

_____

2. Some children in the countryside will be bussed to the primary school. They live far away from the town. This will last until they go to middle school.

_____

3. My sister is young. She is impressionable. She is quick to learn. She loves sports very much.

_____

4. Her new boyfriend is going bald. He's a twenty-five-year-old manager. He couldn't care less about going bald.

_____

5. Tina went swimming in the pond. Lily went with her. They did this despite the cold water. They did it at midnight. They did it for fun.

_____

E. Rewrite the following sentences to make them more concise. Try not to change their basic meaning.

1. My father was annoyed by the fact that I arrived late instead of being on time.

_____

2. I spotted a butterfly which was green in color; I would have caught it in my net if it had not been for a log which caused me to tip.

_____

3. I admired his writing not only for its terse conciseness but also for the fact that its ideas were expressed in a clear, lucid, straightforward manner.

_____

4. The thing that caused the failure of the army to avoid defeat was the nature of its leadership, which was not competent.

_____

5. As a result of the fact that he had never learned the basic fundamentals of algebra, he found calculus difficult to such an extent that he had to withdraw from the course.

_____

6. The smoke was moving in such a way as to cover up the level prairie, until soon nothing was visible to our eyes except for a thick blanket of dense smoke.

_____

7. Sociologists have tried to make a determination as to why so many people who grow up in the upper classes have a tendency to become the sort of people who consistently ignore and break the law.

_____

8. To pay the tuition fees, students can ask their parents for money, or they can borrow it from them now, and return it back after graduation.

_____

F. Correct the sentence fragments and the run-on sentences in the following passage.

The Key to Comfort

Rooms often portray a person's character and personality your character is displayed in the way you keep your room in order. Whether it is neat or disorganized. To me my room is the most important room in the house, the way it is kept shows the kind of atmosphere I want it helps me seclude myself when the going gets too rough at home.

The atmosphere I try to have in my room is one of solitude. I think that comes because of the way my room is decorated. Soft walls in an off-white color. Nothing but my mirror hanging on the walls. A high dark brown dresser. The desk in the far corner is walnut on the top books stand in piles. Which I keep very neat and orderly. The stereo set and my collection of albums and tapes are in the far corner. Next to my amorphous black leather reclining chair. My room is the only room in the house that is so relaxing.

Because the surroundings are so restful. I found that it served as an important place one February evening last year. When my house was filled with guests from a card party my mother was having. I had my final examination in history the next day, I knew if I did not find a quiet place to study I would fail. I excused myself from the incessant noise of my mother's guests and determined to get peace and quiet. Marched upstairs to my room. Upon opening the door to my room. I had almost given up hope. There was so much noise. Loud roars of laughter. People chattering. Dimes and nickels clinking on the table. I quickly slammed the door with me inside the room suddenly the noise was outside, I was trapped in a welcome silence. Because of the solitude in my room I was able to study, passed the final exam.

Rooms help people relax and find quiet. And the appearance of a room sets the scene for relaxation. If more people would set aside certain amount of time each day to solve their problems in a serene room of their choice. The mental pressures that many Americans suffer might disappear. Most people try to relax in an atmosphere that is more distracting than peaceful, to me, the quiet well-decorated, well-kept room is the key to comfort.

The Paragraph

When we group several sentences in some logical order together to discuss one main idea, for the sake of information, persuasion or entertainment, we have a paragraph. While paragraphs have no specific length and no required number of sentences, they do conventionally have three characteristics: they are unified, coherent, and adequately developed. That is, a paragraph presents a single thought, all its parts are clearly related to one another, and its main point is sufficiently supported by details, examples, or explanations. In formal academic English, paragraphs have three principal parts: the topic sentence, body/supporting sentences, and the concluding sentence.

19

The Topic Sentence

A topic sentence states the main point of the paragraph. It expresses a view about the topic and informs the reader of the main idea in the paragraph. In other words, the topic sentence introduces an overall idea or makes an abstract point that the writer discusses in the paragraph. The topic sentence usually but not always appears as the first sentence in the paragraph, though not all paragraphs have clear-cut topic sentences.

A Good Topic Sentence

● includes a subject and a controlling idea,
● is limited enough to be developed in one paragraph,
● prepares the reader for the rest of the paragraph,
● and is a complete thought that lends itself to development.

A Valid Topic Sentence Consists of Two Parts

1. **The Topic/Subject:** the idea that the paragraph is about.
2. **The Main/Controlling Idea:** the statement that makes a point about the topic.

    e.g.: <u>Time management</u> is *a vital skill for college students.*

       (topic)   (main/controlling idea)

      Rather than a creature of endless vacillation, <u>Hamlet</u> is a man of *action.*

                              (topic)   (main idea)

Remember:

- The topic sentence narrows the topic down, makes ONE assertion, and provides a preview of the upcoming point in the paragraph. Because the reader expects that a paragraph will explore ONE idea, it's important that a topic sentence isn't too ambitious. If a topic sentence points to two or three ideas, it is necessary to consider developing more paragraphs.
- By placing the topic sentence at the beginning of the paragraph, the writer lets the reader know where the paper is headed. The topic sentence is an effective signal that keeps both the reader and the writer on track.

Most of the time a topic sentence comes at the beginning of a paragraph. If a writer is going to place it elsewhere, he needs to have a good reason and a bit of skill. He might justify putting the topic sentence in the middle of the paragraph, for example, if he has information that needs to precede it. He might also justify putting the topic sentence at the end of the paragraph, if he wants the reader to consider his line of reasoning before he declares his main point, or he uses specific details to lead up to a generalization.

 ## At the Beginning of the Paragraph

20

> The intelligence of dolphins is well documented by science. Studies show that dolphins are able to understand sign language, solve puzzles, and use objects in their environment as tools. Scientists also believe that dolphins possess a sophisticated language: numerous instances have been recorded in which dolphins transmitted information from one individual to another. A recent experiment proved that dolphins can even recognize themselves in a mirror—something achieved by very few animals. This behavior demonstrates that dolphins are aware of their individuality, indicating a level of intelligence that may be very near our own.

 ## In the Middle of the Paragraph

> When most of us think about language, we think first about words. Thus, the hardest part of learning a foreign language may see to be memorizing its vocabulary; when we observe a child first acquiring speech, we talk of his or her progress as a matter of learning new words. We are also likely to feel that the adult speaker with the largest vocabulary has the best command of English. To think of a language as just a stock of words is, however, quite wrong. Words alone do not make a language; a grammar is needed to combine them in some intelligible way. Moreover, words are relatively easy to learn, and indeed all of us go on learning them all our lives. They are also the least stable part of language. Words come into being, change their pronunciations and meanings, and disappear completely—all with comparative ease.

At the End of the Paragraph

Vocabulary

If we try to recall Boris Karloff's[1] face as the monster in the film of *Frankenstein*[2] (1931), most of us probably think of the seams holding the pieces together, and if we cannot recall other details we assume that the face evokes horror. But when we actually look at a picture of the face rather than recall a memory of it, we are perhaps chiefly impressed by the high, steep forehead (a feature often associated with intelligence), by the darkness surrounding the eyes (often associated with physical or spiritual weariness), and by the gaunt[3] cheeks and the thin lips slightly turned down at the corners (associated with deprivation or restraint). The monster's face is of course in some ways shocking, but probably our chief impression as we look at it is that <u>this is not the face of one who causes suffering but of one who himself is heroically suffering</u>.

1. Boris Karloff: 英国电影演员 William Henry Pratt (1887—1969) 的艺名, 以其在好莱坞恐怖电影中的角色著称。
2. *Frankenstein*: 根据英国作家玛丽·雪莱同名小说改编的电影, 又译《科学怪人》。
3. gaunt: *adj.* thin and bony

21

 ## Paragraph with an Implied Topic Sentence

Vocabulary

Employees with burnout[1] feel tired all the time, and they often show symptoms of depression. The likelihood of burnout is increased if they feel trapped in the job. Burnout can also occur if the job demands an overload of work. Ongoing lack of social support, rigid rules, and unkind bosses also lead to burnout.

1. burnout: *n.* 精力耗尽

The implied topic sentence: Several factors can cause employees to burn out.

Exercises

1. Write a topic sentence for the following topics. Remember to focus your controlling idea on one aspect of the topic.

   (1) My hometown
   (2) My university
   (3) My best friend
   (4) iphone
   (5) Traffic jam

2. Can the two sentences below be used as topic sentences?

    (1) My hometown is famous because it is located by the Yangtze River near the town of Fengdu, known as "city of the ghost."

    (2) There are two reasons why some people like to buy cars with automatic transmission and two reasons why others like cars with manual transmission.

3. Underline the sentence which best expresses the main idea in each paragraph.

Vocabulary

(1) While my gender is extremely important to me, I first identify myself as a scholar because intellect does not have a sex. Knowledge transcends[1] gender. Therefore, I am a thinker, a learner, and a scholar. To me, the process of learning is religious. Words are my "bible," while teachers are my "priests." I respect and revere words like others respect, revere, and fear the idea of God. I understand that words are alive and I must wrestle them down and tame them in order for them to become my own. Hence, I make it a habit to collect words. Then, like bangles[2] and crystals that possess psychedelic[3] and prismatic[4] qualities, I hang the words in my mind for illumination. The meaning of my precious words are revealed to me by teachers—not just those who have a "teaching certificate," but those who awaken my mind, who ignite my senses, who alter my perception of the world; together, as Walt Whitman says, we "roam in thought over the universe," seeking to enlighten ourselves and one another.

1. transcend: *v.* to go beyond

2. bangle: *n.* 手镯
3. psychedelic: *adj.* 产生迷幻效果的
4. prismatic: *adj.* 折射光的，耀眼的

(2) Wearing a Qipao nowadays has turned into something of a vogue, both at home and abroad. Due to its elegance and classical looks the Qipao becomes a source of inspiration for fashion designers. World-renowned brands like CD, Versace, and Ralph Lauren have all cited some Qipao elements in their designs. Many foreign women are eager to get themselves a Qipao should they visit China. Qipao is no longer a garment particular to Chinese women, but is adding to the vocabulary of beauty for women the world over.

(3) In the past, workers with average skills, doing an average job, could earn an average lifestyle. But, today, average is officially over. Being average just won't earn you what it used to. It can't when so many more employers have so much more access to so much more above average cheap foreign labor, cheap robotics, cheap software, cheap automation and cheap genius. Therefore, everyone needs to find their extra — their unique value contribution that makes them stand out in whatever is their field of employment. *Average is over.*

Supporting Sentences

The supporting sentences follow the topic sentence. They are so called because they explain the idea expressed in the topic sentence. They serve to fully and adequately back up, clarify, illustrate, explain or prove the point the writer makes in the topic sentence is true or important. The supporting sentences can be interesting specific facts, illustrations, examples, quotes, citations, reference, etc.

The Concluding Sentence

A concluding sentence summarizes the information in the paragraph, and therefore it is often similar to, but not exactly the same as, the topic sentence. Not every academic paragraph contains a concluding sentence, especially if the paragraph is rather short.

The following paragraph shows how a paragraph is formed. At the beginning, a topic sentence introduces the subject of "universal primary education" and the controlling idea of "stunning progress." In the middle, two supporting sentences are organized from specific to general to prove the topic sentence. At the end of the paragraph, a concluding sentence is given to restate the controlling idea.

[1]Since the turn of the millennium, the world has made stunning progress toward the goal of universal primary education. [2]In sub-Saharan Africa, enrollment in primary school has risen by 18 percentage points; in Asia and Latin America there has been more limited progress. [3]While globally, 69 million school-age children do not attend school now, in 1999 that figure was 106 million. [4] This is a huge achievement.	1 a topic sentence 2—3 supporting sentences 4 a concluding sentence

Exercise

Identify the topic sentence, the supporting sentences, and the concluding sentence in the follow paragraph.

> Most societies have some means of law enforcement. For example, in the less populated regions of the world such as tribal areas, laws or customs may be enforced by a council of elders or by a strong chief or leader of the tribe much in the same manner of a father who decides what behavior is best for his children. As another example, in the sparsely populated great open land of places like Australia, Canada, Siberia, and Brazil, a few policemen must travel great distances to enforce laws made to protect people and property. In countries where most of the people live in crowded urban areas, on the other hand, law enforcement is usually in the hands of large numbers of police who are directly responsible to the chief governmental official for that area. As still another instance, countries have cooperated in establishing various organizations and methods, including military or police action, to enforce the rules and laws agreed to by a majority of the cooperating nations. Although vastly different in form and in circumstances, most cultures have ways of enforcing laws agreed upon by society.

24

Paragraph Unity

Unity is the quality of sticking to *one* idea in a paragraph. It means that all supporting sentences in the paragraph directly and clearly illustrate, clarify, and/or explain the main idea set forth in the topic sentence. To achieve paragraph unity, a writer must ensure two things. First, the paragraph must have a single generalization that serves as the focus of attention, that is, a topic sentence. Secondly, every other sentence in the body of the paragraph not only maintains the same focus of attention as the topic sentence, but also contains more specific information than the topic sentence.

A sentence that does not support the topic sentence destroys unity of the paragraph and becomes an irrelevant sentence:

> (1) Fishing is one of the most popular recreational sports in China. (2) More people become involved in it every year. (3) Moreover, it is an activity that attracts participants from every geographic region of the country. (4) Unfortunately, water pollution poses a serious threat to some lakes and streams. (5) In short, people from all walks of life, old and young, are catching more fish every year.

Sentence (4) is irrelevant because it draws attention away from the main idea of the paragraph.

Underline the irrelevant sentence(s) in the next paragraph.

> A vegetarian diet benefits one's health, one's wellbeing, and even the environment. First, a low-fat vegetarian diet can prevent heart disease and help lower blood pressure, as well as fight diabetes. Not many people realize that almost six percent of Americans are diabetic and that there is no cure. Muscles, strength, and endurance are also enhanced by a vegetarian diet. In addition to the health benefits, vegetarians say they feel better about themselves spiritually than they did when they were eating meat. It is as if people discover a greater awareness of their connection with the plant and animal world. This awareness is related to the satisfaction of knowing that vegetarianism benefits the environment. Less water is used in the cultivation of vegetables than in the production of livestock, and much more fossil fuel is required to produce the same amount of protein from beef as from grain. Given the benefits, it is no wonder over twelve million Americans today consider themselves vegetarians.

Paragraph Coherence

An effective paragraph is not only unified but also coherent. Ideas can't be convincing unless they are properly connected so that readers can move easily from one thought to another. Coherence means that all the information of the paragraph is well-organized, logically ordered and easy to follow. Each sentence in such a paragraph should naturally grow out of each previous sentence in developing the central idea. Ideally, there should be a sense of movement or flow, a going forward and building on what has been said before. The paragraph achieves coherence and a good flow by the use of appropriate transition signals, linking words and phrases, or parallel structures, by having the supporting sentences in logical order, and by making the supporting sentences explain the topic sentence.

Transitional Words

Transitional words can be used to link ideas from different sentences. A conjunction or conjunctive adverb, for example, links sentences with particular logical relationships. Transitional words like "therefore," "moreover," "however" signal the type of relationship one sentence has to another. However, transitional words must appear naturally where they belong and shouldn't be overused.

- Words indicating sameness:

  that is, that is to say, in other words...
- Words indicating contrast:

  but, yet, however, nevertheless, still, though, although, whereas, in contrast, rather, on

the other hand, instead, on the contrary...
- Words indicating addition or continuation:

  and, too, also, furthermore, moreover, in addition, besides, in the same way, again, another, similarly, a similar, the same, likewise...
- Words indicating cause and effect:

  therefore, so, consequently, as a consequence, thus, as a result, hence, it follows that, because, since, for, accordingly...
- Words indicating a summary:

  in summary, in brief, on the whole, in short, in other words, in any event...
- Words indicating a logical connection of an unspecified type:

  in fact, indeed, now, of course...
- Words indicating a willingness to consider the other side:

  admittedly, I admit, true, I grant, of course, naturally, some believe, some people believe, it has been claimed that, once it was believed...
- Words indicating a shift from a more general or abstract idea to a more specific or concrete idea:

  for example, for instance, after all, an illustration of, even, indeed, in fact, it is true, of course, specifically, to be specific, that is, to illustrate, truly, namely...
- Words indicating the chronological order:

  first, then, soon, after, before, later, subsequently, immediately, currently...
- Words indicating the order of place:

  in front of, to the side, adjacent to, in the distance, above, below, here, there..

Notice: Where transitional adverbs (conjunctive adverbs) such as however, therefore, consequently, nevertheless, furthermore, moreover, etc. are inserted within a sentence, they are set off between commas.

e.g.: Her hair, however, was stringy.

Where such a transitional word begins a sentence, it is usually separated by a comma. Where the word occurs between two independent clauses and it goes with the second clause, the two clauses are separated with a semicolon and the transitional word with a comma.

e.g.: His hair was black and wavy; however, it was false.

Exercises

1. Identify transitional words and discuss how they keep the paragraph coherent.

(1) Fast food restaurants have several advantages. First of all, their big draw is the time saved. Customers can walk in the door, walk up to the counter, place an order, and have their lunch in a matter of minutes. If customers prefer to remain in their cars, they can go through the drive-in window and eat in the automobile. In addition, the quality of the food is consistent; people can learn which items on the menu suit them and which ones they

can count on. Best of all, the prices are usually unbeatable. Consequently, fast food restaurants are attracting more and more customers.

(2) Choosing a college or university can be difficult. The most difficult part is finding a university that prepares you well for your future career. In order to get a good job, the curriculum that is taught must be thorough and up-to-date. In addition, the professors must be highly qualified and respected in their fields. Another difficulty in choosing a university or college is affordability. You need to be able to pay the tuition fees and living expenses. Some institutions might be able to offer you scholarships if you cannot afford the fees. A good location is also very important when choosing a school. The environment should be safe and quiet to facilitate studying. Moreover, there should be possibilities near the school for part-time or summer jobs in your major, so you can get some practical work experience. You should consider all of these points carefully so you can choose the most appropriate college or university for you.

2. Fill in the blanks with appropriate transitional words.

Teachers of foreign languages should be extremely well-qualified in order to carry out their duties properly. _____, a teacher should possess a minimum of a graduate degree from a certified education school or institute if he is to teach high school or below. _____ the academic degree, teachers should not consider teaching only as an occupation for earning money; they should also be interested in teaching. It was _____ necessary that teachers be knowledgeable in their major fields, _____ they should be skillful as well. _____, the language teacher must know the target language well enough to be imitated by his students. Proficiency in the target language includes four skills: understanding, speaking, reading, and writing. A teacher should _____ know the linguistic facts of the language of the students in order to understand the problems they will have in learning the target language. _____ the teacher must be familiar with audio-lingual techniques. Knowing all this will help the students to learn correctly and quickly.

Pronouns and Repetition of Words

Key words can be repeated throughout the paragraph as markers to link sentences. One of the simplest tactics is to interweave pronouns along with the subject, as pronouns make explicit reference back to a noun mentioned earlier. Another tactic is the repetition of nouns. Controlled repetition keeps the reader's attention focused. However, repetition shouldn't be overworked to become redundant and obtrusive.

Gold, a precious metal, is prized for two important characteristics. First of all, gold has a lustrous[1] beauty that is resistant to corrosion[2]. Therefore, it is suitable for jewelry, coins, and ornamental purposes. Gold never needs to be polished and will remain beautiful forever. For example, a Macedonian[3] coin remains as untarnished[4] today as the day it was minted[5] twenty-three centuries ago. Another important characteristic of gold is its usefulness to industry and science. For many years, it has been used in hundreds of industrial applications. The most recent use of gold is in astronauts' suits. Astronauts wear gold-plated heat shields for protection outside the spaceship. In conclusion, gold is treasured not only for its beauty but also for its utility.

1. lustrous: *adj.* bright, shining
2. corrosion: *n.* 侵蚀
3. Macedonia: *n.* 马其顿古国
4. tarnish: *v.* lose brightness
5. mint: *v.* make a coin

28

Synonyms

Synonymous words can be used in several sentences to avoid monotony in the repetition of the same word. This strategy is called "elegant variation." The following example abounds in synonyms for "fruitful, rich, and productive":

> The land was fruitful, rich, and productive. It had a tropical climate and a generous amount of rainfall. There was a lot of vegetation and everything was green and flowering. The rivers ran abundantly with water and the mountains were thick with trees. The mornings were immaculate, very sunny and clear, and the fields were richly cultivated and filled with wildflowers. The fecundity of the land produced a diverse fauna that included all sorts of small reptiles such as lizards and snakes, insects such as crickets and dragonflies, and wild animals such as monkeys, wildcats, and coyotes.

Parallel Sentence Structure

Parallel sentence structure ensures coherence in that similar ideas are expressed in outwardly similar sentences. The likeness of form enables the reader to recognize more readily the likeness of content and function.

> We hold these truths to be self-evident, that all men are created equal, that they are endowed by their Creator with certain unalienable Rights, that among these are Life, Liberty, and the pursuit of Happiness. That to secure these rights, Governments are instituted among Men, driving their just powers

from the consent of the governed. That whenever any form of government becomes destructive of these ends, it is the Right of the People to alter or to abolish it, and to institute new government, laying its foundation on such principles and organizing its power in such form, as to them shall seem most likely to effect their Safety and Happiness.

Logical Order in Organization

Putting information in logical order contributes to coherence.

- **Order of importance** is one of the most useful ways of arranging ideas in a paragraph. It can be arranged in two ways: by beginning with the most important idea and proceeding to the least important, or vise-versa.
- **General to specific** is a common type of paragraph order. This arrangement begins with a topic sentence that makes a general statement followed by supporting sentences which supply details, examples, and facts.
- **Specific to general/deductive** reverses the above order. It presents details, examples, facts, impressions or observations, and ends with a generalization or conclusion, usually the topic sentence. It can hold a conclusion in suspense that might be contrary to what the reader believes or expects.
- **Spatial order** is very effective to describe a place. The writer tries to create word picture from a particular point of view and moves outward, from left to right, from right to left, from near to far, from far to near, etc.
- **Chronological order** means that events and details are arranged in the order of time, usually moving from the first or earliest to the last or latest.
- **Simple to complex** begins with the simple information and proceeds to the complex. The way, the writer leads the reader to see the process of reasoning.
- **Cause to effect** starts with the cause and follows with the possible effects of the cause. It can be applied in a situation that a single cause leads to several effects. The cause at the beginning is the topic sentence of the paragraph.
- **Effect to cause** reverses the above one. This pattern begins with an effect and follows with possible causes of the effect. It can be used in a situation that a single effect results from many causes. The effect at the beginning is the topic sentence of the paragraph.
- **Questions to answer** begins with one or a series of questions for the reader to think about. It can arouse the reader's interest to read. With answers to the questions, the paragraph can be well developed.

Writers always combine various devices to make paragraphs coherent.

29

Exercise

Find out as many as possible devices that make the following paragraph coherent.

Each of the U.S. manned space exploration projects had specific major goals. For example, the Mercury project was designed to test whether or not human beings could survive and function in outer space. In addition, the Mercury project tested rockets with the new Mercury space capsule, which could hold one person. As another example, the Gemini project was intended to find out whether two people could work in the weightless environment of space. One way of doing this was by having Gemini astronauts take "spacewalks." That is, they floated outside their spacecraft in a spacesuit, connected to it by a tether. Gemini astronauts also tried out new flying skills. For example, some astronauts flew two spacecraft extremely close together; this procedure was called "rendezvous." On some Gemini flights, astronauts physically linked two spacecrafts together. This linking, or "space docking," was a major goal of the Gemini program. Finally, the Apollo project, with three astronauts, had the goal of testing spacecraft and skills so that people could actually fly to the Moon and land on it. Other goals included performing scientific experiments on the lunar surface and collecting rocks for study on Earth.

30

Paragraph Structure

1. Coordinate Structure

In the coordinate structure, all the sentences are equal to each other and each is a comment on or illustration of the topic sentence. If any of the supporting sentences is removed, it won't make the paragraph incoherent, but it might cause the paragraph underdeveloped.

For example

Topic sentence:

[1]My hometown is famous for several amazing natural features.

Supporting sentences:

[2]*First*, the Wheaton River is very wide and beautiful, on whose either side, which is 175 feet wide, are many willow trees which have long branches that can move gracefully in the wind.

[3]*Second*, Wheaton Hill is unusual and steep, but climbing this hill is not dangerous, because there are some firm rocks along the sides that can be used as stairs.

[4]The *third* amazing feature is the Big Old Tree, two hundred feet tall and about six hundred years old.

Supporting sentences 2, 3 and 4 are equal to support the topic sentence. Their order can be changed because of their equality. If one of them is removed, the paragraph is not fully developed.

2. Subordinate Structure

In the subordinate structure, each supporting sentence adds only to the sentence before it. If any sentence, except the last one, is removed, the paragraph will become incoherent and lack unity.

For example

Topic sentence:

[1]The garlic *bulb*, often rejected by picky eaters as bad-smelling and common, is one of nature's greatest gifts.

Supporting sentences:

[2]The *bulb* breaks into a dozen or more *cloves*, each shaped somewhat like a tear and covered with a paper shell.

[3]Each *clove* releases a powerful *aroma and taste*, a warm, friendly taste of home and familiar things.

[4]This wonderful garlic *flavor* is used by most of the people of the world to spice up the taste of bland food.

In the subordinate structure, supporting sentence 2 comments on the topic sentence, providing a detail of the garlic bulb in sentence 1. Sentence 3 adds to 2, giving a detail about the garlic cloves mentioned in 2; sentence 4 adds to 3, giving a detail about the flavor of garlic mentioned in 3. If one of them is removed, it will cause incoherence and the lack of unity.

3. Mixed Coordinate-Subordinate Structure

The supporting sentences added directly to the topic sentence form a coordinate structure; those added to each other form a subordinate structure. Coordinate structure is good for listing examples, details, and so on; subordinate structure is good for analyzing objects, events and so on. But the most common type of paragraph mixes coordinate and subordinate structures together. Because the sentences are held together in one or the other structure, the paragraph becomes a unit. Because the sentences are related to each other, the reader can follow a flow of information from one sentence to another.

31

For example

    Topic sentence:

[1]Despite this need for public approval, football does not demand a discriminating public.

    Supporting sentences:

[2]The football fan, compared to *the baseball fan* or the tennis fan, is an absolute fool.

    [3]The baseball fan is a man of *high perceptivity and learning*.

        [4]He can *recognize* each player and know every game held last year in detail.

[5]The football fan knows nothing.

    [6]He can't recognize one player from another, except by the number on the uniform.

    [7]All he can do is to follow the ball and he can't often even do that.

All the supporting sentences illustrate the topic sentence, supporting the way that football does not demand a discriminating public. Coordinate sentences 2 and 5 list sub-points. Sentence 3 supports 2; 4 supports 3. Sentences 6 and 7, which are parallel sentences, explain and support Sentence 5.

32

With these three structures, you can generate very complex paragraphs. To ensure the unity and coherence of a paragraph, any sentence that does not relate to the topic sentence or does not grow out of the previous one should be deleted.

Exercise

Are the following unified and coherent paragraphs? What is the topic sentence in each? What logical order of organization or the structure does each use?

Vocabulary

(1) It is commonly recognized that dogs have an extreme antagonism[1] toward cats. This enmity[2] between these two species can be traced back to the time of the early Egyptian dynasties. Archaeologists in recent years have discovered Egyptian texts in which there are detailed accounts of canines[3] brutally mauling[4] felines[5]. Today this type of cruelty between these two domestic pets can be witnessed in regions as close as your own neighborhood. For example, when dogs are walked by their masters, and they happen to catch sight of a stray cat, they will pull with all their strength on their leash until the master is forced to yield; the typical result is that a feline is chased up a tree. The hatred between dogs and cats has lasted for so many centuries; it is unlikely that this conflict will ever end.

1. antagonism: *n.* 敌对
2. enmity: *n.* 敌意

3. canine: *n.* 犬科动物
4. maul: *v.* injure by tearing the flesh
5. feline: *n.* 猫科动物

(2) A painting, among other things, is a controlled or confined space, and our appreciation of a painting partially depends on how well we perceive the spatial relationships employed by the painter. To begin with, our vision is restricted or directed by the outer limits of the painting, a frame in most instances. We may perceive the painting as a "whole," but most often our eyes are directed by the painter to a focal point or center of interest. The focus of the picture alone would not hold our attention, however. We are led to it by the painter because of its significance through its relation to other objects in the painting. We might, for example, notice an outstanding face in the background in the midst of dark clothing and shadows. Or we see figures in the distance in the perspective of the painting, in contrast to a flat silhouette[1] in the foreground that frames them. We are compelled to look at the clouds in the sky because our eyes are lifted upward by the lines of the trees or mountains in the painting. We observe that a large brown field in the lower left is balanced with a small, colorful cluster of trees on the right. In the end — especially in traditional or representational painting — we always return to the center of interest, which has been intensified for us by our taking in the details which visually support it.

1. silhouette: *n.* 侧影

33

(3) As cellphones have gotten smarter, they have become less like phones and more like computers, and thus susceptible[1] to hacking[2]. But unlike desktop or even most laptop computers, cellphones are almost always on hand, and are often loaded with even more personal information. So an undefended or carelessly operated phone can result in a breathtaking invasion of individual privacy as well as the potential for data corruption and outright theft. Cellphones can be hacked in several ways. A so-called man-in-the-middle attack[3] is when someone hacks into a phone's

1. susceptible: *adj.* accessible to some influence
2. hack: *v.* 对系统进行修改
3. 简称"MITM攻击"——一种将受入侵终端虚拟在网络连接中的两个终端之间的"间接"入侵攻击。

operating system and reroutes data to make a pit stop at a snooping[4] third party before sending it on to its destination. That means the hacker can listen to your calls, read your text messages, follow your Internet browsing activity and keystrokes and pinpoint[5] your geographical location. A sophisticated perpetrator[6] of a man-in-the-middle attack can even instruct your phone to transmit audio and video when your phone is turned off, so intimate encounters and sensitive business negotiations essentially become broadcast news.

4. snoop: v. 窥探

5. pinpoint: v. 准确确定
6. perpetrator: n. 作案者

Homework 1

Write a paragraph on your family, your hometown, your best friend, the mobile phone, traffic jam or environmental pollution in your place, or any topic of your own choice. Discuss your writing with your partner, revise it and hand it in to your instructor.

34

Paragraphs in an Essay

An essay might be said to be an extended paragraph: Just as several sentences discussing one main idea in some logical order make a paragraph, when several paragraphs discussing one subject come together, we have an essay. The same way as sentences play different functions in a paragraph, paragraphs in different positions of an essay have different roles to play. In a well-written essay, each paragraph supports the thesis sentence; each is directly linked to the thesis and is clearly related to other paragraphs in the essay. Body paragraphs develop the thesis to make the essay interesting, informative, and/or convincing.

The Introductory Paragraph

The introductory paragraph presents the subject of the essay, narrows that subject down, and introduces the thesis statement. A great difference lies between a topic sentence and the thesis statement. A topic sentence only controls one paragraph and one essay with several paragraphs can have several topic sentences, but the thesis statement controls the whole essay and one essay can only have one thesis statement.

✿ Characteristics of an Effective Thesis Statement

◆ **Specific and limited:** It should serve to focus the entire essay. A vague or general thesis will lead to an unfocused, meandering essay.

Compare:

A. This city is a great place to live in.

B. One reason to live in this city is access to many wonderful places to visit.

◆ **Assertive:** It states the main idea with a strong sense of belief.

Compare:

A. Though there is no proof, communication by email, blog or IM may be better ways of communication than face-to-face communication.

B. Neurobiologists have found out that no form of communication can replace face-to-face communication.

◆ **Arguable:** It is not something that everyone is likely to agree upon; otherwise, the essay may lack energy and interest.

Compare:

A. The average temperature for the island in winter is 5°C and in summer is 25°C.

B. The climate in the island is ideal for outdoor sports.

◆ **Unique:** It should make an original assertion about the subject.

Compare:

A. In William Faulkner's story, "A Rose for Emily," Emily represents the deteriorating American Southern aristocracy.

B. In William Faulkner's story, "A Rose for Emily," the narrator represents the real protagonist of the story and his relationship with Emily is at least as important as her relationship with her former lover, Homer Barron.

To be successful, an introductory paragraph should create interest in the essay and give much helpful information that the reader will need in order to appreciate or understand ideas. In order to grab the reader's attention, writers often begin the introductory paragraph in the following ways:

1. Make the thesis statement directly.
2. Provide background information or interesting details.
3. Raise a question (and answer it with key terms).
4. Give a quotation.
5. Use a shocking or dramatic statement.
6. Provide a definition, preferably not a dictionary one.
7. Tell an anecdote.
8. Cast a glance at the opposition.
9. Combine two or more of this list.

35

Exercise

Read the following introductory paragraphs, find out the thesis statement and comment on the way each paragraph is started.

> (1) One of the enduring pieces of folk wisdom was uttered by the 19th century humorist Artemus Ward, who warned his readers, "It ain't what you don't know that hurts you; it's what you know that just ain't so." There is good advice in that warning to some of television's most vociferous critics.

> (2) "When China awakes," Napoleon is said to have warned, "the world will tremble." For more than a century and a half after his time, that prospect seemed remote. China was devastated by flood, famine, rebellion, warlordism, invasion, civil strife and, finally, a disastrous "Cultural Revolution." It's all the more of a shock, then, that the sleeping dragon has now awoken with a vengeance.

> (3) The birth of American democracy has often been associated with the Mayflower Compact. The compact, to be sure, demonstrated the Englishman's striking capacity for self-government. And in affirming the principle of majority rule, the Pilgrims showed how far they had come from the days when the king's whim was law and nobody dared say otherwise. But the emphasis on the compact is misplaced. Scholarly research in the last half century indicates that the compact had nothing to do with the development of self-government in America. In truth, the Mayflower Compact was no more a cornerstone of American democracy than the Pilgrim hut was the foundation of American architecture. As Samuel Eliot Morison so emphatically put it, American democracy "was not born in the cabin of the *Mayflower*."

Body Paragraphs

The body of an essay consists of several well-developed paragraphs, each beginning with its own topic sentence that, ideally, reveals the organization not only of the essay and but also of the paragraph it introduces. Development of the body paragraphs should be organized, thorough, and unified. There exist some general "modes of arrangement" for arranging information within an essay: examples and illustrations, data, facts, historical or personal details, narratives, description, comparison and contrast, process analysis, definition, division and classification, cause and effect. Major modes of arrangement will be further explained in the following chapters.

The Concluding Paragraph

The concluding paragraph consists of a restatement of the thesis, a few sentences that present a broadening discussion of the subject of the essay and a closing statement. By restating the thesis, the conclusion presents once again the essay's subject. In this way, the reader is reminded of the essay's controlling idea, what the writer has been trying to inform or to persuade the reader about.

An effective concluding paragraph does not introduce an entirely new idea nor does it insert and begin to discuss a new point. Instead, an effective conclusion may reinforce the thesis in a new way (restate the thesis statement in slightly different words, refer to an idea or a detail from the beginning paragraph), draw an inference not yet explicitly expressed, see the material in a fresh perspective, appeal to the reader to act or consider the thesis, warn the reader of possible consequences, make a potential prediction, quote from some authority to enhance the argument, or point to related topic areas. Occasionally, in some persuasive writings, the conclusion may even contain a delayed statement of the thesis.

Exercise

Read the following concluding paragraphs and comment on the method of conclusion.

(1) The issue here is not about class envy. Rather, it's a perception that government policies are skewed toward helping the already wealthy and powerful. While a December Gallup poll found few respondents wanting the government to attempt to reduce the income gap between rich and poor, 70 percent said it was important for the government to increase opportunities for people to get ahead. What the public wants is not a war on the rich but more policies that promote opportunity.

(2) Christians honor the Pilgrim settlers as devout believers and champions of religious freedom, and they have good reason to do so. But the evidence is clear—despite the importance of the *Mayflower Compact*, it was never intended to stand with the *Declaration of Independence* or the *U.S. Constitution* as a cornerstone of American democracy.

(3) 50% of all fatal traffic accidents involve intoxicated drivers, according to the National Highway Traffic Safety Administration. They say that intoxicated drives cost them somewhere between 11—24 billion dollars each year. It is time to give drunk drivers a message: "Stay off the road. You are costing us pain, injury, and death, and no one has the right to do that."

Ⓐ Sample Essay of Five Paragraphs

The birth of American democracy has often been associated with the *Mayflower Compact*. The compact, to be sure, demonstrated the Englishman's striking capacity for self-government. And in affirming the principle of majority rule, the Pilgrims showed how far they had come from the days when the king's whim was law and nobody dared say otherwise. But the emphasis on the compact is misplaced.

The introductory paragraph casts a glance at the opposition and then makes the thesis statement, expressed in four different ways with more and more emphasis, ending with a quotation.

Scholarly research in the last half century indicates that the compact had nothing to do with the development of self-government in America. In truth, the *Mayflower Compact* was no more a cornerstone of American democracy than the Pilgrim hut was the foundation of American architecture. As Samuel Eliot Morison so emphatically put it, American democracy "was not born in the cabin of the *Mayflower*."

The Pilgrims indeed are miscast as heroes of American democracy. They spurned democracy and would have been shocked to see themselves held up as its defenders. George Willison, regarded as one of the most careful students of the Pilgrims, states that "the merely glance at the history of Plymouth" shows that they were not democrats.

The mythmakers would have us believe that even if the Pilgrims themselves weren't democratic, the *Mayflower Compact* itself was. But in fact the compact was expressly designed to curb freedom, not promote it. The Pilgrim governor and historian, William Bradford, from whom we have gotten nearly all of the information there is about the Pilgrims, frankly conceded as much. Bradford wrote that the purpose of the compact was to control renegades aboard the *Mayflower* who were threatening to go their own way when the ship reached land. Because the Pilgrims had decided to settle in an area outside the jurisdiction of their royal patent, some aboard the *Mayflower* had hinted that upon landing they would "use their owne libertie, for none had power to command them." Under the terms of the compact, they couldn't; the compact required all who lived in the colony to "promise all due submission and obedience" to it.

Furthermore, despite the compact's mention of majority rule, the Pilgrim fathers had no intention of turning over the colony's government to the people. Plymouth was to be ruled by the elite. And the elite wasn't bashful in the least about advancing its claims to superiority. When the *Mayflower*

The 2nd paragraph makes a claim as the first proof for the thesis. Unfortunately, historical evidence about what kind of people the Pilgrims were in the Plymouth is not provided.

The 3rd paragraph strongly supports the thesis with concrete evidence.

The 4th paragraph, an echo to the 2nd paragraph, provides more evidence for the thesis.

Compact was signed, the elite signed first. The second rank consisted of the "goodmen." At the bottom of the list came four servants' names. No women or children signed.

Whether the compact was or was not actually hostile to the democratic spirit, it was deemed sufficiently hostile that during the Revolution the Tories put it to use as "propaganda for the crown." The monarchists made much of the fact that the Pilgrims had chosen to establish an English-style government that placed power in the hands of a governor, not a cleric, and a governor who owed his allegiance not to the people or to a church but to "our dread Sovereign Lord King James." No one thought it significant that the Tories had adopted the principle of majority rule. Tory historian George Chalmers, in a work published in 1780, claimed the central meaning of the compact was the Pilgrims' recognition of the necessity of royal authority. This may have been not only a convenient argument but a true one. It is at least as plausible as the belief that the compact stood for democracy.

The concluding paragraph provides more evidence for the thesis and restates the thesis in different terms.

[H]omework 2

Elaborate on the paragraph you've written. Extend your topic sentence into a brief introductory paragraph, list your main points (topic sentences for the supporting paragraphs), and write a brief concluding paragraph. Discuss your writing in your group.

The Narrative Essay

Tuning-in Activities

Choose one of the activities for group discussion; if none of them interests you, create your own narrative prompts.

Activity 1

Tell a story to your group. The following prompts may be helpful.

Prompt A: Think about a time when you faced a challenge. Tell how you dealt with the challenge and what its outcome was. Narrate the event or a series of events with specific details so that the reader can follow your story.

Prompt B: Think about a time when you visited someone you care about. It might have been a relative who lives far away. It might have been a friend that you go to school with. It might have been someone in the hospital. Tell what happened and how you felt about it.

Prompt C: Think about a time you were afraid. You might have been afraid during a storm or a time you tried something new. Tell what happened and how you felt about it.

Prompt D: Think of a person who has been important to you. He/she might be a real person or a character in fiction. Describe why he/she made such an impression on you or made a difference in your life.

Activity 2

Reconstruct a fairy tale from a different point of view. For instance,

- *Sour Grape (Esope's fable)*
- *Snowwhite and Seven Dwarfs*
- *Cinderella*
- *Ugly Duckling*

OR, use *any example* you like.

Activity 3

Tell a story beginning with **one** of the following:

- Annoying!

- At last!
- If I were /had ...
- My first memory
- "All right. So you want to..."
- You won't believe it, but ...

🎵 Activity 4

Read the following incomplete story and discuss all kinds of possibilities to complete the story.

Vingo

On a crowded bus all the passengers were chattering joyfully except Vingo. He sat in the front dressed in a plain, ill-fitting suit, never moving, his dusty face masking his age. He kept chewing the inside of his lip a lot, frozen into complete silence.

As the bus went on, people began to notice him. Some young people near him were whispering, wondering about his life: perhaps he was a sea captain, a runaway from his wife, or an old soldier going home. After a long while the young people were overcome by their curiosity, and one of the girls moved near and introduced herself.

"We're going to Florida," she said brightly. "I hear it's really beautiful."

"It is," he said quietly, as if remember something he had tried to forget.

"Want some wine?" she suggested. He smiled and took a swig from the bottle. He thanked her and retreated again into his silence. Then Vingo nodded in sleep, and the girl went back to the others.

At noon, the bus pulled into a roadside restaurant. Everybody got off the bus and went in. The girl insisted that Vingo join them. He seemed very shy, and ordered black coffee and smoked nervously as the young people chattered about sleeping on beaches. When they returned to the bus, the girl sat near Vingo again, and after a while, slowly and painfully, he began to tell his story. He had been in jail in New York for the past four years ...

🎵 Activity 5

- Tell the story in the drawing.

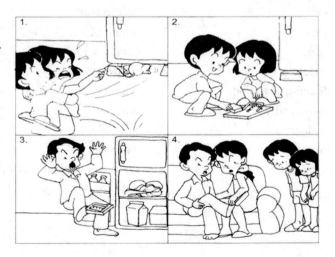

● Use your imagination to create details for the story.

42

Vocabulary: You may find the following list helpful in constructing details in your story. Look the words up if you don't know them and use as many as you can.

 Word list

Shirley Temple	blond
curl	hairdresser
tangled	a mop of
tease	beauty salon
rollers	permanent
burning sensation	whining
hysterically	tantrum
badger	adorable
maturity	overreact
grow up	want ... more than anything

Introduction

A narrative essay tells a story, and therefore involves all the elements of a story: time, place, character and plot. Essentially, it explains about something that happened, relates or recounts an experience, an event, a sequence of events or actions, out of observation or imagination. While telling the story, the narrative writing conveys some meaning, makes a point, teaches a lesson, or says something significant about life, and entertains the reader by appealing to their emotions. Narrative writing can support an analysis and has broad utility in academic writing as a critical skill.

A narrative essay usually begins with an introduction to an event or recurring activity, a personal experience, an observation or imagination, and a particular point of view. One narrative, for example, begins this way:

> *It is hard enough to swallow our own failures; it is even more difficult to tolerate one's friend's undeserved success—especially when you know that you unwittingly helped him to that perch from which he now crows over you.*

It introduces the subject of the essay (a friend's success of some kind with the writer's unwitting help), foreshadows a personal experience and a humorous tone.

The immediate purpose of narration is to bring the story alive to the reader's imagination. For this purpose, narration relies on concrete, sensory details to convey its point, for the reader to form a clear picture of the events and to share the writer's experience. These details should create a unified, forceful effect. The author gives sufficient details about the people, place and events so that the reader gets a clear idea of what's going on and how the author feels about them. For instance,

> *She led him along a dark, narrow passage and up some wooden stairs. The house was filled with junk: broken TV sets and old bicycles, piles of books and empty bottles. The stair rails were covered in cobwebs. They went into a small room at the top of the house.*

Here is a sample story written for Tuning-in Activity 5-B. See if the writer gives sufficient details for the reader.

43

Sample 1

The Road to Adulthood

Like most little girls, I thought it would be very grown up to get my hair done in a beauty parlor instead of by my mother or older sister as it had been done for years. I also knew that at a beauty parlor I could get my limp dull hair changed into shining curls, and I wanted curls more than anything. I was positive that blond waves were just what I needed to acquire the maturity[1] of popularity so essential in the third grade.

For a month I cried and badgered[2] my family, promising everything if they would only let me get my hair done as I wished. Finally, after hearing enough of my whining[3], my mother gave in and made an appointment for me. I was sure I was on my way to become an adorable Shirley Temple[4].

Things didn't turn out quite the way I imagined. To begin with I was not taken to one of the fashionable beauty houses I had often seen on my way home from school, but rather to the oldest salon[5] in town. Its outdated interior hosted only a few older women getting their thin hair inexpertly teased over their visible pink scalps. I should have suspected then and there that things would not be the way I dreamed, but still, naïve, I waited for my transformation.[6] I sat through my appointment nutmeat[7] never questioning the mass of hair that fell to the floor nor the burning sensation as the rollers were pulled tight against my head. In fact it wasn't until I arrived home that I was able to take a good look in the mirror to see what had happened. Looking back at me was not a reflection of a cute curly top, but instead a mop of indescribable frizz[8]: the classic example of the overworked permanent.[9]

Needless to say I overreacted and spent the remaining part of the day washing and re-washing my hair to remove the tangled mess. When this did little to improve the situation, I cried hysterically[10] for hours, my head well hidden beneath a pillow. It

1. maturity: *n.* 成熟

2. badger: *v.* harass or pester persistently

3. whine: *v.* utter a plaintive, high-pitched, protracted sound, as in pain, fear, supplication, or complaint

4. Shirley Temple: 秀兰·邓波儿,生于1928年,6岁时即出演美国歌舞片,大获成功。她的演唱、舞蹈、灿烂的笑容和卷曲的金发使无数人为之倾倒。

5. salon: *n.* a commercial establishment offering a product or service related to fashion: a beauty salon

6. transformation: *n.* marked or drastic change in appearance

7. nutmeat: *adv.* stupidly

8. frizz: *n.* 卷发

9. permanent: *n.* a series of waves in the hair made by applying heat and chemicals

10. hysterical: *adj.* frantic, crazy

44

took a week until I would see anyone without a towel over my head and a month before I could look at someone without feeling that they were making fun of me the minute I turned my back.

When I think about how silly I behaved, I always laugh. Now it seems easy to accept such small disappointment, but if you had asked me then I would have assured you that nothing could possibly have been worse. In a way I feel that such a fruitless journey to the hairdresser actually helped me a bit further along the road to adulthood since it was a perfect example of a disappointing obstacle that can be improved only by time and patience, not by tantrums[11] or senseless worrying.

11. tantrum: *n.* 发脾气

The writer tells a retrospective story: the adult tells a story of the past. In all but the last paragraph, however, she tells the story from the experiencing self—the point of view of an innocent little girl. She chooses details adequate to the little girl to appeal to the reader. In the final paragraph, the writer reflects on the larger meaning or importance of the experience described. She concludes that the fruitless journey to the hairdresser was "a perfect example of a disappointing obstacle that can be improved only by time and patience, not by tantrums or senseless worrying." This lesson is meaningful to all people, children on their way to adulthood in particular, and thus makes a good point of the story.

Homework 1

Decide on a story you're going to tell, write an introduction to it and list as many details as you can. Bring the story to class next time for further discussion. Don't worry about the language mistakes such as grammar errors and misspellings. Focus on the content of the story.

Narrative Writing Skills

Format: As mentioned above, the story should have an introduction that clearly indicates what kind of narrative essay it is (an event or recurring activity, a personal experience, or an observation), the setting and the plot. The story begins in a certain place at a certain time with a character or some characters. In the beginning paragraph, we need to catch the reader's interest so that they will want to continue with the story, and to give them enough information to understand the following actions. Many stories end with a conclusion that makes a point. But the meaning can be implied or left to the reader.

Order: A narrative essay is to move an event through time. It generally follows a chronological order to make it easy for the reader to follow, although sometimes writers choose to withhold certain information from the reader, or to use flashback, in order to create suspense and make the story more interesting.

Narrator: The person telling the story is the point of view of the narrative. The most commonly used points of view are (1) the third person and (2) the first person. Each has its advantage and disadvantage. A first-person narrative may be more graphic and lifelike, because it gives the reader the impression that it is what the writer has seen or experienced. But the scope of the narrative may be limited, for it is difficult to recount events that happen in different places at the same time. A third-person narrative is free from this limitation. And it may seem more objective, but it is not easy to put in good order things that happen to different people in different places. Beginner writers are encouraged to stick to one point of view throughout the story.

Character: The character refers to the person or something with human characteristics. The main character in a story faces a problem against another character, a difficult situation or an idea and has to take some action. He/she may win, lose or tie and may learn from the experience or miss the point. Characters in a story become believable with their realistic actions, speech and feelings. For example,

> *The anger inside her went boiling and boiling, and as she lay in bed that night she made a decision. She decided that every time her father or her mother was beastly to her, she would get her own back in some way or another. A small victory or two would help her to tolerate their idiocies and would stop her from going crazy.*

Plot: Plot is the plan for the development of the actions, or the way we arrange how the conflict begins, how it develops and finally how it is resolved in the story. When actions in a story take place in relation with one another, plot is established. As the British novelist E. M. Forster illustrates, the sentence, "The king died, and then the queen died." narrates just a sequence of events in chronological order, while the sentence, "The king died, and then the queen died of grief." contains a plot.

Conflicts: The most essential element of plot is conflict. In a story, the characters are always involved in some kind of struggle, which sets in motion their actions. This struggle is called the conflict. There are normally three kinds of conflicts: between one character and another; between a character and himself/herself, or between a character and the environment (nature or society). The conflict and its consequent tension lead to a climax, a crucial point of inevitability and no return, to be followed by a resolution, actions that bring the story to a conclusion.

Exercise

Read the following samples carefully and review the narrative skills.

46

Vocabulary

Purchasing the Wedding Ring

The nervous-looking young man hesitated for a few moments outside the jeweler's before summoning up[1] the courage to enter. He was cordially[2] greeted by a young assistant who offered to help him. James felt a rush of blood to his face as he explained he would be bringing in his fiancée[3] to choose an engagement ring later that day. The assistant listened attentively and assured him that the best way to proceed would be to make up a couple of trays of rings which would suit both the young man's pocket and the young lady's tastes. James visibly calmed down a little, worried about overspending. Getting married was an expensive business but hopefully it would be a once-in-a-life time occasion. After some discussion as to a suitable price-range and the variety of styles and materials which his fiancée might like, the sales assistant showed him a couple of dozen rings and offered to set them aside. James approved her choice and, much relieved[4], left the shop promising to return at five o'clock. When, half an hour later than planned, he finally did return to the shop, accompanied by his fiancée, Laura, the assistant acted as if she had never seen him before. On being asked to show them some engagement rings she first brought out a rather inexpensive selection, giving the couple the opportunity to reject them before showing them the two trays she had prepared. A choice was soon made and the couple went away satisfied. James would certainly come here when it was time to buy the wedding ring!

1. summon up: take effort to bring out, muster
2. cordially: *adv.* warmly
3. fiancée: *n.* 未婚妻

4. relieved: *adj.* feeling happy because no longer worried about something

47

Sample 3

Monday dawned warm and rainless. Aurelio Escovar, a dentist without a degree, and a very early riser, opened his office at six. He took some false teeth, still mounted in their plaster mold, out of the glass case and put on the table a fistful of instruments which he arranged in size order, as if they were on display. He wore a collarless striped shirt, closed at the neck with a golden stud[1], and pants held up by suspenders. He was erect and skinny, with a look that rarely corresponded to the situation, the way deaf people have of looking.

When he had things arranged on the table, he pulled the drill toward the dental chair and sat down to polish the false teeth. He seemed not to be thinking about what he was doing, but worked steadily, pumping the drill with his feet, even when he didn't need it.

After eight he stopped for a while to look at the sky through the window, and he saw two pensive buzzards[2] who were drying themselves in the sun on the ridgepole[3] of the house next door. He went on working with the idea that before lunch it would rain again. The shrill voice of his eleven-year-old son interrupted his concentration.

"Papa."

"What?"

"The Mayor wants to know if you'll pull his tooth."

"Tell him I'm not here."

He was polishing a gold tooth. He held it at arm's length, and examined it with his eyes half closed. His son shouted again from the little waiting room.

"He says you are, too, because he can hear you."

The dentist kept examining the tooth. Only when he had put it on the table with the finished work did he say:

"So much the better."

1. stud: *n.* 领扣

2. buzzard: *n.* type of large hawk
3. ridgepole: *n.* 栋梁

48

He operated the drill again. He took several pieces of a bridge out of a cardboard box where he kept the things he still had to do and began to polish the gold.

"Papa."

"What?"

He still hadn't changed his expression.

"He says if you don't take out his tooth, he'll shoot you."

Without hurrying, with an extremely tranquil[4] movement, he stopped pedaling the drill, pushed it away from the chair, and pulled the lower drawer of the table all the way out. There was a revolver. "O.K.," he said. "Tell him to come and shoot me."

He rolled the chair over opposite the door, his hand resting on the edge of the drawer. The Mayor appeared at the door. He had shaved the left side of his face, but the other side, swollen and in pain, had a five-day-old beard. The dentist saw many nights of desperation in his dull eyes. He closed the drawer with his fingertips and said softly:

"Sit down."

"Good morning," said the Mayor.

"Morning," said the dentist.

While the instruments were boiling, the Mayor leaned his skull on the headrest of the chair and felt better. His breath was icy. It was a poor office: an old wooden chair, the pedal drill, a glass case with ceramic[5] bottles. Opposite the chair was a window with a shoulder-high cloth curtain. When he felt the dentist approach, the Mayor braced[6] his heels and opened his mouth.

Aurelio Escovar turned his head toward the light. After inspecting the infected tooth, he closed the Mayor's jaw with a cautious pressure of his fingers.

"It has to be without anesthesia,"[7] he said.

"Why?"

"Because you have an abscess."[8]

The Mayor looked at him in the eye. "All right," he said, and tried to smile. The dentist did not return the smile. He brought the basin of

4. tranquil: *adj.* calm, peaceful and relaxed

5. ceramic: *n.* 瓷

6. brace: *v.* press against sth. in order to keep steady

7. anesthesia: *n.* 麻醉剂
8. abscess: *n.* 脓肿

sterilized instruments to the worktable and took them out of the water with a pair of cold tweezers[9], still without hurrying. Then he pushed the spittoon[10] with the tip of his shoe, and went to wash his hands in the washbasin. He did all this without looking at the Mayor. But the Mayor didn't take his eyes off him.

It was a lower wisdom tooth. The dentist spread his feet and grasped the tooth with the hot forceps[11]. The Mayor seized the arms of the chair, braced his feet with all his strength, and felt an icy void in his kidneys, but didn't make a sound. The dentist moved only his wrist. Without rancor[12], rather with a bitter tenderness, he said:

"Now you'll pay for our twenty dead men."

The Mayor felt the crunch[13] of bones in his jaw, and his eyes filled with tears. But he didn't breathe until he felt the tooth come out. Then he saw it through his tears. It seemed so foreign to his pain that he failed to understand his torture of the five previous nights.

Bent over the spittoon, sweating, panting, he unbuttoned his tunic[14] and reached for the handkerchief in his pants pocket. The dentist gave him a clean cloth.

"Dry your tears," he said.

The Mayor did. He was trembling. While the dentist washed his hands, he saw the crumbling ceiling and a dusty spider web with spider's eggs and dead insects. The dentist returned, drying his hands. "Go to bed," he said, "and gargle[15] with salt water." The Mayor stood up, said goodbye with a casual military salute, and walked toward the door, stretching his legs, without buttoning up his tunic.

"Send the bill," he said.

"To you or the town?"

The Mayor didn't look at him. He closed the door and said through the screen:

"It's the same damn thing."

---

9. tweezers: *n.* 镊子
10. spittoon: *n.* 痰盂

11. forceps: *n.* 钳子

12. rancor: *n.* 积怨

13. crunch: *n.* 嘎吱嘎吱的声音

14. tunic: *n.* 紧身短上衣

15. gargle: *v.* wash one's mouth by filling it with liquid, tilting one's head back, and breathing out, making a bubbling noise

Make the Story Vivid and Lively

Using specific, concrete details

An essay with many vague or abstract sentences will leave the reader confused and without a clear understanding of your topic. Instead, your writing should contain specific, concrete details to help the reader visualize what you are discussing and hold the reader's attention. Using the RENNS model, developed by Lynn Quitman Troyka, can help you make your writing more specific.

RENNS stands for <u>R</u>easons, <u>E</u>xamples, <u>N</u>ames, <u>N</u>umbers, <u>S</u>enses (sight, sound, smell, taste, touch).The following examples illustrate how you can use this device.

REASONS (Why?)

General	Specific
Student parking is becoming an important issue on many college campuses.	**Because of the increasing numbers of students commuting to college,** parking is becoming an important issue.

EXAMPLES (What?)

General	Specific
The handbook is a good guide for using documentation.	The **MLA** handbook provides a guide for **documenting works cited.**

NAMES (Who?)

General	Specific
The governor of Minnesota enacted legislation that decreased the amount of aid available to college students.	The governor of Minnesota, **Arne Carlson**, enacted legislation that decreased the amount of aid available to **middle-income** college students.

NUMBERS (How many?)

General	Specific
Even though many members of the student congress were absent, the motion still passed.	Even though **thirteen** members of the student congress were absent, the motion still passed.

SENSES

Sight

General	Specific
After we viewed the movie about nuclear destruction, we better understood the devastating effects of this type of warfare.	After we viewed the **enormous mushroom cloud** produced by a nuclear bomb, we better understood the devastating effects of this type of warfare.

Sound

General	Specific
The music was very loud at the rock concert last night. ·	**My ears are still ringing today** because the music was very loud at the rock concert last night.

Smell

General	Specific
Through the use of aromatherapy, many retail stores are trying to enhance their customers' moods to increase business.	By using **floral perfumes or outdoor scent**s, many retail stores are trying to make their customers feel like they are in a **natural setting**.

Taste

General	Specific
The university sponsored a festival which featured Japanese foods.	The university sponsored a festival featuring **hot, spicy Japanese foods.**

Touch

General	Specific
The Braille system of communication uses touch to convey a message.	The Braille system of communication requires a person to touch **a series of raised dots** to convey a message.

A narrative is a moving picture. It needs to have a rich texture of details so that the reader is seeing, hearing, smelling, and touching. Often these details should suit the purpose of the narration and create a unified, forceful effect, a **dominant impression**. The reader should experience the story, not simply hear it. For example:

He sat in the front dressed in a plain, ill-fitting suit, never moving, his dusty face masking his age. He kept chewing the inside of his lip a lot, frozen into complete silence.

Exercise

Work in pairs. Go back to the readings to find out detailed descriptions of people, the environment, and attitudes. Then tell your partner the impressions they leave on you.

✿ Using verbs

Verbs are vivid and precise.

Exercises

1. Write down as many sensory verbs and related words as possible.

    hear, _____

    see, watch, peep, glance, look, _____

    smell, _____

    taste, bit, swallow _____

    feel, touch _____

2. Fill in the blanks with words meaning "*look*."

The life of a sentence depends to a great extent on its verbs, the word that directs the action. In the sentence " The professor looked at the student", the verb is general and lifeless, and therefore should be substituted with some other verbs; _____ suggests a lengthy look, perhaps at some wrongdoing; _____, a steady look, maybe of admiration or appreciation; _____, a quick look, probably as a check; and _____, a searching look, probably through glasses or with squinting eyes.

✿ Using dialogs

Dialogs help show the conflict, describe action, foretell events and bring life to the character, giving the character breath and reality. Wisely used dialog adds vividness and liveliness. However few stories are written entirely in dialog. Rather it is used only in appropriate places and for legitimate reasons, often to dramatize events or reveal characters convincingly. There should be a satisfying balance between narration and dialog. Too much dialog runs the risk of monotony. At the same time, the speaker's language should be suitable for his status as it tells much about his education, intelligence, attitude and character.

> *I crashed right into someone and sent them flying. It was old Mrs. Jeeves from across the road. "Sorry," I said. "Gee, I'm sorry." I helped her stand up. She was a bit short sighted and it was dark. She hadn't noticed that I didn't have clothes on. Then the moon came out — the blazing moon. I tried to cover my nakedness with my hands, but it was no good. "Disgusting," she screeched. "Disgusting. I'll tell your father about this."*

✿ Paragraphing

In order to maintain the *unity* in each paragraph in the narrative writing, you should follow certain rules to begin a new paragraph. Here are some points where you might start a new paragraph.

● The time or place changes in the story.

● Another person appears.

- Something important happens in the story.
- Another person speaks in a conversation.
- You stop telling the story and begin to interpret it.

Note:

There are two extremes to avoid in writing a narrative. First, you simply tell the story, event by event, without giving it any texture because you leave out descriptive details and dialogs. At the opposite extreme is a narrative that attempts to tell everything, painting detailed descriptions of every scene, quoting everything that is said, even speculating about the thoughts of the characters. A good narrative has texture, but it is suggestive rather than exhaustive. After all, the reader's imagination needs some room to fill in details. Giving too many details not only overwhelms the reader's imagination, but also slows the pace of the narrative.

To summarize, the narrative essay

- is told from a particular point of view;
- makes and supports a point;
- is filled with precise details;
- uses vivid verbs and modifiers;
- uses conflict and sequence as does any story;
- may use dialogs.

54

Exercises

1. Correct the inconsistency in point of view in the following narratives

Often it took a teacher no more than few minutes to conceive a raging dislike for me. I recalled the instructor in elementary French who shied a textbook at my head the very first day you went to his class. We had never laid eyes on each other until fifteen or twenty minutes before he assaulted me. I no longer remember what, if anything, provoked him to violence. It is possible that one said something that was either insolent or nothing at all. Even your silence, your humility, your acquiescence, could annoy your teacher. The very sight of me, the mere awareness of my existence on earth, could be unendurable irritating to them.

2. How will the sentences be affected if the italicized words or phrases are replaced by those in the ensuing brackets?
   (1) When he *closed* (shut, banged) the door, the girl *cried out* (screamed, shrieked, yelled).
   (2) That day I *saw* (noticed, observed, watched, witnessed) them *walking along* (doddering along, trudging along, strolling about, trotting along) the streets.
   (3) What he had *done* (performed, achieved, executed, fished for) made his colleagues and friends *surprised* (alarmed, startled, irritated, baffled).

3. Put each verb, in its appropriate form, into one of the spaces in the following sentences.

jump, fly, stagger, sprint, hop, slip, wade, shuffle, limp, toddle

(1) The runners _____ to the finishing-post.

(2) I could tell he was drunk because he was _____ from one side of the road to the other.

(3) The baby _____ across the room towards his mother.

(4) I'll be back in a moment. I must just _____ down to the shop for some sugar.

(5) The poor old man _____ down the road.

(6) She had hurt her ankle, and _____ painfully into the room.

(7) There was no bridge, but luckily the river was not deep and we would be able to _____ across.

(8) Ten people were trapped in the burning building, and they _____ into blankets held by firemen in the street below.

(9) When she heard the postman arrive, she _____ down the stairs as she was expecting a letter from her fiancé.

(10) He could only find one shoe, so he _____ across the room on one foot.

4. Put each noun, in its appropriate form, into one of the spaces in the following sentences.

place, location, site, position, neighborhood, territory, land, premises, plot, zone

(1) When I retire I want to live in the country, and I have already bought a _____ of land by the sea where I am going to build a house.

(2) This hotel is built on the _____ of an old monastery.

(3) The police have not yet been able to find the exact _____ of the crime.

(4) It is regarded as a _____ of great natural beauty, and people often come here to paint.

(5) My grandfather's house stood in a very exposed _____, on the top of a hill.

(6) The _____ between the two frontiers is No-Man's land.

(7) The 'Green Dragon' is the most popular pub in the _____.

(8) No unauthorized people are allowed on the _____.

(9) The plains are arable _____ but the hills are not cultivatable.

(10) Those islands are still British _____, but the hills are not cultivated.

5. Read and discuss the story.

Sample 4

Fragile: Please Touch

As she sat in the cafeteria of the psychiatric[1] hospital, Jean felt as old as twice her forty years. She was angry. She was sitting across the table from a woman who had killed her own child. Jean knew all about it; she had read the newspaper.

"Hi," the woman said.

"Hi," Jean mumbled[2], looking at the floor.

"This coffee is terrible..." The woman tried again, her soft, child-like voice willing a response.

Jean slowly lifted her gaze—past the slippered feet and the drab, mustard-yellow hospital robe, up to a pretty face with a fleeting smile, framed by thick blonde hair carelessly tied into a ponytail. She studied the shimmering[3], young blue eyes that simultaneously searched Jean's older stony gray ones.

Unperturbed[4] by the glare, the woman continued: "My doctor said to try to get to know you because you are a nice lady."

Jean thought: "I am a nice lady. I don't kill children." But she said: "My name is Jean."

"Hi," the woman repeated.

A cold silence followed. Jean wondered how she could continue. She knew this woman had killed her own child. From the moment Jean had read about her in the paper she had hated this woman. She should be in jail. Jean wanted to scream at the woman, to shake her, to ask her "why? ... how?" But instead she just tried to sip coffee from her clumsy institutional cup that trembled in her hands. The bitterness forced her to agree: "You are right, this coffee is terrible."

The woman looked past Jean towards the rain that was starting to spatter[5] on the nearby window. Tears welled up in her eyes. "I have just suffered a terrible loss," she began, "My little girl is gone. She was only three."

Jean looked towards the face once more, this

1. psychiatric: *adj.* 精神病的

2. mumble: *v.* to speak indistinctly, almost to an unintelligible extent

3. shimmer: *v.* to gleam faintly

4. perturb: *v.* to disturb or disquiet greatly in mind

5. spatter: *v.* to strike or dash in small drops

time glimpsing part of her own reflection in the brimming[6] tears.

"I'm so sorry for you," Jean responded instinctively. "I lost a child, too, but she..." Jean couldn't believe what she was saying ... sharing with someone like this ... "but she died before she was born ... I just can't imagine..." Jean couldn't say any more. The ache in her throat choked[7] the words.

The woman reached across the table to hold Jean's hand. Jean felt the warm, smooth fingers as they gently covered her own. Briefly she let the old pain surface, allowing it to be soothed[8] by the touch of another who truly understood. But then the horror returned. This was different! This woman killed her child! It wasn't right to hold a killer's hand. Jean pulled away, embarrassed that she had momentarily forgotten...

But the woman kept on: "I am sick, you know, mentally sick, but I am all right if I take medicine. We wanted to have another baby, and I stopped taking my pills. I was O. K., really I was O. K., until, well... until she died..." The woman looked away. Jean just sat and waited, repulsed[9] but curious.

Slowly the woman's words began again. Frightened, small words: "I don't remember what happened. I don't really know ... I just know that she is dead. I wish I was dead."

Jean didn't want to believe that it was possible to kill your own child and not even remember, but she knew that mental illness could be that profound. "It must be very frightening to forget..." Jean thought aloud.

The woman was crying openly now, sobs racking[10] her body. Her hands covered her face. Jean could remember the intensity of the pain of losing a child, especially when it was so fresh and new. Impulsively[11] Jean needed to hug her. She rose and moved closer, gently placing her hands on the quivering shoulders. She cooed[12] and caressed until the young mother was able to stop

6. brim: *v.* to be completely full

7. choke: *v.* to suppress

8. soothe: *v.* to tranquilize or calm; relieve

9. repulse: *v.* to repel with denial, discourtesy; refuse or reject

10. rack: *v.* to torture; distress acutely; torment

11. impulsively: *adv.* act suddenly without thinking about the sensibility, results, etc.

12. coo: *v.* speak softly and lovingly

57

crying. Then the woman stood, whispered a quick: "Thank-you," and walked away.

Jean was left standing, looking out the window at the rain swept fields beyond. She wished she had hugged her.

"How could you do that?" came a voice from behind.

Startled, Jean turned. "Do what?"

"Touch her, even look at her!" The voice insisted. "Don't you know what she has done?"

Thoughtfully, Jean smoothed her own hospital robe with her offending hands. "Yes, I know ..."

"Then, how could you touch her?" the voice persisted.

Jean explained: "She touched me!" Then she added as she walked away:

"...Twice!"

Questions for Consideration

1. How do you like the title? Is there anything unusual about it?

2. In what sense is Jean "touched" twice?

3. Underline the verb meaning "to shine" or "to glow" and try to tell their shades of meaning.

4. How does the story reflect the characters' psychology with description of their action?

5. Does the story make a point? If not overtly, is there a point in the story? What is it?

Sample 5

Vocabulary

Wen Ping and his company pursued Zhao Zilong till they saw Zhang Fei's bristling[1] mustache and fiercely glaring[2] eyes before them. There he was seated on his battle steed, his hand grasping his terrible serpent spear, guarding the bridge. They also saw great clouds of dust rising above the trees and concluded they would fall into an ambush[3] if they ventured across the bridge. So they stopped the pursuit, not daring to advance further.

In a little time Cao Ren, Xiahou Dun, Xiahou Yuan, Li Dian, Yue Jing, Zhang Liao, Xu Chu, Zhang He, and other generals of Cao Cao came

1. bristle: *v.* stand stiffly on end
2. glare: *v.* stare fixedly and angrily

3. ambush: *n.* 埋伏

up, but none dared advance, frightened not only by Zhang Fei's fierce look, but lest they should become victims of a ruse[4] of Zhuge Liang. As they came up, they formed a line on the west side, halting till they could inform their lord of the position.

As soon as the messengers arrived and Cao Cao heard about it, he mounted and rode to the bridge to see for himself. Zhang Fei's fierce eye scanning the hinder position of the army opposite him saw the silken umbrella, the axes and banners coming along, and concluded that Cao Cao came to see for himself how matters stood.

So in a mighty voice he shouted: "I am Zhang Fei of Yan. Who dares fight with me?"

At the sound of this thunderous voice, a terrible quaking fear seized upon Cao Cao, and he bade[5] them take the umbrella away.

Turning to his followers, he said, "Guan Yu had said that his brother Zhang Fei was the sort of man to go through an army of a hundred legions[6] and take the head of its commander-in-chief, and do it easily. Now here is this terror in front of us, and we must be careful."

As he finished speaking, again that terrible voice was heard, "I am Zhang Fei of Yan. Who dares fight with me?"

Cao Cao, seeing his enemy so fierce and resolute, was too frightened to think of anything but retreat.

Zhang Fei, seeing a movement going on in the rear, once again shook his spear and roared, "What mean you? You will not fight nor do you run away!"

This roar had scarcely begun when one of Cao Cao's staff, Xiahou Jie, reeled and fell from his horse terror-stricken, paralyzed with fear. The panic touched Cao Cao and spread to his whole surroundings, and he and his staff galloped for their lives. They were as frightened as a suckling babe at a clap of thunder or a weak woodcutter at the roar of a tiger. Many threw away their spears,

4. ruse: *n.* 策略;花招.

5. bid: *v.* order

6. legion: *n.* 军团;部队

59

dropped their casques[7] and fled, a wave of panic-stricken humanity, a tumbling mass of terrified horses. None thought of ought but flight, and those who ran trampled the bodies of fallen comrades under foot.

7. casque: *n.* 盔

(From *Romance of the Three Kingdoms* by Luo Guanzhong, translated by C. H. Brewitt-Taylor
http://threekingdoms.com/042.htm)

What makes this episode vivid and lively?

Homework 2

Write your first draft of the narrative essay and ask two students to read and to offer suggestions.

Polish Your Story

Activity 1

Work in groups and correct the errors in each of the following sentences.

(1) They saw a very sick old beggar in the street and they sent him to the hospital, the doctor said he needed an operation.

(2) The poor old man has no relation in this town.

(3) ... he ate the medicine.

(4) I really love Bob but I can't receive the money (Bob left for her before he went to the war).

(5) He had no money to afford to the hospital.

(6) He had enough funds to make it (his dream) true.

Hint: Look up the word in an English-English dictionary to get a good understanding of the **connotation** and **usage** of the words: *send, relation, eat, afford* and *fund*.

Activity 2

The following are Chinese English sentences. Did you make the same kinds of mistakes? If so, put your sentences on the blackboard and ask the whole class to help you improve them.

(1) He studied in a rich school. (他在一所贵族学校读书。)

(2) A businessman gave a high price to buy it. (一个商人出很高的价买了它。)

(3) They knocked at her door but nobody opened the door. (他们敲她的门但是没有人来

开门。)
(4) Some students waste time talking about love in the classroom. (有的学生浪费时间，在教室里谈恋爱。)

Activity 3

Some sentences are not wrong in terms of grammar but inefficient because of wordiness. Try to improve the following sentences, and then improve your wordy expressions in the second draft.

(1) She was affected by a kind of poison. (Abstract modifier)

(2) This machine was jointly designed by the old engineer in collaboration with some of his young colleagues. (Repetition of words with the same meaning)

(3) In my opinion, I think your plan is feasible. (Repetition of words with the same meaning)

(4) When you come to the second traffic light, turn right. (Conciseness can sometimes be achieved by changing the sentence structure: when you can use a phrase, don't use a sentence.)

(5) *Moby Dick* is a book. It is a long book. It is about a whale. A man named Ahab tries to kill it. Herman Melville wrote it. (Combine the sentences using the same structure: Subject +Verb.)

(6) There was an oak tree that stood like a giant at the entrance of the village. It towered over the trees and houses around it. ("There be ..." structure sometimes can be wordy.)

(7) The doctor examined the patient and the operation began. (Changing the subject makes the sentence neither coherent nor concise.)

Activity 4

Make the following sentences concise.

(1) In the year of 1939, the Second World War broke out.

(2) He returned back home after he graduated from university.

(3) The cause of the flood was due to the heavy rain in late spring.

(4) He opened the door. He went into the kitchen. He baked the potatoes.

(5) The work was repetitious. The boredom made me desperate.

(6) A Stone that is rolling gathers no moss.

(7) If there is no software, the computer would be useless.

(8) The problem is that enough food should be provided.

(9) He did not tell the truth with an honest attitude.

(10) There are a number of students who want to join the drama club.

(11) She was kind enough to let me share the umbrella with her.

(12) He asked the teacher to repeat the question again.

Activity 5

Discuss the problematic words and expressions from the students' writing.

Homework 3

Work in groups of three or four to have your first draft and the instructor's comments and suggestions read and discussed for improvements. Here are some questions you may ask in your discussion:

1. Does the narrative tell a significant main event? Is the main event told through a mixture of action, description, dialogue, thoughts and feelings?
2. How is the narrative organized?
3. Does the beginning grab the reader's attention and introduce the reader to the story?
4. Does the narrative elaborate on characters, settings, and objects through the senses?
5. Does the narrative have a suspense or tension?
6. How is the ending? Does it express a view or a feeling that is meaningful to other people?

Revise your essay on the basis of your discussion.

Analysis of Students' Writing

Student's Free Writing

My National Holiday

My National holiday came to an end yesterday. My first taste of Liaoning was refreshing. I enjoyed several relaxing days with my classmate in her hometown, Yingkou. I really appreciate her treat.

Yingkou is located at the coastal areas of Bohai bay. So, seafoods are available there and we did a whole lot of eating.

The food in Yingkou is amazing. We had a seafood buffet. BBQ there is sort of different from Tianjin; We also tried Hot Pot there. Hot pot is a typical Northern dish. So we had to try. It is really nice, especially when put some pickles into the pot.

Let me tell you more about my trip there.

I am thankful that her mother drove us to the mountain to pick some apples. I like the experience very much, because I can pick up fruits on my own and also learn some skills of farming.

My classmate took me to the sea as well. I think it should be the first time that I see the sea with a beach. Faced the coming waves, I was satisfied. So I took off my shoes, walked along the beach. The feeling is exactly relaxed.

I'd like to sum up by saying: this vacation was special, and I was fortunate enough to experience the life in the Northeast of China. I like there and I really appreciate my classmate's treat.

Comments

In the free writing, the student just wrote what occurred to her when she reflected on her last holiday experience, with little consideration for structure, grammar and spelling. Upon reading her free writing and discussing it in her group, she discovered that she talked about three activities: enjoying seafood, walking on the beach and picking apples, that it had been a pleasant and relaxing experience, and that she was grateful to her friend for the experience. She decided to highlight her feelings and structure the essay by the activities.

Student's First Draft

A Trip to Yingkou

I had a relaxing and refreshing trip to my friend, Yalan's home at Yingkou, Liaoning Province during the National Day holidays.

We ate a lot amazing seafood in Yingkou. Yingkou located at the coastal areas of Bohai bay and so is rich in seafood. We ate all kinds of seafood. I especially like the seafood barbecue there: Many people sat around a table, in a small peaceful yard. We chatted casually while roasted seafood together. Seafood also served in a hot pot. They taste delicious, especially when pickles are put in the pot.

I relaxed myself on the beach. Yalan took me to the seaside. It was my first time to stand on so beautiful a beach. The delicate sand and gentle waves invited me. So I took off my shoes, walked along the beach. It was a very exciting and relaxing experience.

Picking apples was another thrilling experience. Yalan's mother drove us to the mountain to pick apples. We went to an orchard and picked up two baskets of apples. I learned some farming skills and ate two fresh apples from the tree.

I'll never forget my trip to Yalan's home at Yingkou.

63

Comments

This draft is unified and structurally well organized, with a thesis statement in the beginning, three supporting paragraphs with a topic sentence in each, and a concluding sentence/paragraph to echo the beginning, but it is a rather dull narrative that few people will choose to read.

The direct opening explains the impact of the experience on the writer, but can hardly attract the reader's attention. The three supporting paragraphs make some relevant reference to her thesis, but vague terms and scant details make them boring. In addition, grammatical errors in the second paragraph interfere with meaning and further distract the reader's attention. The concluding paragraph tries to convey a strong emotion to reinforce the thesis, but without prior details, it's little more than a slogan, hardly convincing.

The writing could be improved by emphasizing on one of the events with more vivid details to convey the emotional impact of the event and to capture the reader's interest.

Student's Third Draft

Friendship Warming up while Apples Cooling Off

My friendship with Yalan warmed up during the National Day break when she took me to her hometown at Yingkou, Liaoning Province.

Yalan and I made friends about one month after we became classmates in TFSU in spite of our different characters: She is proper and hardworking, while I'm talkative and brash at times. Mutually attracted to the other by what is absent in ourselves, we often hang together. Her invitation for me to visit her family, however, came as a surprise at the beginning of our second fall semester. I accepted it all too eagerly though.

Yalan is a good host and her parents are very nice to me. We enjoyed the sandy beach, and at her encouragement, I ventured some queer seafood. However, the most exquisite experience was picking apples in Mount Chi.

On Oct. 5, Yalan's mother drove us for nearly two hours to an orchard at the foot of Mount Chi in Gaizhou, "the county af apples." It was a slightly foggy day, but the view of colorful orchards was breathtaking. Apples ranging from pink, shining red, crimson, dark brown, to green, lemony yellow and golden yellow smiled at me and resonantly pronounced autumn to me! I plunged into an orchard of yellow-green apples with orange and red stripes. For a moment, I was simply bewildered in the sweet aroma, at a loss as what to do. Then I remembered Yalan had told me I could eat my fill in any of the orchards for free, and we could just pay for the apples we take away. So I reached out to a big apple with lovely pink speckled over yellow-green and pulled it off from the branch. The pink flush and the skin texture felt clean and moist. I brushed it after a fashion with my hand and took a deep bite.

It was disappointing! The apple was crisp and juicy, but not as sweet and refreshing as I expected.

"Fuji tastes the best when slightly chilled," Yalan joined me. "You can just let it cool off a bit. Come on, I'll find you a better one to eat fresh off the tree! The Yellow Banana."

Yalan then told me a lot about apples and apple picking as we strolled through the orchard. She told me that the farmer, rather than the color, is more dependable to tell whether an apple is ripe, since the farmer knows when the trees bloomed. "The Fuji you took just now for example," she explained, "ripens in around 150 days and the 'Yellow Banana' in 140 since the tree bloomed." She also told me not to pull an apple straight from the tree, but to roll it upwards off the branch and give a little twist. She talked slowly in her soft voice, leaving me in wonder about her orchard expertise.

"How come you understand so much?" I asked in admiration.

She stopped, turned around to look at me in the eye and admitted timidly, "I only read about apples from the Internet last night."

I understood it was her way to say I could have done the same. That way, she made sure I got her message without getting embarrassed.

Two hours later, we were on our way home, with two full baskets of different apples to cool off and a friendship substantially warmed up.

Comments

This is a good piece of narrative. The opening sentence engages the reader's interest by piquing the reader's curiosity. Background information in the second paragraph reveals the "good-but-not-best" friendship between the writer and her friend. The last two sentences in the paragraph set the narrative to motion. The third paragraph, a condensation of the first draft, transfers a general coverage of her holiday to a specific event. The fourth paragraph uses vivid details and figurative language to describe the orchard. The writer shows her excitement without using such vague words as *amazing*, *thrilling* and *relaxing* that she used in the first draft. The anti-climax in the fifth paragraph creates suspense and catches the reader by surprise. Realist dialogue in the sixth paragraph not only advances the plot, but alludes to the title/main idea and foreshadows the ending at the same time. Details in the seventh paragraph are informative. Technical as they are, they are necessary for the message the writes intends to convey—the lesson she learned from her friend and further understanding of her friend. The last paragraph winds up the narrative — making the trip to the orchard complete, with more explicit statement of the title.

Further Reading

Read the following models and observe how unity and coherence are preserved and how vividness and liveliness are achieved.

Passage 1

Downtown

She was always worried about walking home at night. The city had grown so much, and downtown wasn't as friendly as it used to be. It was Monday night, the streets were empty, only the occasional taxi passed her by as she walked along the road trying to remain as inconspicuous as possible. She hated her job, not so much the actual work, but the fact that she got off so late frightened her. In the distance the motor of a larger vehicle could be heard, mixed in with the deep sound of bass pulsating though the night. She began to shiver, probably another group of teenagers that will zoom by hollering things at her. The vehicle was getting closer, she could now see the headlights through the windows of an office building ahead of her. She kept as far away from the street as possible, hoping they wouldn't see her. As they passed her, the motor leveled off and the bass ceased. She sped up. From the corner of her eye she noticed they were driving along side of her. She refused to look over, refused to make eye contact. She wished another car would pass by, maybe then they would stop. This was worse than just driving by, what were they doing? She could hear them talking, calling to her. Ignoring them, she was almost jogging now, her heels echoing in the street. The vehicle accelerated and caught up to her. She began to cry, she wished she was at home. Up ahead was an intersection, the lights were flashing red, almost warning her about what was to come. She approached the intersecting street, hoping to see someone. The only sight was the glare of the headlights still. She broke into a full out run. Only two blocks from home. The vehicle remained next to her. Every move she made was followed. She could see her apartment building in the distance, it seemed so far away. She could still hear them talking. Probably laughing at her. She approached her building, she could hear them clearly now. They must have their window down. She reached the steps of the apartment. She could hear the squeak of the vehicles brakes, as it came to a halt. She turned around to get a quick look. A movement in the corner of her eye caught her attention, as she stared at the vehicle. She turned. Three shadows disappeared into the night.

"You're lucky you live this close," a voice called from the vehicle. The voice sounded friendly, but she wasn't sure. "Those three were following you since you left that other building."

Passage 2

16th January[1]

I was walking through our little village last Sunday morning, when suddenly I found my attention drawn to a small cottage sandwiched between the butcher's and the blacksmith's shop. I stopped at the gate. I looked at the familiar, whitewashed wall with its rather slovenly roofing of thatch, and I tried to discover what it was that attracted me to it. Was it its garden? I looked at the clumps of wallflowers, the few unstaked chrysanthemums and the tiny untended lawn, and I realized that its garden was in no way different from a dozen others I had just passed.

Then I remembered that on other Sunday mornings on the same walk home from the church to my farm I had paused at this same gate. This realization perturbed me. Had I, I wondered, some sinister subconscious attraction to its owner? Then I remembered who lived there, and smiled at the very idea. For the cottage belonged to an old crone of seventy winters—she never had a summer—a woman who earns her living plucking fowls. They say she talked her husband into his grave; though, personally, I believe he

---

1 The journal was written by Ronald Duncan, first published as "Jan's Journal" in the *Evening Standard* on Saturdays for more than five years beginning from 25th May, 1946. Some extracts were later published in a book entitled *The Blue Fox* in 1951.

perished from exasperation; for it's a frustrating business trying to answer back when the woman's as deaf as a post.

Ah! That was it. I now realized what it was that had drawn me to the cottage and held me at the gate. It was its silence. It was the only cottage in the entire village which was not belching forth the flat facetiousness of some Yorkshire comedian. Every other house was sunk in this horrid hypnotic and noisy trance, like a lot of rabbits before a barrel-organ.

I walked on, cursing the Box which has destroyed our peace and reduced every village to passive listening to distant blather. I turned into the "Blue Fox" intending to drink a pint and improve my temper. But as I opened the bar door, the same northern accent barked at me. There sat Amos and the Colonel as silent as stuffed owls, forced to listening to this piffle. There was a time when, of a Sunday, we would sit and tell each other stories. They may not have been true. They may not have been witty. But they were our own. And talking to a person at least gives one the impression that one is not entirely alone. ...

"Good morning, Colonel," I said affably.

He did not hear me.

The radio continued to bellow. I then waited until the recorded laughter followed the recorded joke, giving the false impression of spontaneous hilarity as the workers enjoyed this horrid playtime; and then, when this entertainment was at its noisiest, I slowly but loudly offered Amos a double Scotch. Of course, he could not hear. So I stalked out unnoticed. When I am in one of these moods, I just follow my feet.

They led me past my own farm, where the dinner was being cooked to the accompaniment of Radio Luxembourg and a cow was chewing the cud to the same rhythm. I strode on as if pursued. Fortunately, an Atlantic gale was blowing up, and the combined musical boxes of the village were soon lost in the noise of the wind.

My feet sought the woods, and I stood and listened to all those sounds which are so delicate that, added together, they give the impression of silence and a feeling of solitude which is not loneliness. The scrub oaks strained and creaked as the gale combed the tips of their branches. The rain fell softly on the leafless limbs. A few wood-pigeons cooed as sweetly as doves. And everything moved, yet the whole was still.

And, as I stood at the foot of a tree, I wondered when science would drive me to seek refuge up it.

I tell you, it brought us down as monkeys and it will drive us up as men—and in my time, too!

Passage 3

I[1] wandered into a retreat by accident. Signs with arrows around the barbecue pit pointed MEN, WOMEN, CHILDREN toward fading lanes, grown over since last year. Feeling ages old and very wise at ten, I couldn't allow myself to be found by small children squatting behind a tree. Neither did I have the nerve to follow the arrow pointing the way for WOMEN. If any grownup had caught me there, it was possible that she'd think I was being "womanish" and would report me to Momma, and I knew what I could expect from her. So when the urge hit me to relieve myself, I headed toward another direction. Once through the wall of sycamore trees I found myself in a clearing ten times smaller than the picnic area, and cool and quiet. After my business was taken care of, I found a seat between two protruding roots of a black walnut tree and leaned back on its trunk. Heaven would be like that for the deserving. Maybe California too. Looking straight up at the uneven circle of sky, I began to sense that I might be falling into a blue cloud, far away. The children's voices and the chick odor of food cooking over open fires were the hooks I grabbed just in time to save myself.

Grass squeaked and I jumped at being found. Louise Kendricks walked into my grove. I didn't know that she too was escaping the gay spirit. We were the same age and she and her mother lived in a neat little bungalow behind the school. Her cousins, who were in our age group, were wealthier and fairer, but I had secretly believed Louise to be the prettiest female in Stamps, next to Mrs. Flowers.

"What you doing sitting here by yourself, Marguerite?" She didn't accuse, she asked for information. I said that I was watching the sky. She asked, "What for?" There was obviously no answer to a question like that, so I didn't make up one. Louise reminded me of Jane Eyre. Her mother lived in reduced circumstances, but she was genteel, and though she worked as a maid I decided she should be called a governess ... Louise was a lonely girl, although she had plenty of playmates and was a ready partner for any ring game in the schoolyard.

Her face, which was long and dark chocolate brown, had a thin sheet of sadness over it, and light but as permanent as the viewing gauze on a coffin. And her eyes, which I thought her best feature, shifted quickly as if what they sought had just a second before eluded her

She had come near and the spotted light through the trees fell on her face and braids in running splotches. ...

She looked up—"Well, you can't see much sky from here." Then she sat down, an

---

1 This is an excerpt from Chapter 20 of *I Know Why the Caged Bird Sings*, the first of a five-volume autobiographical series by Maya Angelou. Maya Angelou was born Marguerite Johnson. Her parents divorced when she was three. At eight, when staying with her mother, she was first sexually assaulted and later raped by her mother's boyfriend. At her testimony, her mother's family lynched the rapist. Haunted by the trauma and feeling guilty for another person's death, Maya withdrew into herself and silence, speaking only to her brother Bailey and matured her beyond her years. Later, while staying with her paternal grandmother—referred to as "Momma," at Stamps, Arkansas, she met Mrs. Flowers, who enlightened her into the beauty and power of words. Louise was the first childhood friend Maya made herself outside her family. The friendship provided Maya with her first opportunity to experience and enjoy her girlhood.

arm away from me. Finding two exposed roots, she laid thin wrists on them as if she had been in an easy chair. Slowly she leaned back against the tree. I closed my eyes and thought of the necessity of finding another place and the unlikehood of there being another with all the qualifications that this one had. There was a little peal of a scream and before I could open my eyes Louise had grabbed my hand. "I was falling"—she shook her long braids—"I was falling in the sky."

I liked her for being able to fall in the sky and admit it. I suggested, "Let's try together. But we have to sit up straight on the count of five." Louise asked, "Want to hold hands? Just in case?" I did. If one of us did happen to fall, the other could pull her out.

After a few near tumbles into eternity (both of us knew what it was), we laughed at having played with death and destruction and escaped.

Louise said, "Let's look at that old sky while we're spinning." We took each other's hands in the center of the clearing and began turning around. Very slowly at first. We raised our chins and looked straight at the seductive patch of blue. Faster, just a little faster, then faster, faster yet. Yes, help, we were falling. Then eternity won, after all. We couldn't stop spinning or falling until I was jerked out of her grasp by greedy gravity and thrown to my fated below—no, above, not below. I found myself safe and dizzy at the foot of the sycamore tree. Louise had ended on her knees at the other side of the grove.

This was surely the time to laugh. We lost but we hadn't lost anything. First we were giggling and crawling drunkenly toward each other and then we were laughing out loud uproariously. We slapped each other on the back and shoulders and laughed some more. We had made a fool or a liar out of something, and didn't that just beat all?

In daring to challenge the unknown with me, she became my first friend. We spent tedious hours teaching ourselves the Tut language. You (Yak oh you) know (kack nug oh wug) what (wack hash a tut). Since all the other children spoke Pig Latin, we were superior because Tut was hard to speak and even harder to understand. At last I began to comprehend what girls giggled about. Louise would rattle off a few sentences to me in the unintelligible Tut language and would laugh. Naturally I laughed too. Snickered, really, understanding nothing. I don't think she understood half of what she was saying herself, but, after all, girls have to giggle, and after being a woman for three years I was about to become a girl.

69

The Descriptive Essay

𝕋uning-in Activities

Activity 1

Try to describe something/somebody of your interest on campus, a canteen, a shop, a tree, a statue, a professor, etc., and identify a dominant impression and give some details in support of the impression.

Activity 2

Try to describe one of these pictures or pictures of the instructor's or students' choice:

- What is the dominant impression you have about the picture?
- What are the details to support your impression?
- What's unusual about the picture?
- What adjectives, nouns, adverbs, and verbs can you use to convey your impression to your reader?
- What sights, smells, sounds, and tastes are in the picture?
- Do the sights, smells, sounds, and tastes remind you of anything?

Introduction

Description represents what the five senses experience about persons, places, objects or feelings in vivid language. In other words, the main purpose of a descriptive essay is to recreate/paint in words a scene which appeals to the writer's senses and to present the sensory details vividly to the reader, who will imaginatively share the writer's experience or feelings. When describing a bus tour to the countryside in spring, for example, we may show what we saw, touched, smelled, tasted and heard:

> *A vast expanse of yellow rape flowers danced gently in the breeze.*
> *The open window allowed a cool spring breeze to caress my cheeks.*
> *A fully loaded truck spluttered along in front of us spewing out nauseous black clouds of exhaust.*
> *The bitter taste of the pre-trip travel sickness pill still clung to back of my throat.*
> *The screeching siren of a police car forced us to pull in and wait till it passed.*

Though description seldom stands alone in the development of an essay, it is heavily relied upon in other expository modes of writing. In a narrative, for example, description can make the setting or characters more vivid; in an analysis, description can help us highlight the essential differences between two items we are discussing; in an argument, description can make a position more persuasive. In fact, much of a writer's success depends on his/her ability to provide readers with detailed descriptions. Moreover, it is possible to use description as the primary method of development for an essay.

Purpose of Description

Although we can describe anything under the sun, the description must relate to something of consequence and must be purposeful. Writing must always be directed towards the reader and hence writers must have a good reason for describing something or someone. Keeping this reason in mind can help us focus our description and imbue our language with a particular perspective or emotion.

Suppose someone wants to describe his grandfather. The person has decided to write about his grandfather's physical appearance and his grandfather's way to interact with

71

people. However, rather than providing a general description of these aspects, he wants to convey his admiration for his grandfather's strength and kindness. This is actually his reason for writing the descriptive essay. To achieve this, the person might focus one of his paragraphs on describing the roughness of his grandfather's hands, roughness resulting from the lifetime labor of work, but he might also describe how his grandfather would hold his hands so gently with those rough hands when having a conversation with him or when taking a walk. Similarly, someone describing a lonely beach may want to persuade the reader to consider the importance of peace and solitude in this busy world, and another one describing a room may be providing details for the reader to understand more about the owner of the room, rather than introduce the room for its own sake.

Finding a Subject for Description

Since we are trying to present our subject of description in sensory details, the more strongly we feel about and the more intimately connected we are to the subject, the easier it will be to arouse our reader's interest. A person whose characteristics stand out, like Samuel Beckett, will probably be of greater interest to the reader and more meaningful to describe than an ordinary person.

Recall an experience of being impressed by natural scenery, a person, an object or an animal, make a list of all the details that made you feel the way you did. Explore the list through each of the five senses: what did you see, smell, taste, touch, and hear? Be specific. Try to describe in such way that they burn a lasting impression in your mind. It might be of help to learn that some of the most interesting subjects for description express surprising contrasts —

- the homeless man who, though uneducated, makes a profound statement
- the elegant restaurant that served the worst meal you've had
- the unheated, leaking cottage that you remember with great fondness
- the brand new expensive imported mobile phone that is a constant source of headaches

Option A: Describing a Place

This can be your favorite place, your least favorite place, a place you often visit, a place where you spend a lot of your time, a place that you have only seen once, a place that you never want to return to again, a place that holds happy or sad memories for you, or a place that you dream about. It can be your bedroom, your house, your classroom, a street corner, a beach, a library, a grocery store, a park, a museum, a city, or any other place you can think of.

Option B: Describing a Person

This can be a person you know well, a person you only met yesterday, a person you love, a person you despise, a person you would like to meet, or a person you hope you will never meet. It can be someone you remember fondly from childhood, someone who made you afraid, someone you had a crush on, or someone who hurt you. It can be your mother, your best friend, your roommate, your next-door neighbor, an interesting stranger you saw on the bus this morning, your ideal husband or wife, the worst or best teacher you've ever had, or anyone else you can think of.

Option C: Describing an Object

This can be an object you see often, an object you love, an object you wish didn't exist, an object you can't live without, or an object you wish you had. It can be your most valuable possession, something you can't get rid of, something you inherited, something your boyfriend or girlfriend gave you, something you have had since you were a child, or something you have had for only a week. It can be your car, your favorite shirt, a gift your mother gave you, a painting you love, a trophy you won, or any other object you can think of.

Option D: Describing an Animal

This can be your favorite type of animal, an animal that you cannot stand, an animal you think is beautiful, or an animal that you think is ugly. It can be an animal that you have raised, an animal that makes a good pet, an animal that would not make a good pet, or an animal that you have strong memories about, or any other animal you can think of.

73

Option E: Describing a Picture/Painting/Drawing

This can be a famous painting like *Mona Lisa*, or a picture in the media or a picture you took yourself.

◎bjective and Subjective Description

A descriptive essay can be objective or subjective, giving the author a wide choice of tone, diction and attitude. Objective description focuses on facts, statistics, and observable details. For instance, an objective description of one's dog would mention such facts as height, weight, coloring and so forth. Since objective description avoids emotion, sensationalism, or subjective interpretation, vague adjectives such as *good, lovely, exciting, interesting,* etc. sound hollow. Writers choose nouns to make the reader see and verbs to make the reader feel.

Sample 1

Beijing's Siheyuan

Courtyard houses of north China, with Beijing's Siheyuan (courtyard with houses on all sides), being the highest level and most typical, are the outstanding representatives of traditional residences of China's Han nationality.

Beijing's Siheyuan, seated in the north of the compound and facing south, mostly consist of inner and outer yards. The Outer yard is horizontal and long; the main door opens to the southeast corner, conducive[1] to maintaining the privacy of the residence and increasing spatial change.

After entering the main door and turning westward into the outer yard, one finds there are guest rooms, servant's room, a kitchen and toilet. Going northward from the Outer yard through an exquisitely[2] shaped and quite beautiful floral-pendant[3] gate, one enters the square, spacious main yard. The principal room in the north is the largest, erected with the tablets of "heaven, earth, monarch, kinsfolk and teacher," which is for holding family ceremonies and receiving distinguished guest.

The left and right sides of the principal room are linked to aisles inhabited by family elders. In front of the aisle there is a small corner yard which is very quiet and is often used as a study. Both sides of the main yard have a wing room serving as living rooms for the younger generations. Both the principal room and the wing rooms face the yards which have front Porches. Verandahs[4] are used to link the floral-pendant gate and the three houses, so that one can move along or sit in them to enjoy the flowers and trees in the courtyard. Behind the principal room, sometimes, there is a long row of "Hou Zhao Fang (back illuminated room)" serving either as a living room or utility room.

Beijing's Siheyuan is cordial and quiet with a strong flavor of life. The courtyard is square and

1. conducive: *adj.*
   contributive; helpful;
   favorable

2. exquisite: *adj.* 精美的;精致的
3. pendant: *n.* 悬吊装置

4. verandah: *n.* 外廊;长廊

74

vast and of a suitable size. The courtyard is planted with flowers and set up with rocks, providing an ideal space for outdoor life, and making it seem to be an open-air large living room, drawing heaven and earth closer to people's hearts and therefore most favored by them. The verandah divides the courtyard into several big and small spaces, which, however, are divided but not distant from each other; instead, they penetrate each other and increase the levels, setting off the void and the solid and the contrast of shadow. They also make the courtyard better conform to the standards of daily life. Family members can have an exchange of views here, creating a cordial temperament and interest in life.

In fact, the centripetal[5] and cohesive atmosphere displayed by Beijing's Siheyuan, with strict rules and forms, is precisely a typical expression of the character of most Chinese residences. The courtyard's pattern of being closed to the outside and open to the inside can be regarded as a wise integration of two kinds of contradictory psychology: On the one hand, the self-sufficient feudal families needed to maintain a certain separation from the Outside world; on the other hand, the Psychology deeply-rooted in the mode of agricultural production makes the Chinese particularly like to get closer to nature. They often want to see the heaven, earth, flowers, grass and trees in their own homes.

The square courtyards of an appropriate size of Beijing's Siheyuan are helpful to take in sunshine in winter. In areas south of Beijing, the setting sun in summer is quite strong, so the courtyards there become narrow and long on the north-south side, so as to reduce the sunshine.
(http://www1.chinaculture.org/library/2008-01/16/content_38954.htm)

5. centripetal: *adj.* 向心性的

75

A subjective description, on the other hand, is personal and would not only include details, but also stress the author's feeling toward the object, together with its personality and habits in some cases. Rather than focusing on factual details, subjective description

Unit FourUnit Four

seeks to create powerful impressions. You might describe your dog as your friend, full of consideration for you, or as your spoilt cousin on whom you lavish your attention and allowance, but not just in cold, technical details from head to tail without a dominant impression. Since subjective description often relies on emotion to convey its point, writers choose verbs, adverbs, and adjectives, rather than nouns, to create and convey the emotion to the reader.

Sample 2

The thick, burnt scent of roasted coffee tickled[1] the tip of my nose just seconds before the old, faithful alarm blared[2] a distorted top-forty through its tiny top speaker. Wiping away the grit[3] of last night's sleep, the starch[4] white sunlight blinded me momentarily as I slung[5] my arm like an elephant trunk along the top of the alarm, searching for the snooze[6] button. While stretching hands and feet to the four posts of my bed, my eyes opened after several watery blinks. I crawled out of the comforter, edging awkwardly like a butterfly from a cocoon[7], swinging my legs over the side of the bed. The dusty pebbles on the chilled, wood floor sent ripples[8] spiraling from my ankles to the nape[9] of my neck when my feet hit the floor. Grabbing the apricot, terri-cloth robe, recently bathed in fabric softener and October wind, I knotted it tightly at my waist like a prestigious coat of armor and headed downstairs to battle the morning.

Vocabulary

1. tickle: *v.* produce an irritating but sometimes pleasant feeling in a part of the body by touching it lightly
2. blare: *v.* make loud harsh unpleasant sounds
3. grit: *n.* 沙砾
4. starch: *n.* 淀粉；生硬
5. sling: *v.* put carelessly
6. snooze: *n.* 瞌睡
7. cocoon: *n.* 茧
8. ripple: *n.* 涟漪；波纹
9. nape: *n.* 项，后颈

The descriptive essay can either be objective or subjective by nature. The emotion that needs to be evoked determines the outcome. An objective essay is precise and clinical in approach while a subjective essay has a personal touch. Writers often blend objective and subjective description to balance factual detail with the power of emotional impressions. By blending objective and subjective elements, writers can provide readers with both logical and emotional appeals. The one we're trying to write is subjective-oriented description.

The Dominant Impression

A (subjective) descriptive essay conveys one clear dominant impression to help realize the purpose of the description. In describing a snowfall, for example, we need to decide and to let our reader know if it is threatening or lovely; in order to have one dominant impression it cannot be both. The dominant impression guides the writer's selection of detail and is made clear to the reader in the thesis statement. For example, in "The Fall of the House of Usher," Edgar Allan Poe describes the physical oppression of the weather in an opening sentence. Through descriptive details, Poe creates "a sense of insufferable gloom" and thus conveys an emotional oppression.

Sample 3

Vocabulary

During the whole of a dull, dark, and soundless day in the autumn of the year, when the clouds hung oppressively low in the heavens, I had been passing alone, on horseback, through a singularly dreary tract of country; and at length found myself, as the shades of the evening drew on, within view of the melancholy[1] House of Usher. I know not how it was—but, with the first glimpse of the building, a sense of insufferable gloom pervaded my spirit. ... I looked upon the scene before me—upon the mere house, and the simple landscape features of the domain—upon the bleak walls—upon the vacant eye-like windows—upon a few rank sedges[2]—and upon a few white trunks of decayed trees—with an utter depression of soul which I can compare to no earthly sensation more properly than to the after-dream of the reveller[3] upon opium—the bitter lapse into everyday life—the hideous dropping off of the veil. ... I reined my horse to the precipitous[4] brink of a black and lurid tarn[5] that lay in unruffled[6] lustre[7] by the dwelling, and gazed down—but with a shudder even more thrilling than before—upon the remodeled and inverted images of the gray sedge, and the ghastly tree-stems, and the vacant and eye-like windows.

1. melancholy: *n.* 忧郁, 愁思

2. sedge: *n.* 莎草, 苔草

3. reveller: *n.* 寻欢作乐的人

4. precipitous: *adj.* 陡峭的
5. tarn: *n.* 池塘, 湖
6. ruffle: *v.* 弄皱
7. lustre: *n.* 光泽

Questions for Consideration

1. What is the dominant impression that Poe creates about the House of Usher?
2. What details does Poe use in support of his impression?
3. What mood is suggested in such phrases as "I found myself," "I had been passing alone," "found myself within view of..."?

Homework 1

Decide on a topic for description and use pre-writing techniques of listing, clustering, freewriting, etc. to work out a dominant impression.

Details in Description

Descriptions are made to involve the reader enough so he/she can actually visualize the thing being described. Therefore, once we decide on a dominant impression, we can evaluate the subject in terms of visual, auditory, and other sensory details. We need to think in concrete terms.

Every person, place, or thing has its special characteristics, and it is up to us to discover what sets this subject apart from others like it. Then, we must select the concrete words that will enable our readers to see, hear, taste, touch, or smell what we are describing. We should try to incorporate words (verbs, adjectives, adverbs, and nouns) that build an emotional state, reflective of our experience and knowledge of the world.

Show, don't tell!

Description *shows* attributes of a topic through sensory details. To *show* "sweat dripped from his forehead," conveys much more effectively than the vague telling that "he was nervous." If someone says "*I grew tired after dinner*", he simply *tells* the reader about his feeling. However, if he writes,

> *As I leaned back and rested my head against the top of the chair, my eyelids began to feel heavy, and the edges of the empty plate in front of me blurred with the white tablecloth.*

He *shows* the reader how he feels. The most effective descriptive essays are loaded with such *showing* because they enable readers to imagine or experience something for themselves.

78

Exercise

1. Compare the following pairs of sentences:

   a. It was a nice day.

   b. The sun was shining and a slight breeze blew across my face.

   a. The food was unappetizing.

   b. The stew congealed into an oval pool of muddy-brown fat.

   a. The empty room smelled stale and was devoid of furniture or floor covering; the single window lacked curtains or blinds of any kind.

   b. The apartment smelled of old cooking odors, cabbage, and mildew; our sneakers squeaked sharply against the scuffed wood floors, which reflected a haze of dusty sunlight from the one cobwebbed, gritty window.

Which sentence in each pair do you like better?

What makes you like the sentence better than the other in the same pair?

What makes one sentence more vivid than the other?

You may have noticed that the first sentence in each pair uses vague or ambiguous words to make a general statement about a situation, whereas the second sentence shows the *sights, touches, textures, smells,* and *sounds* of the situation with specific details.

Use action verbs!

Well chosen verbs, especially action verbs, enhance descriptive writing because they describe the action with the senses of sight, sound, smell, taste, and feel. Consider this sentence: *The petite woman walks in the park.* If we change the verb "walks" to "ambles," we will create a more vivid image of the woman. However, if we use one of these verbs instead—strides, stumbles, limps, races, or jogs—we will see a completely different picture. Compare:

Weak:	She *walked* casually into the room and deliberately *tried* not to pay attention to their stares.
Strong:	She *strolled* into the room and *ignored* their stares.
Weak:	The wind *blew* through the trees.
Strong:	The wind *roared* through the trees.
Weak:	He *makes* his point well.
Strong:	He *hammers* home his point.
Weak:	They *began* their work without caution or hesitation.
Strong:	They *plunged into* their work.
Weak:	The water *ran* out of the fountain.
Strong:	The water *gushed* out of the fountain.
Weak:	The rain *fell* down from the heavens.
Strong:	The rain *spilled* down from the heavens.
Weak:	There was *quaking*, the sea *tossed* and *turned*, and there was lots of lightening and fire, not to mention the ash that *fell* from the sky.

Strong: We saw the sea *sucked away* by the *heaving* of the earth... a fearful cloud forked with great tongues of fire *lashed* at the heavens and torrents of ash began to *pour* from the sky.

We can always learn ingenious use of verbs from professional writers. Look at how Ralph Ellison uses verbs in the famous battle royal scene of *Invisible Man*.

Sample 4

I *lunged*[1] for a yellow coin lying on the blue design of the carpet, *touching* it and *sending a surprised shriek* to join those rising around me. I tried frantically to remove my hand but could not let go. A hot, violent force *tore* through my body, *shaking* me like a wet rat. The rug was electrified. The hair *bristled*[2] up on my head as I shook myself free. My muscles *jumped*, my nerves *jangled*[3], *writhed*[4]. But I saw that this was not stopping the other boys. Laughing in fear and embarrassment, some were holding back and *scooping*[5] *up* the coins *knocked off* by the painful contortions[6] of the others. The men *roared*[7] above us as we *struggled*.

Vocabulary

1. lunge: *v.* dart; move suddenly and clumsily in order to catch something or hit someone
2. bristle: *v.* rise away from the skin because of cold, fear or anger
3. jangle: *v.* rattle
4. writhe: *v.* twist and turn violently
5. scoop: *v.* pick sth. up by putting hands under it and lifting it quickly
6. contortion: *n.* 扭曲
7. roar: *v.* laugh very noisily

Avoid weak verbs such as "to be," "to become," "to get," "to do," "to make," and "to have" because they do not generate motion or action. Compare:

Weak: The keys *became stiff*.

Strong: The keys *stiffened*.

Weak: She *consumed the remainder of the coffee in* her cup.

Strong: She *drained* her coffee cup.

Weak: The injury *deprived* him *of the use of his leg*.

Strong: The injury *lamed* him.

Weak: He *got* to the door *before* me.

Strong: He *beat* me to the door.

Weak: She *got quickly out of the way of* the bus.

Strong: She *dodged* the bus.

Weak: The audience *was* irate. People *were* jumping out of their seats and *were coming into* the aisles.

Strong: The irate audience *jumped* out of their seats and *flooded* the aisles.

Weak: The waves *were so high* that the boat *was nearly tipping* on end. The wind *felt rough,* and the salt spray *became so strong* that we *felt* our breath would be cut off. I *was afraid.*

Strong: The waves *towered* until the boat *tipped* on end. The wind *lashed* our faces, while the salt spray *clogged* our throats and *cut off* our breath. Panic *gripped* me.

Clearly, verbs of action invigorate and shorten the sentences.

Use precise nouns!

Nouns can also be general or precise. A dog can be a puppy, a cur, a wolf or a Chihuahua, a house can be a mansion, a villa, a castle, a palace, or a chateau, a woman can be a blonde, a matron or a crone, and happiness can be cheer, delight, ecstasy, elation or gratification. Note the different mental pictures we associate with the specific nouns as opposed to the general word of dog, house, woman or happiness. When we use specific, concrete nouns, our writing comes to life and we help the reader to pin down details, as in

*The swollen **mass** teemed forwards like a seething **colony** of crawling **ants**.*

Towards the end of Chapter 9 in *Life on the Mississippi,* Mark Twain employs rich language to detail the Mississippi river at sunset.

81

Sample 5

Vocabulary

Now when I had mastered the language of this water and had come to know every trifling feature that bordered the great river as familiarly as I knew the letters of the alphabet, I had made a valuable acquisition. But I had lost something, too. I had lost something which could never be restored to me while I lived. All the grace, the beauty, the poetry had gone out of the majestic river! I still keep in mind a certain wonderful sunset which I witnessed when steamboating was new to me. A broad expanse of the river was turned to blood; in the middle distance the red hue[1] brightened into gold, through which a solitary log came floating, black and conspicuous; in one place a long, slanting[2] mark lay sparkling upon the water; in another the surface was broken by boiling, tumbling[3] rings, that were as many-tinted[4] as an opal[5]; where the ruddy[6] flush was faintest, was a smooth spot that was covered with graceful circles and radiating lines, ever so delicately traced; the shore on our left was

1. hue: *n.* 色彩
2. slant: *v.* lie along a line that is neither horizontal nor vertical
3. tumble: *v.* roll and swirl
4. tinted: *adj.* colored, especially with a pale or weak color
5. opal: *n.* 蛋白石；乳色玻璃
6. ruddy: *adj.* reddish

densely wooded, and the sombre[7] shadow that fell from this forest was broken in one place by a long, ruffled[8] trail that shone like silver; and high above the forest wall a clean-stemmed dead tree waved a single leafy bough[9] that glowed like a flame in the unobstructed[10] splendor[11] that was flowing from the sun. There were graceful curves, reflected images, woody heights, soft distances; and over the whole scene, far and near, the dissolving lights drifted steadily, enriching it, every passing moment, with new marvels of coloring.

I stood like one bewitched. I drank it in, in a speechless rapture...

7. sombre: *adj.* dark and dull
8. ruffle: *v.* ripple, cause the surface to become uneven and wavy
9. bough: *n.* 树枝
10. obstruct: *v.* block
11. splendor: *n.* 光辉;绚丽

Questions for Consideration

1. Underline the precise nouns used in the passage and explain how they help to make the description vivid.
2. What other devices does Mark Twain use to make the description vivid?
3. What is the dominant impression of the description?

Use adjectives and adverbs selectively!

Adjectives and adverbs can help if they add content, but they work best when they support the carefully chosen nouns and verbs. In other words, use adjectives and adverbs only to enhance those words that in themselves really do need extra description. Words like "fabulous," "exciting," "cool", "cute", "very," "good" and "lovely" have little meaning and may therefore do without.

Sample 6

Vocabulary

The once fertile valley is now a dusty moonscape of dry riverbeds, broken earth, and skeletons. Hundreds of men and women die of thirst, hunger, and disease in the heat and dust of the hopeless refugee camps. Emaciated[1] orphans wander along the highway, lifting bony, empty hands to passing drivers. Scarred by hunger and loss, their young faces are old with death.

1. emaciated: *adj.* extremely thin from lack of food or illness

It was a cold grey day in late November. The weather had changed overnight, when a backing wind brought a granite[1] sky and a mizzling[2] rain with it, and although it was now only a little after two o'clock in the afternoon the pallor[3] of a winter evening seemed to have closed upon the hills, cloaking[4] them in mist. It would be dark by four. The air was clammy[5] cold, and for all the tightly closed windows it penetrated the interior of the coach. The leather seats felt damp to the hands, and there must have been a small crack in the roof, because now and again little drips of rain fell softly through, smudging[6] the leather and leaving a dark-blue stain like a splodge[7] of ink. The wind came in gusts, at times shaking the coach as it travelled round the bend of the road, and in the exposed places on the high ground it blew with such force that the whole body of the coach trembled and swayed, rocking between the high wheels like a drunken man.

The driver, muffled[8] in a greatcoat to his ears, bent almost double in his seat in a faint endeavour to gain shelter from his own shoulders, while the dispirited horses plodded[9] sullenly[10] to his command, too broken by the wind and the rain to feel the whip that now and again cracked above their heads, while it swung between the numb fingers of the driver.

The wheels of the coach creaked and groaned as they sank into the ruts[11] on the road, and sometimes they flung up the soft spattered[12] mud against the windows, where it mingled with the constant driving rain, and whatever view there might have been of the countryside was hopelessly obscured.

1. granite: *n.* very hard grey rock
2. mizzle: *v.* drizzle
3. pallor: *n.* paleness
4. cloak: *v.* hide, cover
5. clammy: *adj.* unpleasantly wet, cold and sticky
6. smudge: *v.* smear
7. splodge: *n.* a large mark in irregular shape
8. be muffled (up): wear a lot of heavy clothes with very little of the body or face visible
9. plod: *v.* trudge
10. sullen: *adj.* silent and cheerless
11. rut: *n.* 车辙
12. spatter: *v.* sprinkle

83

Sample 8

When I pulled the trigger I did not hear the bang or feel the kick—one never does when a shot goes home—but I heard the devilish roar of glee[1] that went up from the crowd. In that instant, in too short a time, one would have thought, even for the bullet to get there, a mysterious, terrible change had come over the elephant. He neither stirred nor fell, but every line of his body had altered. He looked suddenly stricken, shrunken, immensely old, as though the frightful impact of the bullet had paralysed[2] him without knocking him down. At last, after what seemed a long time—it might have been five seconds, I dare say—he sagged[3] flabbily[4] to his knees. His mouth slobbered[5]. An enormous senility[6] seemed to have settled upon him. One could have imagined him thousands of years old. I fired again into the same spot. At the second shot he did not collapse but climbed with desperate slowness to his feet and stood weakly upright, with legs sagging and head drooping[7]. I fired a third time. That was the shot that did for him. You could see the agony of it jolt[8] his whole body and knock the last remnant of strength from his legs. But in falling he seemed for a moment to rise, for as his hind legs collapsed beneath him he seemed to tower upward like a huge rock toppling[9], his trunk reaching skyward like a tree. He trumpeted[10], for the first and only time. And then down he came, his belly towards me, with a crash that seemed to shake the ground even where I lay.

Vocabulary

1. glee: *n.* 高兴，欢欣
2. paralyse: *v.* cause... to have no feeling and unable to move
3. sag: *v.* hang down loosely
4. flabby: *adj.* not firm but loose or soft
5. slobber: *v.* (liquid) fall from the mouth
6. senility: *n.* 衰老；老态龙钟
7. droop: *v.* hang downwards with no strength
8. jolt: *v.* move suddenly and violently
9. topple: *v.* become unsteady and fall over
10. trumpet: *v.* (elephant) bellow, make a sound

Questions for Consideration

1. Underline the verbs, adjectives and adverbs the writers use in the three passages. Do the writers use more adjectives or adverbs than verbs? Do the adjectives and adverbs enhance the words they modify and contribute to the dominant impression?

2. In Sample 6, what kind of image do such adjectives as "dusty," "dry," "broken," "hopeless," "emaciated," "bony" and "empty" create as a whole?

3. In Sample 7, how does Daphne du Maurier use adjectives, verbs and adverbs for effect in the excerpt from *Jamaica Inn*?

4. In Sample 8, how does George Orwell in "Shooting an Elephant" convey immense emotional impact in the act of shooting?

5. How long might the actual shooting have taken? What is George Orwell's purpose, to show the process of shooting and dying of the elephant or to highlight the dignity of life?

Exercise

Choose the most suitable adjective for each sentence.

1. The forest is bursting with_____pine. (aromatic, smelly, tasty, pretty)
2. He dislikes going to those_____basketball games. (interesting, playful, rowdy, colorful)
3. I love the sound of thunder on_____ summer afternoons. (clammy, bright, humid, busy)
4. Everyone pushed his way into the_____ subway car. (crowded, unbearable, dramatic, ancient)
5. Winning the championship was the most_____surprise of all. (curious, coveted, unbelievable, embarrassing)

Use figurative language!

Sensory description can be achieved using figurative language, a way of saying something other than the literal meaning of the words, like similes and metaphors—explicit (with "as" or "like") or implied comparisons (without "as" or "like") between two objects or ideas that are different, such as

> Her cheeks glowed **like** the ripest of strawberries. (simile)
> The multitude of creatures created a **cacophony** of calls that **assaulted** our ears. (metaphor)

Exercise: Identify similes and metaphors.

1. The swollen mass teemed forwards like a seething colony of crawling ants.
2. The mingling spices tingled our senses to create a glorious surge of appetite.
3. The flashes of lightning flooded the land with a fearful display of Nature's power.
4. The children were like bundles of concentrated energy exploding with delight.
5. The darkening sky ushered in a forbidding, sombre mood that set the scene for the grim news lying in wait for us.
6. Our noses were assaulted by the putrefying smell of rotting flesh. It was like a wall of evil.
7. The evening was aflame with the glorious sunset.
8. In the Reserve I have sometimes come upon the Iguana, the big lizards, as they were sunning themselves upon a flat stone in a river bed. They are not pretty in shape, but nothing can be imagined more beautiful than their colouring. They shine like a heap of precious stones or like a pane cut out of an old church window. When, as you approach, they swish away, there is a flash of azure, green and purple over the stones, the colour seems to be standing behind them in the air, like a comet's luminous tail. (from Isak Dinesen's *Out of Africa*)

Here are a few more common "figures of speech" to achieve figurative language:

Personification:	the attribution of distinct human qualities, e.g., honesty, emotion, volition, etc., to an animal, object or idea, as in *The wind whispers and the cold creeps.*
Hyperbole:	a bold, deliberate overstatement or exaggeration not intended to be taken literally, as in *The skin on her face was as thin and drawn as tight as the skin of onion and her eyes were gray and sharp like the points of two picks.*
Synecdoche:	the use of a part of something to suggest the whole or the whole to represent a part, as in *And let us mind, faint heart n'er wan* *A lady fair*
Metonymy:	the substitution of one word or phrase for another with which it is closely associated or the indirect reference of something to things around it, as in *The suits on Wall Street walked off with most of our savings.*
Paradox:	a statement that contains apparently contradictory or incompatible elements, but on closer inspection may be true as in *The child is father of the man.*

Exercise: Compare the following pairs of sentences.

a. The sun was going down beyond the lake. The sky was beautiful. Shades of purple and pink, orange and red, a few really dark blotches, and a bit of yellow were reflected in the water.

b. The sleeping water reflected the evening sky. The angels must have spilled their jam, because the sunset was a mixture of grape with strawberry, apricot and raspberry, clumps of blueberry, and a little melted butter.

a. It was hot. It was too hot. The girl stood beside the road and waited. She was so uncomfortable that she lifted her hair off her neck to cool down. She began to sweat.

b. Humidity breathed in the girl's face and ran its greasy fingers through her hair. As she stood looking down the long, deserted road, she could see heat vapor rising in the distance, creating a rippled, watery effect. She frowned and lifted her hair off her neck. A drop of perspiration slid down her spine.

Which sentence in each pair is more figurative?

What makes the sentence more figurative?

Make static images dynamic!

Description of an object with specific nouns can instill a strong image. However, to maximize the effect of the image it must not remain static. The image must assume activity to ensure its survival. Manipulated correctly, a clinical detachment of painterly precision can be transformed into a sudden burst of vivid animation within the image through the use of a simple change in verb choice. But verb choice alone cannot propel the image into a dynamic change. Something such as choice of nouns with varying interpretations and figurative language must continue that momentum. Simile, for example, assumes the weight of responsibility when the pool's surface is equated to a bracelet shaken in a dance. Without this transformation from static to dynamic, the image is either lost in the blandness of clinical description, or moving too quickly to appreciate the object in motion. Wallace Stevens, in "Study of Two Pears," combines static description and dynamic motion with technical grace to enhance one from the other.

Sample 9

Vocabulary

STUDY OF TWO PEARS

Wallace Stevens

I

Opusculum paedagogum.[1]
The pears are not viols,[2]
Nudes[3] or bottles.
They resemble nothing else.

II

They are yellow forms
Composed of curves
Bulging[4] toward the base.
They are touched red.

III

They are not flat surfaces
Having curved outlines.
They are round
Tapering[5] toward the top.

IV

In the way they are modelled
There are bits of blue.
A hard dry leaf hangs
From the stem.[6]

V

The yellow glistens.[7]
It glistens with various yellows,
Citrons[8], oranges and greens
Flowering over the skin.

VI

The shadows of the pears
Are blobs[9] on the green cloth.
The pears are not seen
As the observer wills.

1. Opusculum paedagogum: *n.* 拉丁文,两种梨的名字
2. viol: *n.* 中世纪的提琴
3. nude: *n.* 裸体

4. bulge: *v.* protrude, stick out

5. taper: *v.* become smaller

6. stem: *n.* 树干

7. glisten: *v.* (sth. smooth, wet, or oily) shine or sparkle
8. citron: *n.* 枸橼

9. blob: *n.* 一团,黑乎乎的一堆

87

In this poem, Stevens comes closely to still life and makes it dynamic. According to Thomas Cain, the 13 sentences in the poem stretch in 24 lines, with each line of an average of 4 words. The second, third and first half of the fourth stanza describe the pears in terms of shape and primary colors. The pears have no action and nothing acts upon them. "They are yellow forms...They are touched red...They are not flat...They are round...There are bits of blue." This clinical description comes to an end at the second half of the fourth stanza with a simple active verb— "hard leaf hangs / from the stem." This dramatic shift in verb choice forces the study of the two pears to suddenly have an activity, and therefore a life within them. In this course of change from inactive to active, the image assumes vitality.

Those innate colors suddenly come to life, "The yellow glistens." No longer is the color a description, but it has become a subject of a transitive verb. It "Glistens with various yellows, / Citrons, oranges and greens / Flowering over the skin." The flat affect of the painting has become alive through colors. While citrons and oranges are colors, they are also fruits, living fruits; the same goes with the use of greens as both colors and names for various vegetables. Underscoring this burst of life in colors is the gerund phrase "Flowering over the skin." At this stage in the poem we have moved from the scientific Latin names of the fruit through a geometrical description and have blossomed into vibrant living colors. Using contrast with vibrancy, the next line reflects on the background, "The shadows of the pears / Are blobs on the green cloth." The dramatic slip back into a passive verb form, with the shapeless colorless shadows as blobs on a once vibrant color of green, enhances the skin colors of the pears.

Take interest in words!

Description relies heavily on vocabulary. After all, a writer paints with words. As language learners, we need to be observant and reflective all the time, particularly when we are reading.

Searching for and discovering the fitting word or phrase rewards with "a bit of perfection in a world of pain." To experience pleasure from the treasure of words, students of English should always keep an English-English dictionary and a thesaurus handy and use them not only to understand the meaning of words, but also to come to the understanding of their usage and to find the right word. However, it is important to keep in mind that a writer's goal is to find a word that nails down the meaning for the reader, not one that merely attracts attention to the writing. Overuse of exotic synonyms corrupts style and tone of writing.

Be selective of details!

One important thing in writing description is to realize that not all details relating to the topic are equally useful or desirable. Only those **details** that **add to the dominant impression** should be included—human attention is selective after all. Effective description is **finely detailed** but **very carefully focused**. As writers, we have the license to omit details which are incongruent with the dominant impression unless the dominant impression is one which points out the discrepancies. For example, in describing a man's face to show how angry he was, we would probably describe the movement of his nose and hair, but not the shape of his nose or the color of his hair. The point is to use only those specific details that are relevant to our purpose.

In the following extract from *Hard Times*, Charles Dickens selects details to create, in subtle and compelling ways, layers of meaning that add to the dominant impression.

Sample 10

[Coketown] was a town of red brick, or of brick that would have been red if the smoke and ashes had allowed it but as matters stood it was a town of unnatural red and black like the painted face of a savage[1].

It was a town of machinery and tall chimneys, out of which interminable[2] serpents of smoke trailed[3] themselves for ever and ever, and never got uncoiled[4]. It had a black canal in it, and a river that ran purple with ill-smelling dye, arid[5] vast piles of building full of windows where there was a rattling and a trembling all day long, and where the piston[6] of the steam-engine worked monotonously[7] up and down, like the head of an elephant in a state of melancholy[8] madness. It contained several large streets all very like one another, and many small streets still more like one another, inhabited[9] by people equally like one another, who all went in and out at the same hours, with the same sound upon the same pavements, to do the same work, and to whom every day was the same as yesterday and tomorrow, and every year the counterpart of the last and the next...

Vocabulary

1. savage: *n.* 野人
2. interminable: *adj.* never-ending
3. trail: *v.* move slowly
4. coil: *v.* curve into a continuous series of loops or into the shape of a ring
5. arid: *adj.* dull and uninteresting
6. piston: *n.* 活塞
7. monotonous: *adj.* dull, boring
8. melancholy: *adj.* sad, gloomy
9. inhabit: *v.* live, dwell

Questions for Consideration

1. What is the dominant impression created by the description?
2. What details does Dickens select to add to the dominant impression? Do the details enhance that impression?
3. What is the quality of life like in the town?
4. What attitude of the writer can you identify towards the people living in the town?

Homework 2

Develop your topic into the first draft with a dominant impression and specific details.

Organizing a Descriptive Essay

Extended description that lacks organization has a confusing, surreal quality and easily loses readers' interest. While details are important, the way they are presented is going to decide whether the readers opt in or out. We therefore need to choose an organizational plan. We can use whatever progression seems logical—spatial order, chronological order, climatic/emphatical order or classification order. We can also combine different methods of organization, but the shift should be logical. For example, it does not make sense to describe a person's facial features and hair, then his sonorous voice and impressive vocabulary, and then return to details about his eyebrows and glasses. The particular organizing scheme we choose depends upon the dominant impression we want to convey, our thesis, our purpose and audience.

 ## Spatial Order

One option for organizing a descriptive essay is spatial: top to bottom, bottom to top, inside to out, outside to in, left to right, right to left, clockwise, counterclockwise, near to far, etc. Prepositional phrases and other references to relative positioning are common in the spatial order description.

Sample 11

Invasion of the English Teacher's Classroom

As we enter the corner classroom, we immediately know that it belongs to an English teacher. In the front of the room, the chalkboard reports the SAT[1] Word-of-the-Day and critical announcements, while an overhead projector beams instructions for the day's objectives and the night's homework. To the left, a chalk board stretches across the light beige[2]

Vocabulary

1. SAT: 美国学习能力倾向测试 Scholastic Aptitude Test 的缩写。指根据美国大学入学考试委员会编的试题进行的高等学校入学前的预测性考试。

2. beige: *n.* 米色

90

wall and displays important information about class activities; in addition, a laminated[3] large poster offers a time line on American authors. Bulletin boards flank[4] each end of the chalkboard and hold information and illustrations about an author and his works. On the back wall, warped[5] bookshelves overflow with dictionaries, literature books, and bulging writing folders. Locked blue closets, also in the back, contain secret devices that only an English teacher could disclose. The right wall should support large sparkling windows which would brighten the attractive room and nourish[6] flowering pink begonias[7] or delicate purple violets[8] with the warm afternoon sunshine; however, worn bricks shadow the room. Bulletin boards on this wall honor commendable student writing and again trap a chalk board to which ancient remains of yellow dust cling with boredom. In the middle of the area, rows of neatly arranged dark brown desks and sky blue chairs foretell of students reading Shakespeare's sonnets[9], composing creative essays, or punctuating complicated sentences. In addition, the teacher's desk, located near the right front of the room, conceals tests and lesson plans for the day. Finally, even the bluish gray carpet marks an English teacher's presence, as it muffles[10] harsh voices and secludes fallen paper clips and hole punchings which nestle[11] in the crevices[12] of the rough fabric. As we silently exit the room, we extinguish[13] the banks of harsh florescent[14] lights which clutter the ceiling, leaving no evidence of our invasion of the English teacher's domain.[15]

3. laminated: *adj.* covered with a thin sheet of clear plastic
4. flank: *v.* be on the side(s) of
5. warp: *v.* bend, twist

6. nourish: *v.* provide for
7. begonias: *n.* 秋海棠
8. violet: *n.* 紫罗兰

9. sonnet: *n.* 十四行诗

10. muffle: *v.* deaden
11. nestle: *v.* be in a position that seems safe and sheltered
12. crevice: *n.* 裂缝
13. extinguish: *v.* put out

14. florescent: *adj.* bright
15. domain: *n.* 领地

Questions for Consideration

1. What is the dominant impression of this room?
2. Underline all location phrases.
3. Circle all action verbs.
4. Underline descriptive adjectives twice.
5. What keeps the description coherent?

Chronological Order

It is possible to organize a description according to the time order in which an observer might see each part of the place. This works particularly well if we observe a place during an extended period of time. A description of the first day on a new job, for example, can start with how the person feels the first hour on the job and proceeds through the rest of the day. Similarly, a description of a large place can be arranged in the order of what the viewer sees at different times of the day.

 ## Climatic/Emphatical Order

Many writers try to save the best details for last and arrange details from least important to most important. In a description about a bout with the flu, a writer might arrange details emphatically, beginning with a description of the low-level aches and pains and concluding with an account of the raging fever.

Classification Order

With some description topics, it may be possible to group together things that are related. Similar items can be placed in the same group and described together even if they are not located near each other. We can, for example, classify things in a park into such groups as plants, facilities, trails, and people. Or we can group things together according to our sensory impressions when describing a cafeteria.

 ## Combination of Different Methods

Sometimes two or more methods of organization can be combined effectively. For example, if a writer is describing a fairly large area that he is observing over a period of time, he might combine spatial order and chronological order. In this case, he could write as an observer moving through the area and describing things in different locations as he sees them. Whether it is one or the other, the body of the essay needs to be correctly segmented. While giving details, we need to set the different aspects off in different paragraphs depending on its content. This way the essay reads well, has coherence and is meaningful.

Ⓗomework 3

Work in groups of three or four to have your first draft and the instructor's comments and suggestions read and discussed for improvements. Here are some questions you may ask in your discussion.

1. Have you created dominant impressions? Do you avoid overly general terms and focus on specific impressions? Is the dominant impression stated or implied? Should it be made more obvious or more subtle?

2. Is the essay primarily objective or subjective? Should the essay be more personal and emotionally charged or less so?

3. Are sensory details included more than sight? Can you add impressions of taste, touch, sound, and smell? Which descriptive details don't support the dominant impression? Should they be deleted, or should the dominant impression be adjusted to encompass the details?

4. Do you *show* rather than *tell*? Can you add action to your description to keep it from being static?

5. How are the essay's descriptive paragraphs organized? Would another pattern be more effective?

Revise your essay on the basis of your discussion.

Ⓐnalysis of Students' Writing

1. A Writer's Face

I was at the Smithtown Public library. I saw a picture of someone with a face like I don't see every day. It was a writer named Samuel Beckett. His face made me stop to look at it real close.

Mr. Beckett's hair was gray, short on the sides, and longer on top. You could hardly tell that his eyes were blue because they were so light. His forehead had deep wrinkles, and his eyebrows were bushy and his nose was like a beak.

Beckett reminded me of some kind of angry bird. His face made me sort of think of that. But maybe he couldn't help it.

2. A Look on a Book

After school, at the Smithtown Public Library, I noticed a book on the table. It showed a picture of the author Samuel Beckett. His face practically jumped out at me, so I stopped, and looked closer.

Beckett had silver hair, which was cut short above his ears. On top it was longer and scrunched up, like a crown of feathers. His forehead had rows of wrinkles across it. His eyebrows stuck out like another set of plumes. His pale blue eyes seemed to be sharply focused on something. His nose was like an enormous beak, and it cast a shadow across his mouth. He was frowning as if he had invented the frown!

I wondered how someone could develop a face like that. What had Mr. Beckett been thinking all his life? He looked like a wild eagle.

93

Comments:

The two passages, taken from *Write! Foundations and Models for Proficiency,* were written by American eighth graders at the prompt: "Write an essay describing a specific person's face." Both pieces connect directly to the prompt, introduce the subject at the beginning, use interesting details and sensory words to represent the subject in the middle and end with a dominant impression.

However, the second piece is more interesting because it uses more verbs of action, more concrete images, the dominant impression of "a wild eagle" in contrast with the vague term of "some kind of angry bird" in the first piece in particular, more figurative language, and a more thought-provoking ending question which may arouse the reader's interest in understanding more about the subject. (For that reason, the ending becomes more effective with the question at the very end, and "He looked like a wild eagle" placed at the beginning of the last paragraph.) The first piece, on the other hand, primarily uses "to be" and vague expressions like "a face like I don't see every day" and "some kind of angry bird" to describe the subject and ends with a rather indifferent attitude towards the subject. Unfortunately, the second piece has a vague title and an indirect wordy beginning. "Samuel Beckett's picture jumped out at me at ..." becomes a much more effective beginning.

Further Reading

Once More to the Lake

E. B. White

(An excerpt)

One summer, along about 1904, my father rented a camp on a lake in Maine and took us all there for the month of August. We all got ringworm from some kittens and had to rub Pond's Extract on our arms and legs night and morning, and my father rolled over in a canoe with all his clothes on; but outside of that the vacation was a success and from then on none of us ever thought there was any place in the world like that lake in Maine. We returned summer after summer—always on August 1st for one month. I have since become a salt-water man, but sometimes in summer there are days when the restlessness of the tides and the fearful cold of the sea water and the incessant wind which blows across the afternoon and into the evening make me wish for the placidity of a lake in the woods. A few weeks ago this feeling got so strong I bought myself a couple of bass hooks and a spinner and returned to the lake where we used to go, for a week's fishing and to revisit old haunts.

I took along my son, who had never had any fresh water up his nose and who had seen lily pads only from train windows. On the journey over to the lake I began to wonder what it would be like. I wondered how time would have marred this unique, this holy spot—the coves and streams, the hills that the sun set behind, the camps and the paths behind the camps. I was sure that the tarred road would have found it out and I wondered in what other ways it would be desolated. [...]

I was right about the tar: it led to within half a mile of the shore But when I got back there, with my boy, and we settled into a camp near a farmhouse and into the kind of summertime I had known, I could tell that it was going to be pretty much the same as it had been before—I knew it, lying in bed the first morning, smelling the bedroom, and hearing the boy sneak quietly out and go off along the shore in a boat. I began to sustain the illusion that he was I, and therefore, by simple transposition, that I was my father. This sensation persisted, kept cropping up all the time we were there. It was not an entirely new feeling, but in this setting it grew much stronger. I seemed to be living a dual existence. I would be in the middle of some simple act, I would be picking up a bait box or laying down a table fork, or I would be saying something, and suddenly it would be not I but my father who was saying the words or making the gesture. It gave me a creepy sensation.

We went fishing the first morning. I felt the same damp moss covering the worms in the bait can, and saw the dragonfly alight on the tip of my rod as it hovered a few inches from the surface of the water. It was the arrival of this fly that convinced me beyond any doubt that everything was as it always had been, that the years were a mirage and there had been no years. The small waves were the same, chucking the rowboat under the chin as we fished at anchor, and the boat was the same boat, the same color green and the ribs broken in the same places, and under the floor-boards the same freshwater leavings and debris—the dead helgramite, the wisps of moss, the rusty discarded fishhook, the dried blood from yesterday's catch. We stared silently at the tips of our rods, at the dragonflies that came and wells. I lowered the tip of mine into the water, tentatively, pensively dislodging the fly, which darted two feet away, poised, darted two feet back, and came to rest again a little farther up the rod. There had been no years between the ducking of this dragonfly and the other one—the one that was part of memory. I looked at the boy, who was silently watching his fly, and it was my hands that held his rod, my eyes watching. I felt dizzy and didn't know which rod I was at the end of.

[...] When we got back for a swim before lunch, the lake was exactly where we had left it, the same number of inches from the dock, and there was only the merest suggestion of a breeze. This seemed an utterly enchanted sea, this lake you could leave to its own devices for a few hours and come back to, and find that it had not stirred, this constant and trustworthy body of water. In the shallows, the dark, water-soaked sticks and twigs, smooth and old, were undulating in clusters on the bottom against the clean ribbed sand, and the track of the mussel was plain. A school of minnows swam by, each minnow with its small, individual shadow, doubling the attendance, so clear and sharp in the sunlight. Some of the other campers were in swimming, along the shore, one of them with a cake of soap, and the water felt thin and clear and insubstantial. Over the years there had been this person with the cake of soap, this cultist, and here he was. There had been no years.

Up to the farmhouse to dinner through the teeming, dusty field, the road under our sneakers was only a two-track road. [...] and something about the way it lay there in the

95

sun reassured me; the tape had loosened along the backline, the alleys were green with plantains and other weeds, and the net (installed in June and removed in September) sagged in the dry noon, and the whole place steamed with midday heat and hunger and emptiness. There was a choice of pie for dessert, and one was blueberry and one was apple, and the waitresses were the same country girls, there having been no passage of time, only the illusion of it as in a dropped curtain—the waitresses were still fifteen; their hair had been washed, that was the only difference—they had been to the movies and seen the pretty girls with the clean hair.

Summertime, oh summertime, pattern of life indelible, the fade proof lake, the woods unshatterable, the pasture with the sweet fern and the juniper forever and ever, summer without end; this was the background, and the life along the shore was the design, the cottages with their innocent and tranquil design, their tiny docks with the flagpole and the American flag floating against the white clouds in the blue sky, the little paths over the roots of the trees leading from camp to camp and the paths leading back to the outhouses and the can of lime for sprinkling, and at the souvenir counters at the store the miniature birch-bark canoes and the post cards that showed things looking a little better than they looked. [...]

It seemed to me, as I kept remembering all this, that those times and those summers had been infinitely precious and worth saving. There had been jollity and peace and goodness. The arriving (at the beginning of August) had been so big a business in itself, at the railway station the farm wagon drawn up, the first smell of the pine-laden air, the first glimpse of the smiling farmer, and the great importance of the trunks and your father's enormous authority in such matters, and the feel of the wagon under you for the long ten-mile haul, and at the top of the last long hill catching the first view of the lake after eleven months of not seeing this cherished body of water. The shouts and cries of the other campers when they saw you, and the trunks to be unpacked, to give up their rich burden. (Arriving was less exciting nowadays, when you sneaked up in your car and parked it under a tree near the camp and took out the bags and in five minutes it was all over, no fuss, no loud wonderful fuss about trunks.)

Peace and goodness and jollity. The only thing that was wrong now, really, was the sound of the place, an unfamiliar nervous sound of the outboard motors. This was the note that jarred, the one thing that would sometimes break the illusion and set the years moving. In those other summertimes, all motors were inboard; and when they were at a little distance, the noise they made was a sedative, an ingredient of summer sleep. They were one-cylinder and two-cylinder engines, and some were make-and-break and some were jump-spark, but they all made a sleepy sound across the lake. The one-lungers throbbed and fluttered, and the twin-cylinder ones purred and purred, and that was a quiet sound too. But now the campers all had outboards. In the daytime, in the hot mornings, these motors made a petulant, irritable sound; at night, in the still evening when the afterglow lit the water, they whined about one's ears like mosquitoes.[...]

We had a good week at the camp. The bass were biting well and the sun shone endlessly, day after day. We would be tired at night and lie down in the accumulated heat of the little bedrooms after the long hot day and the breeze would stir almost imperceptibly outside and the smell of the swamp drift in through the rusty screens. Sleep would come easily and in the morning the red squirrel would be on the roof, tapping out his gay routine. [...] After breakfast we would go up to the store and the things were in the same place—the minnows in a bottle, the plugs and spinners disarranged and pawed over by the youngsters from the boys' camp, the fig newtons and the Beeman's gum. Outside, the road was tarred and cars stood in front of the store. Inside, all was just as it had always been, except there was more Coca Cola and not so much Moxie and root beer and birch beer and sarsaparilla. We would walk out with a bottle of pop apiece and sometimes the pop would backfire up our noses and hurt. We explored the streams, quietly, where the turtles slid off the sunny logs and dug their way into the soft bottom; and we lay on the town wharf and fed worms to the tame bass. Everywhere we went I had trouble making out which was I, the one walking at my side, the one walking in my pants.

One afternoon while we were there at that lake a thunderstorm came up. It was like the revival of an old melodrama that I had seen long ago with childish awe. The second-act climax of the drama of the electrical disturbance over a lake in America had not changed in any important respect. This was the big scene, still the big scene. The whole thing was so familiar, the first feeling of oppression and heat and a general air around camp of not wanting to go very far away. In mid-afternoon (it was all the same) a curious darkening of the sky, and a lull in everything that had made life tick; and then the way the boats suddenly swung the other way at their moorings with the coming of a breeze out of the new quarter, and the premonitory rumble. Then the kettle drum, then the snare, then the bass drum and cymbals, then crackling light against the dark, and the gods grinning and licking their chops in the hills. Afterward the calm, the rain steadily rustling in the calm lake, the return of light and hope and spirits, and the campers running out in joy and relief to go swimming in the rain, their bright cries perpetuating the deathless joke about how they were getting simply drenched, and the children screaming with delight at the new sensation of bathing in the rain, and the joke about getting drenched linking the generations in a strong indestructible chain. And the comedian who waded in carrying an umbrella.

When the others went swimming my son said he was going in too. He pulled his dripping trunks from the line where they had hung all through the shower, and wrung them out. Languidly, and with no thought of going in, I watched him, his hard little body, skinny and bare, saw him wince slightly as he pulled up around his vitals the small, soggy, icy garment. As he buckled the swollen belt suddenly my groin felt the chill of death.

Questions for Close Reading and Consideration
 1. What is the dominant impression or thesis?
 2. White says that he seemed to be living "a dual existence" as a father in the present and as a son in the remembered life of the past. Point to some moments when that dual existence seems most natural and to some when it seems more difficult to maintain. What seems to explain the differences to him and to you?

3. Why does White return to the lake in Maine he had visited as a child? Why do you think he has waited to revisit it until he has a young son to bring along?

4. Several times in the essay, White notes that he felt as if he were his own father—and that his son became his childhood self. What event first prompts this sensation? What actions and thoughts cause it to recur?

5. White overlays two sets of sensory details: those of the present-day lake and those of the lake as it was in his boyhood. Which set of details is more objective? Which seems sharper and more powerful?

6. In what ways do White's physical descriptions of the lake and its surroundings suggest why he loves the place? Analyze an example or two in which emotion is created by style.

7. To describe the lake, White chooses many words and phrases with religious connotation. Give some examples. What might have been his purpose in using such language?

8. In paragraph 12, White uses a metaphor to describe a thunderstorm. To what does he compare a thunderstorm? Why does he make this comparison?

9. What makes the thunderstorm a good episode with which to end the essay? What earlier themes does the moment collect and connect?

10. What do you make of the final sentence of the essay?

98

Unit 5

The Comparison and Contrast Essay

Tuning-in Activities

 Activity 1

Look at the following pictures carefully and match a person in Column A with a dog in Column B according to their similarities in appearance. And then, list the similarities between each pair.

Column A: People	Column B: Dogs	Similarities or differences of the pairs
 A. An old man	 1. A red setter	Pair A:
 B. A young lady	 2. A greyhound	Pair B:
C. A young man	3. A bulldog	Pair C:

Activity 2

Identify as many differences as possible in the different citation styles.

Authors: Peter S. Heikinheimo and Jean M. Schute

Article Title: The Adaptation of Foreign Students: Student Views and Institutional Implications

Journal Title: Journal of College Student Personnel

Volume: 27   **Number:** 5   **Pages:** 399—405

Date: September 1986

APA format:

Heikinheimo, P.S., & Schute, J.M. (1986). The adaptation of foreign students: Student views and institutional implications. *Journal of College Student Personnel*, 27(5), 399—405.

MLA format:

Heikinheimo, Peter S., and Jean M. Schute. "The Adaptation of Foreign Students: Student Views and Institutional Implications." Journal of College Student Personnel 27 (1986): 399—405.

Introduction

We have just compared the appearances of three people with those of three dogs. In fact, we compare and/or contrast things every day: when we have to decide on one of the (two) universities to go, one of the brands of mobile phones to buy or one of the boys/girls to date. Before we make a decision, we **compare to bring out the similarities** between two things, and/or **contrast to emphasize the differences** between them. Comparison and contrast help us to analyze, understand and evaluate two subjects better than we would do if we just examine the two individually. Writing an essay of comparison and contrast is just an extension of this logical thought process.

In writing a comparison and/or contrast essay, we may emphasize either the similarities or the differences between the two subjects, or, we may include both the similarities and differences. No matter what we may emphasize in our essay, we should always keep in mind that we have to **be fair in making the comparison** and that we need to **make a point** in our essay. If the two items are too similar or too different, there won't be any point in comparing or contrasting them. We normally make a comparison and/or contrast for one of three purposes: **to present information** about something unfamiliar by comparing it with something familiar, **to show the superiority** (or our preference) of one thing by comparing it with another, and **to help the reader better understand or evaluate two things** by showing their similarities and differences.

We will communicate more clearly when we keep our **purpose** and **audience** in mind. If our purpose is to provide information about softball, which is not very popular in China, we can show the reader how it is like baseball, focusing primarily about their **similarities**. If our purpose is to convince the reader that the pig is a healthier pet to keep than the dog, we can contrast **differences** between the two animals. If our purpose is to provide information about Jiuzhaigou and Zhangjiajie so that the reader can make a choice for his/her vacation, we need to point out **both similarities and differences** of the two places.

In order for our writing to be as informative or persuasive as it can be, we should carefully consider who our intended **audience/reader** is. We need to consider what the reader already knows about the subject so as to decide what terms to define and how much background information to provide.

Sample 1

Different Roommates
Cecilia Richardson

Vocabulary

I am amazed myself at how little trouble it is living with and liking two such different roommates. Their physical appearances differ greatly. With small brown eyes and straight black hair to her shoulders, Julie is tall, lean and statuesque[1]. Pat, on the other hand, is tiny. Under five feet tall, she keeps her blonde hair short and fluffy[2]. Looking out over a small nose, her large gray eyes are "funny looking," according to her. "They're all right if you like cats," she says grinning.

These two girls also have different kinds of interests. Julie likes reading or relaxing quietly in front of the TV set. She likes talking too; she will speak to me for hours about a feature in *People Magazine* or about a Marx Brothers' film she watched on Channel 4 until dawn. Her voice quivers with excitement. "Just listen to this," she will say, her eyes glowing, her warm fingers pressed to my palm to hold my attention. But for Pat the outdoor life holds more interest than books or screens. At six each morning, in a bright orange sweat suit, she is jogging merrily down University Drive, crunching[3] through leaves for her usual four miles. She swims. She plays tennis. She is a terror at paddleball[4], smashing shots I have to groan to

1. statuesque: *adj.* calmly and grandly beautiful
2. fluffy: *adj.* soft and loose

3. crunch: *v.* make a crushing noise
4. paddleball: *n.* 板手球运动

return.

However, the most interesting difference between them is their approach to schoolwork. Julie grows tense before an exam. At her desk a small fluorescent[5] lamp throws a pale light on her face as she sits for hours glaring nervously at a page in her biology book. She underlines words noisily and scrawls notes to herself in the margin with a yellow felt[6] pen. Her lips say over and over some key words she wants to memorize. Because only "A" grades satisfy her, she works tirelessly. Pat, on the contrary, takes everything easy, and exams are no exception. Sprawled on the red and white print couch, she surrounds herself with cola, corn chips, chocolate bars, apples, and salted nuts. She jabbers[7] endlessly and jumps up every few minutes to stare out the window, to do a few sit-ups or to splash herself with spicy cologne. Without much effort or anxiety she crams[8] enough data into her head to earn grades that keep her happy.

Since I can live in harmony with my roommates in spite of their differences, I am confident that I will be able to get along with most people anywhere.

5. fluorescent: *adj.* 荧光的

6. felt: *n.* 毛毡

7. jabber: *v.* talk quickly but unclearly
8. cram: *v.* fill sth. too full

102

Exercises

1. What do you think is Cecilia Richardson's purpose in writing this essay of contrast?
2. Identify the thesis and supporting details of each paragraph.

Thesis: _____

(1) Topic: _____

    a. Julie _____

    b. Pat _____

(2) Topic: _____

    a. Julie _____

    b. Pat _____

(3) Topic: _____

    a. Julie _____

    b. Pat _____

Generation Next
Nancy Gibbs

Vocabulary

Millennials[1] respect their elders, so why do they say the generation gap is wider than ever?

Today the members of the millennial generation, ages 18 to 29, are so close to their parents that college students typically check in their emails about 10 times a week, and they are all Facebook[2] friends. Kids and parents dress alike, listen to the same music and fight less than previous generations, and millennials assert that older people's moral values are generally superior to their own.

Yet even more young people perceive a gap. According to a recently released Pew Research Center[3] report, 79% of millennials say there is a major difference in the point of view of younger and older people today. Young Americans are now more educated, more diverse, more optimistic and less likely to have a job than previous generations. But it is in their use of technology that millennials see the greatest difference, starting perhaps with the fact that 83% of them sleep with their cell phones. Change now comes so strong and fast that it pulls apart even those who wish to hang together—and the future belongs to the strong of thumb.

But we miss the point, warns social historian Neil Howe, if we weigh only how technology shapes a generation and not the other way around. The millennials were raised in a cocoon, their anxious parents afraid to let them go out in the park to play. So should we be surprised that they learned to leverage technology to build community, tweeting[4] and texting and friending while their elders were still dialing long-distance? They are the most likely of any generation to think technology unites people rather than isolates them, that it is primarily a means of connection, not

1. millennials: *n.* "千禧代"

2. Facebook: *n.* 一个社交网站的名字

3. Pew Research Center: 皮尤研究中心

103

4. tweet: *v.* 网民通过 Twitter ("推特", 国外的一个社交网络及微博服务的网站)来发送信息等

competition.

That hunger for community further distinguishes them from the radical individualists of the baby-boom years. In fact, in some respects the millennials emerge as radically conventional. Asked about their life goals, 52% say being a good parent is most important to them, followed by having a successful marriage, 59% think that the trend of more single women having children is bad for society. While more tolerant than older generations, they are still more likely to disapprove of than support the trend of unmarried couples living together. While they're more politically progressive than their elders, you could argue that their strong support for gay marriage[5] and interracial marriage reflects their desire to extend traditional institutions as widely as possible. If boomers were always looking to shock, millennials are eager to share.

But they are also unconventionally conventional. They are, for example, the least officially religious of any modern generation, and fully 1 in 4 has no religious affiliation at all. On the other hand, they are just as spiritual, just as likely to believe in miracles and hell and angels as earlier generations were. They pray about as much as their elders did when they were young— all of which suggests that they have not lost faith in God, only in the institutions that claim to speak for him.

The greatest divide of all has to do with hope and heart. In any age, young folk tend to be more cheerful than old folk, but the hope gap has never been greater than it is now. Despite two wars and a nasty recession that has hit young people hardest, the Pew survey found that 41% of U.S. millennials are satisfied with how things are going, compared with 26% of older people. Less than a third of those with jobs earn enough to lead the kind of life they want—but 83% are confident that they will one day.

"Youth is easily deceived," Aristotle said, "because it is quick to hope." But I'd rather think

104

5. gay marriage: 指同性婚姻

that the millennials know something we don't about the inventions that will emerge from their networked brains, the solutions that might arise from a generation so determined to bridge gaps and work as a team. In that event, their vision would be vindicated[6], not only for themselves but for those of us who will one day follow their lead.

6. vindicate: *v.* 证明正确或合理

Exercises

1. Identify the main idea and supporting details.

Thesis: _____

1. Similarities

   a. _____

   b. _____

2. Differences

   a. _____

   b. _____

2. Does this essay stress comparison, contrast, or both?

Finding the Topic

It is not difficult to find two things to compare and/or contrast. Two books, movies, mobile phones, cars, seasons, decades, places, people, events, fashions, methods, attitudes, feelings, ideas, etc. can all become our topic for comparison and/or contrast. However, we need a good reason to make the comparison and/or contrast. *Why* should we compare one with the other? Will the comparison actually help anyone's understanding of either one? Can we actually accomplish something important in making the comparison and/or contrast? Can we provide a unique insight into the nature of these two things that the reader would never have discovered otherwise? With these questions in mind, we can decide on our topics, freewrite on them and then work in pairs to discuss whether we have a good reason to make the comparison and/or contrast.

When we are convinced of the reason for the comparison and/or contrast, we may begin to create a list of the potential points for each of our selected subjects, and then organize the points in some logical order.

Understanding Different Patterns of Organization

There are three major ways to organize supporting details in a comparison and/or contrast essay: **point-by-point** pattern, **subject-by-subject** or **block-by-block** pattern and a special kind of comparison: **the analogy**. In long papers, we may mix them, but in the shorter pieces, we will usually select one and make it our basic organizational plan.

Pattern One: Point-by-Point Arrangement

With this scheme we make a point of differences/similarities about the first subject and then treat the corresponding point of differences/similarities about the second subject. We treat the next point about the first subject and follow it with the corresponding point about the second subject. We continue in this alternating fashion until all our points have been presented and developed.

Point 1:	**Subject A**
	Subject B
Point 2:	Subject A
	Subject B
Point 3:	**Subject A**
	Subject B

This way can be used for long, complex essays or essays developed with a great many points, or where the interest of the writer is on the specific aspects of the subject.

Sample 3

Judo versus Wrestling

Ray Jensen

Many people believe judo[1] and wrestling[2] are basically the same because they are both one-on-one contact sports that have pinning[3] and points for the means of winning. However, judo is easier and less dangerous because of the differences in the throws, the pinning techniques, and the scoring system.

One the main differences between judo and wrestling is the throws. In wrestling, there are very few throws that are legal, and most of them are very painful to the receiver. In fact, most of the throws are not intended, and they can result in broken bones. If a throw is done in wrestling, it rarely accomplishes much. However, in judo there are many throws, and the throws are taught as an art. A judo student learns the kata (the motions of the throw) before he learns the actual throw. The judo student is trained to throw his opponent in such a way as to give the least pain and danger. Also, the judo student is trained to fall correctly to avoid hurting himself.

Besides the throws, the pinning techniques make competition in judo easier. In wrestling, the wrestler has to have both shoulders of his opponent touching the mat in order to win. The count is for approximately five seconds, and sometimes the referee does not or cannot see whether or not both shoulders are actually touching. Many times, the wrestler gets his opponent's shoulders on the mat, and just before the count is over, his opponent moves, forcing him to lose all the effort he has put into it. In contrast, the judo student only has to have his opponent in a "controlled hold," which does not require both shoulders touching. It is much easier to get the opponent in a controlled hold for 30 seconds than to try to get both of the opponent's shoulders to touch the mat.

In addition to the throws and pinning techniques, the scoring system in wrestling is more complicated

1. judo: *n.* 柔道
2. wrestling: *n.* 摔跤
3. to pin sb. in a position: to hold the person or press down on him firmly so that the person cannot move.

107

than in judo. In wrestling, for example, the wrestler gets points for a reversal, which means that the wrestler was in a down position but then made a fast move to get out from under his opponent's control and then another move to gain control of his opponent. Other moves that gain points are a takedown, which is when the wrestler forces his opponent to the mat, and an escape, which is when the wrestler escapes from a hold that his opponent puts on him. The scoring system for judo is simpler. The judo student can get a full point, which means a win, if he throws his opponent directly on his back. If the judo student only throws his opponent halfway, he gains half a point, which also allows him to be given five seconds off the time he has to have his opponent in a controlled hold.

108

With all the advantages of the throws, pinning techniques, and scoring system, it is no surprise that judo is easier and less dangerous. More people should try judo for exercise and for the competition.

Questions for Consideration

1. What pattern of organization is used in making the comparison and contrast?
2. Which sentence states the thesis?
3. What is the function of the last paragraph?
4. It is obvious that this essay is well-organized and carefully avoids the choppy seesaw effect. However, as a reader, do you think it lacks vividness in expression? Do you expect more vicarious excitement from it?

Pattern Two: Subject-by-Subject Arrangement

It is a common arrangement. In this scheme, we make all our points of similarities/ differences about the first subject, and then we go on to make all our points of similarities/ differences about the second subject.

Subject A: **Point 1**

Point 2

Point 3

...

Subject B: Point 1

                Point 2

                Point 3

                ...

In general, this way works better in short essays where few aspects are considered, or where the interest of the writer is on the whole. Otherwise, the reader working through our points on the second subject must keep too many points about the first subject in mind.

Sample 4

Shopping in America
Charles M. Bezzler

Since the 1950s, American shoppers have been spending their money in suburban malls instead of in downtown business districts. This is even true of shoppers who have to go out of their way to shop in the malls; they will bypass downtown stores (which they might have gotten to by convenient bus) to drive to the brightly bedecked and weather-free meccas[1] of shopper-heaven. The result, some people claim, is the demise of the central urban commercial district, Downtown, a process leading inevitably toward more widespread urban blight[2]. But why are Americans so easily lured to shop in malls in the first place?

First, Americans don't like weather. They like to be indoors whenever possible, even on nice days, and they're willing to pay a premium[3] to be protected from the elements. If they can find someone who can afford it, they will even put their sports stadiums under a gigantic bowl, and they love to stay indoors for a day of shopping, perhaps never seeing the sun from the time they first enter until they leave, hours later, relieved of money, oxygen, and much money.

Second, Americans love convenience and, except during the crush of major holidays, malls offer plenty of convenient parking. A happy, enormous island of commerce in a sea of asphalt[4], the mall

Vocabulary

1. mecca: *n.* 麦加(伊斯兰教圣地);众人渴望去的地方

2. blight: *n.* ugly or neglected part (esp. of cities)

3. premium: *n.* 保险费;额外费用

4. asphalt: *n.* 沥青

offers plenty of docking point—usually next to major commercial outlet—for cars that circle in search of the closest slot and an easy entrance.

Third, the mall offers an extraordinary variety of products under its one gigantic roof. Specialty stores and boutiques[5] offer items that people don't realize they need until they're put under the spell of brightly lighted, beautifully furnished window after window of beguiling wares. Malls are built to respond to Americans' insatiable desire for stuff; either that, or a generation of Americans has been genetically engineered to respond to the sellers of stuff. Either way, it works.

And finally, the mall feels safe: it is lighted, warm, dry, and busy. Senior citizens are invited to do their walking exercises there in the early hours; physically challenged people easily meander the smooth floors of curbless, stairless businesses in motorized carts; children are amused by clowns and fed at convenient cafeterias in Food Court.

America's Downtown, on the other hand, is often in sad repair. Parking is difficult, if not dangerous, and until you get through the door, it's all outdoors. To get from store to store, you must expose yourself to heat, cold, rain, snow. There are sometimes solicitors to fleece[6] you of change before you even get into a store. If there is a plan here, it is not evident to most shoppers. Where is the information kiosk[7] with a cordial, well-informed attendant to direct you to the nearest clothier, jeweler, fast-food outlet, or bathroom? Is there a bathroom?

What is left in the American Downtown to recommend it to shoppers? Practically nothing. Nothing, that is, unless you regard as important the notion that the businesses you give your money to should be owned by people, families, in your own community. Yes, there may be chain-stores; it seems there has always been a W.T. Grants, a J.C. Penneys, a Whackers. But the people who owned the franchise[8] and worked behind the cash register were people you might meet in your own

110

5. boutique: *n.* 小精品店

6. fleece: *v.* 敲竹杠

7. kiosk: *n.* small open structure where newspapers, refreshments, etc. are sold

8. franchise: *n.* formal permission to sell a company's goods or services in a particular area

neighborhood. When you walk into the Downtown hardware store, you often feel wood, not vinyl linoleum, beneath your feet. And some old guy, who seemed old when he sold your father the hammer you use today, will sell you nails in a paper bag, weighing them out by the handful until you get the exact number you need, not the arbitrary number that comes in a hermetically sealed plastic box[9].

Next door, in the department store, there will be two women who know you by name and who can't wait to help you find what you need or will let you ruminate among the shelves if you want. In the drug store across the street, the pharmacist knows your aches and pains and what you've been taking for them the last five years and what upsets your stomach and knows to call your doctor when the prescription doesn't make sense. If there is a soda fountain there—naah, that's asking too much.

The truth is that the American mall grows where it does because someone with enormously deep pockets decides to plunk it down where there used to be woods or a golf course. He surrounds it with hundreds of acres of parking and waits for people to come spend their money, as he knows they will because people will do what mass advertising tells them to do. Downtown, on the other hand, grew where it did because there was an organic need for it. It was a community's response to a community's needs—neighbors responding to neighbors—and it flourished as the community flourished. If the mall can replace this sense of community, then so be it; it deserves our affection as well as our dollars. If it can't, then we have gained convenient parking and freedom from the weather at an awful price.

9. hermetically sealed plastic box: 密封的塑料盒

111

Exercises

1. What is the thesis? Is it clearly stated or implied?

2. How do you like the essay? Is it interesting? What makes it so?

3. Fill out the following form according to this essay. And then add more rows to the form as you find more categories in which shopping in a modern mall vs. shopping in an old-fashioned downtown store. Comparison and contrast can be made in terms of your own experience.

Category	Shopping in the Mall	Shopping in Downtown

Pattern Three: A Special Kind of Comparison: The Analogy

An ordinary comparison/contrast essay points out similarities and differences between two things of the same class. An analogy is slightly different: it deals only with similarities, not with contrasts, between two things of different classes. The purposes of analogy are to clarify, support, illustrate or simplify an abstract, unfamiliar, or complex subject by comparing it to something that is familiar to the reader, often something that is more concrete or easier to understand. In an analogy, one subject is the main focus of attention.

Sample 5

What True Education Should Do

Sydney J. Harris

Vocabulary

When most people think of the word "education," they think of a pupil as a sort of animate sausage casing[1]. Into this empty casing, the teachers are supposed to stuff "education."

But genuine education, as Socrates knew more than two thousand years ago, is not inserting the stuffings of information into a person, but rather eliciting knowledge from him; it is the drawing out of what is in the mind.

"The most important part of education," once wrote William Ernest Hocking, the distinguished Harvard philosopher, "is this instruction of a man in what he has inside of him."

1. sausage casing: 灌香肠用的肠衣

And, as Edith Hamilton has reminded us, Socrates never said, "I know, learn from me." He said, rather, "Look into your own selves and find the spark of truth that God has put into every heart, and that only you can kindle to a flame."

In the dialogue called the "Meno," Socrates takes an ignorant slave boy, without a day of schooling, and proves to the amazed observers that the boy really "knows" geometry[2]—because the principles and axioms of geometry are already in his mind, waiting to be called out.

2. geometry: *n.* 几何（学）

So many of the discussions and controversies about the content of education are futile and inconclusive because they are concerned with what should "go into" the student rather than with what should be taken out, and how this can best be done. The college student who once said to me, after a lecture, "I spend so much time studying that I don't have a chance to learn anything," was succinctly expressing his dissatisfaction with the sausage-casing view of education.

He was being so stuffed with miscellaneous[3] facts, with such an indigestible mass of material, that he had no time (and was given no encouragement) to draw on his own resources, to use his own mind for analyzing and synthesizing and evaluating this material.

3. miscellaneous: *adj.* of various kinds

Education, to have any meaning beyond the purpose of creating well informed dunces, must elicit from the pupil what is latent in every human being— the rules of reason, the inner knowledge of what is proper for men to be and do, the ability to sift evidence and come to conclusions that can generally be assented to by all open minds and warm hearts. Pupils are more like oysters than sausages. The job of teaching is not to stuff them and then seal them up, but to help them open and reveal the riches within. There are pearls in each of us, if only we knew how to cultivate them with ardor and persistence.

Questions for Consideration
1. How does the writer limit the broad topic to a manageable one for a short essay?
2. What analogies does the writer use and how do they help make the point?
3. What is the tone of the essay?
4. What is the function of the last sentence?

Paragraphs in a Comparison and Contrast Essay

The introductory paragraph

We can introduce a comparison and contrast essay by explaining clearly our purpose for making the comparison and/or contrast, stating our thesis, presenting background information that triggers the essay, or trying to get the reader's attention. Sample 3 begins with a lead-in sentence, followed immediately by a clearly stated thesis, in which the writer not only makes a strong point that judo is easier and less dangerous, but also indicates the structure of the essay by mentioning the three different points between the two sports.

The supporting paragraphs

As in other modes of writing, the supporting paragraphs, the body of the essay, present information to support the thesis. In a comparison and contrast essay, details may mainly be arranged either in subject-by-subject or point-by-point pattern. Sometimes, both patterns are adopted in the same essay when both similarities and differences are highlighted. In Sample 3, the writer employs the point-by-point pattern to explain one difference between judo and wrestling in each paragraph following the order listed in the thesis: the throws, the pinning techniques and the scoring system. Each point made about judo is compared with the corresponding point made about wrestling to argue that judo is easier and less dangerous.

The concluding paragraph

Our conclusion should help our readers to understand our point better. We may connect our main points back to the thesis, restate our purpose in a fresh way, propose an action, stimulate the reader or make a generalization. In Sample 3, the concluding paragraph includes not only a restatement of the thesis, but also a call for action based on the thesis.

Homework 1

Organize the potential points for your subject in one of the three patterns and write the first draft of an essay.

Using Transitional Words or Phrases

Transitions are important in every kind of expository writing. But in writing a comparison and contrast essay, they are especially necessary. A reader needs clear signals in order to follow the many shifts of a writer's thought as he describes the similarities or differences of a subject.

The following words and phrases are often used in writing comparison:

also	in the same way	likewise
similarly	too	at the same time
equally important	like	as
equally		

Other words and phrases that are often helpful when dealing with contrast are these:

on the contrary	yet	different from	but
on the other hand	unlike	in spite of	whereas
despite	in contrast	although	nevertheless
in contrast	however	instead	even so
even though	for all that	still	notwithstanding
conversely	rather than		

Transitional words help the writer to keep his/her ideas flowing and the reader to keep to the writer's idea. They, therefore, come naturally in the text.
For example:

Fire fighting is a very action-oriented profession suited for individuals with a high drive for action. *Similarly*, journalism too calls for action-oriented attitude in work where the journalist follows various happenings around the world and tries to be where the news happens. *However*, the two professions differ when it comes to the level of glamour involved. Journalism carries more glamorous image than the fire fighting profession. Journalists ranging from news anchors to action reporters are constantly in the media lime light. *In contrast*, the fire fighters who put their lives on line to save others are rarely in the public eye on an individual basis.

Translation vs Interpretation
Laura K. Lawless
Most laypeople refer to both translation and interpretation as "translation." Although translation and interpretation share the common goal of taking information that is available in one language and converting it to another, they are in fact two separate processes.

Translation is written—it involves taking a written text (such as a book or an article) and translating it in writing into the target language. *On the other hand*, interpretation is oral—it refers to listening to something spoken (a speech or phone conversation) and interpreting it orally into the target language.

The main difference is in how the information is presented—orally in interpretation and written in translation. This might seem like a subtle distinction, but if you consider your own language skills, the odds are that your ability to read/write and listen/speak are not identical—you are probably more skilled at one pair or the other. So translators are excellent writers, *while* interpreters have superior oral communication skills. In addition, spoken language is quite different from written, which adds a further dimension to the distinction. Then there's the fact that translators work alone to produce a translation, *while* interpreters work with two or more people/groups to provide an interpretation on the spot during negotiations, seminars, phone conversations, etc.

Exercise

Fill in the blanks with the following transitional words or phrases:

even though, rather than, similarly, on the other hand, in contrast, conversely, while, whereas, however, etc.

1. We are taught that a business letter should be written in a formal style _____ in a personal one.

2. On the one hand, my piano teacher always picks on me; _____, she takes a detached view of my performance.

3. Not all business transactions are legitimate _____, not all clients are honest either.

4. The Chinese economy has expanded dramatically, while the American economy, _____ has shrunk.

5. Physicians today still face serious physical and psychological stress on duty; _____ working conditions for most people have been improved greatly.

6. Roosevelt was a more effective president than Wilson not only because of his determination, but also because of his greater enthusiasm. First, President Wilson took a more pessimistic approach to the United States role in World War I, an approach that resulted in some strong opposition to the war. _____ from the very beginning of the United States entry into World War II, President Roosevelt expressed to the nation an encouraging enthusiasm that uplifted the spirits of the American people. For example, in Wilson's war address to Congress, he states rather negatively, "It is a fearful thing to lead this great nation into war, into the most terrible and disastrous of all wars." Roosevelt, _____, in his war address says, "No matter how long it may take us to overcome this premeditated invasion, the American people in their righteous might will win through to absolute victory." Wilson's use of negative words such as "never," "fearful, "terrible," and "disastrous" show his pessimism about the United States' entry into the war. Roosevelt, _____,

uses words that convey a positive, optimistic tone, such as "overcome," "righteous," and "absolute victory." Furthermore, Wilson uses the neutral term "war," _____ Roosevelt characterizes the enemy action (the Pearl Harbor attack) as an "invasion" (even though it has taken place at a great distance from the United States), thus creating a sense of urgency and outrage calculated to stirring up patriotic unity. Wilson refers to the nation with a sonorous abstraction ("great...people") and as being "peaceful," hardly words that would be effective in rallying a war effort. Roosevelt, _____, refers specifically to "the American people," calling on their unified identity, and identifying them not as being "peaceful" but rather as having "righteous might," a term that appeals to their sense of strength. Finally, _____ Wilson's statement focuses on the "terrible and disastrous" war, suggesting a possibly negative outcome, Roosevelt effectively uplifts the nation's spirit with his confidence that America "will win" an "absolute victory."

[H]omework 2

Improve the text organization of your first draft with consideration of the organization pattern and the use of transitional words. Ask two of your classmates to comment on your draft and revise it accordingly.

Tips for revision

1. A useful way to begin writing a comparison-and-contrast essay is to make a chart to put the information in the proper order. Ordering details by importance is often the best plan for the point-by-point pattern. We may wish to discuss in less detail our first point or points so that we can concentrate more fully on the last point, the one that is more important to us.

2. The subtopic sentence helps us introduce each new point of comparison and contrast.

3. A comparison and contrast essay is not two separate essays on related subjects that are then shuffled together. We should NOT assume that our readers will make the comparisons or contrasts we see in the material we've presented. Rather, as writers of the comparison and contrast essays, we are responsible for making the comparisons and contrasts, directly and explicitly. To do so, we should use coherent cues to relate the two subjects and draw the comparisons or contrasts.

4. Writers of comparison-contrast essays usually use a clear, authoritative tone because they want to sound knowledgeable about their subjects. We might decide, however, that a humorous tone is more fitting for our essay. The tone we use depends on the purpose of our writing, on our intended audience, and on the subjects we are comparing and/or contrasting.

Analysis of Students' Writing

Student's first draft

> ### Mount Hua or Qingdao
>
> When I graduated from high school and was waiting to go to college, my parents told me they could take me on a vacation to Mount Hua or Qingdao. They asked me to make the decision. Both places are fun to me. I did a careful comparison of the scenery, activities and convenience for transportation. Then I concluded that Qingdao was better for family vacation.
>
> Sceneries of Mount Hua and Qingdao are very different. Mount Hua is a very famous Taoist Mountain. It is known for its temples and precipitous peaks. Qingdao is a city on the coast. We can enjoy the beautiful beach, Qingdao beer, Western architecture and Mount Lao, which is lower but easier to climb than Mount Hua.
>
> Another difference between Mount Hua and Qingdao is the activities we may take. If we choose Mount Hua, mountain-climbing is the only thing we could do, which may be dangerous for my parents. In Qingdao, we can go to the beach and enjoy the sunshine. I can swim, play volleyball in the sea. We can also go shopping and toke pictures of the Western style architecture.
>
> As for transportation, we live in Kaifeng, Henan Province, between the two places. Qingdao is about 200 kms farther away than Mount Hua from my hometown. However, we could get directly to Qingdao by train in about thirteen hours. On the other hand, we would have to transfer trains to get to the small town of Huayin near Mount Hua, which could take us a longer time.
>
> Taking into consideration of these differences, I decided my family should take the vacation in Qingdao.

Comments

This draft is structurally well organized, with a thesis in the introductory paragraph, three developing body paragraphs on different aspects of contrast, and a conclusion to refer back to the thesis. Moreover, the student makes a point in the comparison. However, the essay can be further improved with more details, consistency of verb tenses and varied sentence structures.

Mount Hua or Qingdao

When I got the admission letter from TFSU, my parents, who were more excited than I, celebrated the occasion with a promise for a family vacation at my choice between Mount Hua and Qingdao. Both places appealed to me. However, a brief comparison of the attractions, activities and convenience for transportation convinced me that Qingdao would make a better destination.

Although both Mount Hua and Qingdao are national summer resorts, they have different attractions for tourists. Mount Hua, a Taoist Mountain, is famous for its magnificent views, precipitous peaks and historical temples. Qingdao, on the other hand, is a coastal city known for, in addition to beer, its sandy beach and clear water, well reserved Western architecture and vibrant life as an international city. As I had been accepted into the English department, Western architecture and tourists from other countries were of greater interest to me than Taoist and Buddhist temples.

My second consideration was what my family could do together—I would like the three of us to communicate as much as possible during the vacation. At Mount Hua, there would be little for us to do except to climb and climb. Knowing how steep and narrow the step paths are, I didn't think we could communicate much climbing, or crawling, up the steps over some perpendicular precipice, particularly in places where people have to get over one by one. Nor did I want to break my mom's back, nor her ankles, to take that adventure with two men at the warmest time in summer. In addition, even if we wanted some adventure, we could take Mount Lao in Qingdao, which is about half the height of Mount Hua and much more accessible. In contrast, at Qingdao, we could go swimming, sun bathe on the beach, catch some rays, knock around in the city, visit museums or shops, and have more choice for food. In most of the activities, we could talk about anything under the sun.

Convenience and comfort came as my third concern. We live in Kaifeng, Henan Province, between the two places, about one third or 200 kilometers nearer to Mount Hua. However, while there was a through train to Qingdao, we would have to transfer trains or take a tour bus to Mount Hua. Though it would take the snail train about thirteen hours to get to Qingdao, since we would each have a berth, it appeared a lesser evil, more tolerable than transferring trains in a strange station or bumping in a bus for seven hours.

My parents had no objection to my decision, and we have never regretted spending five happy days in Qingdao.

119

Comments

This is a good essay, argumentative and convincing, with attempts for humor though not very interesting on the whole.

Homework 3

Revise the second draft according to the professor's comments, and try to avoid organizational, logical and grammatical mistakes.

Further Reading

Passage 1

Knowledge vs. Wisdom

Anne L.

Though knowledge and wisdom may seem alike, they are really very different. As a matter of fact they only have two things in common: both require a brain and both are very hard to obtain.

A knowledgeable person might dress in a fashion that can be accepted by everyone, not too conservative and not too abstract. When a knowledgeable person enters a room, she tries not to make herself too noticed though she does want everyone to acknowledge that she is in the room. A knowledgeable person knows things like times and dates, and just what should happen at this time and who should be where at that time. A knowledgeable student dresses to suit the "norm" of her surroundings and makes an attempt to fit in as best as possible. When entering a classroom, a knowledgeable student always goes directly to her seat and promptly takes out the previous night's lessons so that she might review it once more before the start of class. A knowledgeable student knows things such as the multiplication tables all the way up to twenty, how to diagram every sentence that she hears, and the Japanese alphabets, all three.

A wise person dresses in a fashion that suits her, so that she is conformable, not worrying what everyone else around her thinks. Upon entering a room, a wise person casually greets their friends, engages in a little conversation and then continues on with their business, knowing that it is important to let people know that she always enjoys talking with them. A wise person knows things such as the importance of dates and times and why things should happen. A wise student dresses in what she wants to dress in, regardless of what all of the others wear or believe to be the "norm." A wise student enters a room and jokes with her classmates before settling in their desk to take out her books, knowing that the time she shares with her friends is just as important as the time she uses completing her lessons. A wise student comes to class knowing how to use the multiplication tables in daily life, and why it is so important to know how to diagram sentences, and how to use the Japanese alphabets, all three.

Knowledgeable people spend most of their time planning out exactly when something should happen and just how long it has to take. And after they have completed the task of planning everything they spend the rest of their time accomplishing everything on their list; the only thought in their minds is that everything at one time or another has to be completed. Wise people are aware of the fact that they can only plan so much and the rest should be done when time allows. They know that it is not only impossible to plan every moment that one is awake, but that this is equally an ineffective way to live one's life. Wise people also know that not everything can be done in the time allotted, and that they must use their time for business as well as pleasure.

In summary, knowledgeable people and wise people may have the same amount of intelligence and may be equally smart, but there is still a huge difference between the two. Knowledgeable people know more often when and where, but wise people know more of the reasons, how something happened and why it is significant. For example, in the case of a personal tragedy, a knowledgeable person would know what was supposed to be said and when, but a wise person would know what needed to be said and how, already knowing the why.

The most direct difference between wisdom and knowledge is this: knowledge is only information, until it is successfully retained in one's mind. Without a brain, knowledge is simply information, whereas the application of knowledge, or wisdom, cannot exist without a mind, not being something that one can read about or memorize, because if there is no brain, there is no wisdom.

(From <headroyce.org/research/writing/comparecontrast/cceng11sample.html>)

Passage 2

Born to Be Different?

Camille Lewis

Some years ago, when my children were very young, I cut a cartoon out of a magazine and taped it to my refrigerator. It showed a young couple welcoming friends over for Christmas. The hosts rather proudly announce that instead of dolls, they have given their little daughter her own set of tools. And sure enough, the second panel shows their little girl playing in her room, a wrench in one hand and a hammer in the other. But she's making the wrench say. "Would you like to go to the prom, Barbie?" and the hammer answer, "Oh, Ken! I'd love to!"

Oh my, did that cartoon strike a chord. I grew up with *Ms*. Magazine and the National Organization of Women and a firm belief that gender differences were *learned*, not inborn. Other parents may have believed that pink and baby dolls and kindergarten teaching were for girls, and blue and trucks and engineering were for boys, but by golly, *my* kids were going to be different. They were going to be raised free of all that harmful gender indoctrination. They were just going to be *people*.

I don't remember exactly when I began to suspect I was wrong. Maybe it was when my three-year-old son, raised in a "no weapons" household, bit his toast into a gun shape and tried to shoot the cat. Maybe it was when his younger brother nearly levitated out of his car seat, joyously crowing "backhoe!" upon spotting his first piece of earth-moving equipment. Maybe it was when my little daughter first lined up her stuffed animals and began teaching them their ABC's and bandaging their boo-boos.

It wasn't that my sons couldn't be sweet and sensitive, or that my daughter wasn't sometimes rowdy and boisterous. But I had to rethink my earlier assumptions. Despite my best efforts not to impose gender-specific expectations on them, my boys and my girl were, well, different. *Really* different.

Slowly and hesitantly, medical and psychological researchers have begun confirming my observations. The notion that the differences between the sexes (beyond the obvious anatomical ones) are biologically based is fraught with controversy. Such beliefs can easily be misinterpreted and used as the basis for harmful, oppressive stereotypes. They can be overstated and exaggerated into blanket statements about what men and women "can" and "can't" do; about what the genders are "good" and "bad" at. And yet, the unavoidable fact is that studies are making it ever clearer that, as groups, men and women differ in almost every measurable aspect. Learning about those differences helps us understand why men and women are simultaneously so attracted and fascinated, and yet so frequently stymied and frustrated, by the opposite sex. To dig into what it really means to be masculine and feminine helps to depersonalize out responses to one another's behavior—to avoid the "*My* perceptions and behaviors are normal; and *yours* don't make sense" trap. Our differences are deep-rooted, hard-wired, and present from the moment of conception.

To begin with, let's look at something as basic as the anatomy of the brain. Typically, men have larger skulls and brains than women. But the sexes score equally well on intelligence tests. This apparent contradiction is explained by the fact that our brains are apportioned differently. Women have about 15 percent more "gray matter" than men. Gray matter, made up of nerve cells and the branches that connect them, allows the quick transference of thought from one part of the brain to another. This high concentration of gray matter helps explain women's ability to look at many sides of an argument at once, and to do several tasks (or hold several conversations) simultaneously.

Men's brains, on the other hand, have a more generous portion of "white matter." White matter, which is made up of neurons, actually inhibits the spread of information. It allows men to concentrate very narrowly on a specific task, without being distracted by thoughts that might conflict with the job at hand. In addition, men's lager skulls contain more cerebrospinal fluid, which cushions the brain. Scientists theorize that this reflects men's history of engaging in warfare and rough sports, activities which bring with them a high likelihood of having one's head banged about.

Our brains' very different makeup leads to our very different methods of interacting with the world around us. Simon Baron-Cohen, author of *The Essential Difference:Men, Women and the Extreme Male Brain*, has labeled the classic female mental process as "empathizing." He defines empathizing as "the drive to identify another person's emotions and thoughts, and to respond to these with an appropriate emotion." Empathizers are constantly measuring and responding to the surrounding emotional temperature. They are concerned about showing sensitivity to the people around them.

This empathetic quality can be observed in virtually all aspects of women's lives: from the choice of typically female-dominated careers (nursing, elementary school teaching, social work) to reading matter popular mainly with women (romantic fiction, articles about relationships, advice columns about how people can get along better) to women's interaction with one another(which typically involves intimate discussion of relationships with friends and family, and sympathy for each others' concerns). So powerful is the empathizing mindset that it even affects how the typical female memory works. Ask a woman when a particular event happened, and she often pinpoints it in terms of an occurrence that had emotional content: "That was the summer my sister broke her leg," or "That was around the time Gene and Mary got into such an awful argument." Likewise, she is likely to bring her empathetic mind to bear on geography. She'll remember a particular address not as 11th and Market Streets but being "near the restaurant where we went on our anniversary," or "around the corner from Liz's old apartment."

In contrast, Baron-Cohen calls the typical male mindset "systemizing," which he defines as "the drive to analyze and explore a system, to extract underlying rules that govern the behavior of a system." A systemizer is less interested in how people feel than in how things work. Again, the systematic brain influences virtually all aspects of the typical man's life. Male-dominated professions (such as engineering, computer programming, auto repair, and mathematics) rely heavily on systems, formulas, and patterns, and very little on the ability to intuit another person's thoughts or emotions. Reading material most popular with men includes science fiction and history, as well as factual "how-to" magazines on such topics as computers, photography, home repair, and woodworking. When they get together with male friends, men are far less likely to engage in intimate conversation than they are to share an activity: watching or playing sports, working on a car, bowling, golfing, or fishing. Men's conversation is peppered with dates and addresses, illustrating their comfort with systems: "Back in 1996 when I was living in Boston—" or "The best way to the new stadium is to go all the way out Walnut Street to 33rd and then get on the bypass—"

One final way that men and women differ is in their typical responses to problem-solving. Ironically, it may be this very activity—intended on both sides to eliminate problems—that creates the most conflict between partners of the opposite sex. To a woman, the *process* of solving a problem is all-important. Talking about a problem is a means of deepening the intimacy between her and her partner. The very anatomy of her brain, as well as her accompanying empathetic mindset, makes her want to consider all sides of a question and to explore various possible solutions. To have a partner who is willing to explore a problem with her is deeply satisfying. She interprets that willingness as an expression of the other's love and concern.

But men have an almost completely opposite approach when it comes to dealing with a problem. Everything in their mental makeup tells them to focus narrowly on the issue, solve it, and get it out of the way. The ability to fix a problem quickly and efficiently is, to them, a demonstration of their power and competence. When a man hears his female partner begin to describe a problem, his strongest impulse is to listen briefly and then tell

123

her what to do about it. From his perspective, he has made a helpful and loving gesture; from hers, he's short-circuited a conversation that could have deepened and strengthened their relationship.

The challenge that confronts men and women is to put aside ideas of "better" and "worse" when it comes to their many differences. Our diverse brain development, our ways of interacting with the world, and our modes of dealing with problems all have their strong points.

In some circumstances, a typically feminine approach may be more effective; in others, a classically masculine mode may have the advantage. Our differences aren't going to disappear: My daughter, now a middle-schooler, regularly tells me she loves me, while her teenage brothers express their affection by grabbing me in a headlock. Learning to understand and appreciate one another's gender-specific qualities is the key to more rich and rewarding lives together.

Passage 3

Why Children Need Father-Love and Mother-Love
Glenn T. Stanton

If Heather is being raised by two mommies and Brandon is being raised by Daddy and his new husband-roommate, Heather and Brandon might have two adults in their lives, but they are being deprived of the benefits found in the unique influences found in a mother and father's differing parenting styles. Much of the value mothers and fathers bring to their children is due to the fact that mothers and fathers are different. And by cooperating together and complementing each other in their differences, they provide these good things that same-sex caregivers cannot. The important value of these gender-based differences in healthy child-development will be explored here.

[…]

Mothers and Fathers Parent Differently

This difference provides an important diversity of experiences for children. Dr. Pruett explains that fathers have a distinct style of communication and interaction with children. Infants, by 8 weeks, can tell the difference between a male or female interacting with them. Stanford psychologist Eleanor Maccoby, in her book *The Two Sexes*, explains how mothers and fathers respond differently to infants. Mothers are more likely to provide warm, nurturing care for a crying infant. This diversity in itself provides children with a broader, richer experience of contrasting relational interactions—more so than for children who are raised by only one gender. Whether they realize it or not, children are learning at earliest age, by sheer experience, that men and women are different and have different ways of dealing with life, other adults and their children.

Mothers and Fathers Play Differently

Fathers tend to play with, and mothers tend to care for, children. While both mothers and fathers are physical, fathers are physical in different ways.

Fathers tickle more, they wrestle, and they throw their children in the air. Fathers chase their children, sometimes as playful, scary "monsters." Fathers are louder at play, while mothers are quieter. Mothers cuddle babies, and fathers bounce them. Fathers roughhouse while mothers are gentle. One study found that 70 percent of father-infant games were more physical and action oriented while only 4 percent of mother-infant play was like this. Fathers encourage competition; mothers encourage equity. One style encourages independence while the other encourages security.

[···]

Fathering expert John Snarey explains that children who roughhouse with their fathers learn that biting, kicking and other forms of physical violence are not acceptable. They learn self-control by being told when "enough is enough" and when to "settle down." Girls and boys both learn a healthy balance between timidity and aggression. Children need mom's softness as well as dad's roughhousing. Both provide security and confidence in their own ways by communicating love and physical intimacy.

Fathers Push Limits; Mothers Encourage Security

Go to any playground and listen to the parents. Who is encouraging their kids to swing or climb just a little higher, ride their bike just a little faster, throw just a little harder? Who is yelling, "slow down, not so high, not so hard!" Of course, fathers encourage children to take chances and push limits and mothers protect and are more cautious. And this difference can cause disagreement between mom and dad on what is best for the child.

But the difference is essential for children. Either of these parenting styles by themselves can be unhealthy. One can tend toward encouraging risk without consideration of consequences. The other tends to avoid risk, which can fail to build independence, confidence and progress. Joined together, they keep each other in balance and help children remain safe while expanding their experiences and confidence.

Mothers and Fathers Communicate Differently

A major study showed that when speaking to children, mothers and fathers are different. Mothers will simplify their words and speak on the child's level. Men are not as inclined to modify their language for the child.

Mother's way facilitates immediate communication. Father's way challenges the child to expand her vocabulary and linguistic skills, an important building block of academic success.

Father's talk tends to be more brief, directive, and to the point. It also makes greater use of subtle body language and facial expressions. Mothers tend to be more descriptive, personal and verbally encouraging. Children who do not have daily exposure to both will not learn how to understand and use both styles of conversation as they grow. These boys and girls will be at a disadvantage because they will experience these different ways of communicating in relationships with teachers, bosses and other authority figures.

Mothers and Fathers Discipline Differently

Educational psychologist Carol Gilligan tells us that fathers stress justice, fairness and duty (based on rules), while mothers stress sympathy, care and help (based on relationships). Fathers tend to observe and enforce rules systematically and sternly, which teach children the objectivity and consequences of right and wrong. Mothers tend toward

125

grace and sympathy in the midst of disobedience, which provide a sense of hopefulness. Again, either of these by themselves is not good, but together, they create a healthy, proper balance.

Fathers and Mothers Prepare Children for Life Differently

Dads tend to see their child in relation to the rest of the world. Mothers tend to see the rest of the world in relation to their child. Think about it.

What motivates most mothers as parents? They are motivated primarily by things from the outside world that could hurt their child (i.e., lightning, accidents, disease, strange people, dogs or cats, etc.). Fathers, while not unconcerned with these things, tend to focus on how their children will or will not be prepared for something they might encounter in the world (i.e., a bully, being nervous around the opposite sex, baseball or soccer tryouts, etc.)

Fathers help children see that particular attitudes and behaviors have certain consequences. For instance, fathers are more likely to tell their children that if they are not nice to others, kids will not want to play with them. Or, if they don't do well in school, they will not get into a good college or job. Fathers help children prepare for the reality and harshness of the real world, and mothers help protect against it. Both are necessary as children grow into adulthood.

[…]

Fathers and Mothers Teach Respect for the Opposite Sex

FACT: A married father is substantially less likely to abuse his wife or children than men in any other category. This means that boys and girls with fathers learn, by observation, how men should treat women.

Girls with involved fathers, therefore, are more likely to select for themselves good suitors and husbands because they have a proper standard by which to judge all candidates. Fathers themselves also help weed out bad candidates. Boys raised with fathers are more likely to be good husbands because they can emulate their fathers' successes and learn from their failures.

The American Journal of Sociology finds that, "Societies with father-present patterns of child socialization produce men who are less inclined to exclude women from public activities than their counterparts in father-absent societies."

Girls and boys with married mothers learn from their mothers what a healthy respectful female relationship with men looks like. Girls who observe their mothers confidently and lovingly interacting with their fathers learn how to interact confidently with men.

[…]

Conclusion

To be concerned with proper children development is to be concerned about making sure that children have daily access to the different and complementary ways mothers and fathers parent. The same-sex marriage and parenting proposition says this doesn't really matter. They are wrong and their lack of understanding will hurt children. It will rob children of the necessary and different experiences mothers and fathers expose children

to. As a result, children growing up in mother-only or father-only homes will suffer deeply in terms of lack of confidence, independence, and security. Boys and girls will be at greater risk for gender confusion, abuse and exploitation from other men. They are less likely to have a healthy respect for both women and men as they grow into adulthood.
（From <http://www.family.org/cforum/fosi/marriage/ssuap/a0027554.cfm>）

Unit 6

The Process Analysis Essay

Tuning-in Activities

 Activity 1

Many people look for the steps to happiness. Read the following anonymous poem and the tips given by Dr. Barton Goldsmith, identify the "steps" they suggest we should take for happiness, and then compare the "steps" with the stages of cultural shock identified by Kwintessential Ltd.

Steps to Happiness

Everybody Knows,
You can't be all things to all people.
You can't do all things at once.
You can't do all things equally well.
You can't do all things better than everyone else.
Your humanity is showing just like everyone else's.

So,
You have to find out who you are, and be that.
You have to decide what comes first, and do that.
You have to discover your strengths, and use them.
You have to learn not to compete with others, because no one else is in the contest of "being you".

Then,
You will have learned to accept your own uniqueness.
You will have learned to set priorities and make decisions.
You will have learned to live with your limitations.
You will have learned to give yourself the respect that is due.
And you'll be a most vital mortal.

Believe,

That you are a wonderful, unique person.

That you are a once-in-all-history event.

That it's more than a right, it's your duty, to be who you are.

That life is not a problem to solve, but a gift to cherish.

And you'll be able to stay one up on what used to get you down.

10 Steps to Happiness and Emotional Fulfillment

Barton Goldsmith, Ph.D. in Emotional Fitness

We all want to feel happy, and each one of us has different ways of getting there. Here are ten steps that you can take to increase your joie de vivre and bring more happiness into your life.

1. **Be with others who make you smile.** Studies show that we are happiest when we are around those who are also happy. Stick with those who are joyful and let rub off on you.

2. **Hold on to your values.** What you find true, what you know is fair, and what you believe in are all values. Over time, the more you honor them, the better you will feel about yourself and those you love.

3. **Accept the good.** Look at your life and take stock of what's working, and don't push away something just because it isn't perfect. When good things happen, even the very little ones, let them in.

4. **Imagine the best.** Don't be afraid to look at what you really want and see yourself getting it. Many people avoid this process because they don't want to be disappointed if things don't work out. The truth is that imagining getting what you want is a big part of achieving it.

5. **Do things you love.** Maybe you can't skydive every day or take vacations every season, but as long as you get to do the things you love every once in a while, you will feel greater happiness.

6. **Find purpose.** Those who believe they are contributing to the well-being of humanity tend to feel better about their lives. Most people want to be part of something greater than they are, simply because it's fulfilling.

7. **Listen to your heart.** You are the only one who knows what fills you up. Your family and friends may think you'd be great at something that really doesn't float your boat. It can be complicated following your bliss. Just be smart, and keep your day job for the time being.

8. **Push yourself, not others.** It's easy to feel that someone else is responsible for your fulfillment, but the reality is that it is really your charge. Once you realize that, you have the power to get where you want to go. Stop blaming others or the world, and you'll find your answers much sooner.

9. **Be open to change.** Even if it doesn't feel good, change is the one thing you can count on. Change will happen, so make contingency plans and emotionally shore yourself up for the experience.

10. **Bask in the simple pleasures.** Those who love you, treasured memories, silly jokes,

129

warm days, and starry nights: these are the ties that bind and the gifts that keep on giving.

Happiness and fulfillment are within your grasp, but sometimes just out of reach. Understanding what works best for you is the first step in finding more of it.

(http://www.psychologytoday.com/blog/emotional-fitness/201105/10)

Stages of Cultural Shock
Kwintessential Ltd.

"Culture shock" is used to describe the emotional rollercoaster that someone experiences when living in a new country. Anyone that has worked and lived in a foreign country will experience culture shock of some sort.

Culture shock affects anyone from business personnel and their families, to EFL teachers to sports stars. Recognising culture shock is an important way of being able to deal with it. Dealing with it helps minimise the risk of becoming disillusioned with a new country and the possibility of deciding that a quick return "home" is the only solution.

Experts agree that culture shock has stages and all agree that once people get beyond the initial and most difficult stages, life in a new country becomes a lot better. Outlined below is an example of the stages people go through with culture shock:

Stage 1—Excitement

The individual experiences a holiday or "honeymoon" period with their new surroundings. They:

● Feel very positive about the culture

● Are overwhelmed with impressions

● Find the new culture exotic and are fascinated

● Are passive, meaning they have little experience of the culture

Stage 2—Withdrawal

The individual now has some more face to face experience of the culture and starts to find things different, strange and frustrating. They:

● Find the behaviour of the people unusual and unpredictable

● Begin to dislike the culture and react negatively to the behaviour

● Feel anxious

● Start to withdraw

● Begin to criticize, mock or show animosity to the people

Stage 3—Adjustment

The individual now has a routine, feels more settled and is more confident in dealing with the new culture. They:

● Understand and accept the behaviour of the people

● Feel less isolated

● Regains their sense of humour

Stage 4—Enthusiasm

The individual now feels "at home." They:

● Enjoy being in the culture

- Functions well in the culture
- Prefer certain cultural traits of the new culture rather than their own
- Adopt certain behaviours from the new culture

(http://www.kwintessential.co.uk/cultural-services/articles/cultureshock-stages.html)

Activity 2

Discuss how to make an Internet purchase. Take notes for the later essay writing.

Activity 3

Tell your partner how to
- cook your local dishes, or make your local pickles;
- make a bracelet, make a bag out of your old pants;
- or *something else* you want to share.

Activity 4

Learn to make traditional Chinese knots:

a.    b.    c.

The traditional Chinese knot symbolizes happiness and good luck. Real Chinese knots are tied and plaited instead of being cut. Tying a Chinese knot demands a lot of patience, but with practice, you will eventually learn how to make one of your own. The following example of a simple knot is a good start.

Instructions
1. Stretch out a 20-inch long and 1/8-inch thick red, braided ribbon or string on a level surface, such as a desk.
2. Pick up one end and bring it down and across to the right to form a large loop.
3. Pick up and move the right end of the ribbon or string all the way to the left, beneath the other end of the ribbon or string that is lying in the middle, and take it back beneath that end to the right to form a smaller loop under the bigger one (see a).
4. Take the end of the ribbon or string that is in the middle up across the entire smaller loop under it and feed it into the bigger loop beneath it (see b).
5. Take the same end and bring it down to feed into the smaller loop on top of it (see b).
6. Carefully pull both ends (see c).
   Congratulations! You have created a simple Chinese knot!

Introduction

Process analysis writing is the description of **a series of steps/stages** about how a change takes place (also known as informational process analysis) or how things are done or made (also known as directional process analysis) so that the reader may understand how something works or perform the steps him/herself. The main purpose of an informational process essay is to inform, explain, or analyze a process in which something works, something happened, or something is or was done, as in how World War II broke out or how cloud forms. The purpose of a directional process essay, on the other hand, is to clarify the steps in the procedure so that the reader can re-create the steps and the desired results, as in the case of how to make a Valentine gift. A directional process essay can be informational at the same time. Whether the reader is going to perform the process or not, process analysis helps the reader to understand it so that s/he can judge its reliability, practicality, or efficiency.

The first consideration in a process analysis essay is the audience because it determines the amount of information you should include—you don't want to teach your grandmother to suck eggs. In general, we choose a topic that we assume the reader/audience know little about.

After identifying the audience, we consider the steps for the desired result. We normally describe the process step-by-step, following the order in which the steps are taken. In other words, we put these steps in chronological order. We need to include all the steps and explain why each step is necessary. In the process, we may give advice, provide words of caution, or explain an unfamiliar term. However, if we just or mainly give advice or tips that do not necessarily make a process in chronological order, as Dr. Barton Goldsmith does in "10 Steps to Happiness and Emotional Fulfillment," we are not actually doing a process analysis. If we're writing a directional process essay, we should also offer clear descriptions of the tools or materials needed to carry out the process, and where applicable, provide a way of assessing whether the process has been successfully completed.

In style, the process analysis essay is usually concise, written in simple language. The thesis statement simply informs the reader about the subject; the introductory paragraph briefly describes why the reader should be interested in learning more about the subject; the body paragraphs explain the actual steps; and the concluding paragraph, where necessary, summarizes once again the importance of understanding the process just described.

Learning to Swim

Swimming is good exercise for our health. It does not only strengthen the muscles but also make the body pliable[1] and slender. An increasing number of people realize this now and try to learn swimming. Unfortunately many find it hard and give it up halfway. In fact, as long as you master the preliminary skills of swimming and practice it continually, you'll find swimming easy and enjoyable.

Before going into water, some warm-up exercise on the bank is necessary. You can start from learning to regulate your balance of breath. Draw a deep breath, then breathe it out as slowly as you can. This exercise helps you stay under water longer and prevents drowning. Keep doing this for a few minutes and then combine it with practicing the upper limbs. Take breaststroke for example. Put the palms together in front of your chest and push forward. Part the palms and swing them sideways with your fingers close to each other. That'll bring your palms back to the chest. Repeat the cycle.

Now you are ready to practice the movements in water. You must be brave. Fear of water is the main barrier in learning swimming. To overcome the fear, you can wear a life jacket which can make floating easier. Simply put into practice what you learned with your arms. Breathe in with every pushing forward; breathe out during the course of circling your arms. In the meanwhile, lift your body horizontally[2] and move your legs in the same way as frogs do in water. You may find with a pleasant surprise that you can swim.

Repeat the series of actions until you are confident in throwing away the life jacket. Once you have learned this basic movement, it is easy to try floating on water, a must for a swimmer.

Like other skills swimming requires courage, persistence and practice. "Practice makes perfect."

Vocabulary

1. pliable: *adj.* flexible, shaped

133

2. horizontal: *adj.* flat, level

Unit Six

Usually it takes two weeks to a month to learn swimming. When you can swim freely, you'll enjoy the voluptuous[3] touch of water on your body. But don't forget the tips. Before you become a skilled swimmer, stay in the shallow water. Second, whenever and wherever you swim, be sure to be in the sight of people. After all, safety comes first.

3. voluptuous: *adj.* giving sensual pleasure

Questions for Consideration

1. What is the author's thesis? Try to formulate one sentence that captures the central idea the author tries to convey.

2. Examine the organization of the essay. Try numbering the steps of the process in the margin or on a piece of paper. After that, ask yourself if the process is arranged in time-based order, from the least to the most important point, or along some other lines.

3. Is the essay primarily directional or informational? Explain how the essay differs from the instruction of a swimming coach. Identify the "analysis" in the essay.

Sample 2

134

Adapting to Deafness

Jack Moore

Vocabulary

Young people are adaptable, so I didn't realize that being deaf in one ear was anything to worry about. My friends and family did not treat me any differently. I really didn't pay much attention to the stages I went through in adapting to partial deafness. As I look back over the years, I can see that I developed a conscious process of adapting to deafness. I made physical, mental and social adjustments.

The first step in adapting to deafness was physical. I had to position my body so that I could hear my friends and my family. Since my right ear was my "bad" ear, I learned to tip my head to the right so that the sound entered my left or "good" ear. Over the years it has become such a habit that all my photographs show me with my head tipped to the right. Another way I found that I could position my body was to get on the right-hand side of people. Even today, when I sit on a couch or ride in the back seat of a car, I always get on the "outside" or right-hand side. This sometimes causes me some problems with men who think they should be on the "outside." I never talk when I drive a car because I can't hear well enough to carry on a conversation, without losing track of[1] my concentration.

I realized early that consciously positioning my body to the situation was not enough, so I progressed to the second step—being alert. I knew that I had to concentrate and listen very carefully to those around me. Other people would not go out of their way to help me hear. Besides, I wasn't willing to go around explaining that I heard with only one ear. Who cares! Therefore, I learned that by concentrating I could increase my hearing ability dramatically. By watching faces and lips, I taught myself lip-reading. Today, I can tell what is going on in television show when the sound is off by reading the actor's lips. I also became alert to body language—usually gestures, facial expressions and movements—that helped tell me what people were thinking.

My final step was to adjust my social life to partial deafness. I couldn't have much fun at large parties because the commotion[2] created too much "surface noise" for me to carry on conversation. However, when I was forced into large groups, I tried to figure out the general conversation and make suitable noises like "Oh?" "Is that so?" "Well!" and "I agree." I am afraid there are times when I agreed when I shouldn't have. Occasionally I received some peculiar looks when my pat[3] answer didn't quite fit the discussion.

I am lucky that I became partially deaf when I was very young. I have since met older people who became deaf later in life. Instead of working on the process of hearing, they have become lazy and resentful. They make other people do the work. No one wants to shout while conversing. It is better to answer with an occasional "I agree," even when it doesn't fit, than to be a demanding, irritable deaf person.

1. lose track of: no longer know what is happening, or not to remember something

2. commotion: *n.* a sudden short period of noise, confusion or excited movement

3. pat: *adj.* (answer or remark) sounding previously prepared, rehearsed

135

Points for Discussion

1. What do you think is Jack Moore's purpose of writing, to instruct readers how to adapt to deafness or to inform readers of what he learned from a misfortune or to amuse the readers? How does the writer set the tone? How would you describe the relationship Moore wants to have with the reader?

2. How does he introduce the essay before he gives us "the first step"?

3. Is this process analysis arranged in chronological order or some other order? Can you locate the transitional words or phrases he employs to guide the reader?

4. What do you think of the concluding paragraph?

5. In planning your own essay, make some decisions about your purpose, tone, organization and relationship with your readers. Discuss your plans with a classmate. Listen to your classmate's plans and exchange comments and advice with each other.

You may have noticed that the two sample essays above both follow a fairly well standardized pattern: *an introduction, an overall picture* including a list of the main steps that make up the process, *an explanation of each of the steps listed*, and *a conclusion*.

Introduction of "Learning to Swim" states that swimming is a good exercise for health, is easy to learn, and is enjoyable when learned. The purpose is to persuade readers to learn to swim. Jack Moore introduces his essay by telling readers that he once successfully adapted to partial deafness. In retrospect, he realized that he went through a process in making physical, mental and social adjustments. The casual tone and retrospect view assures readers that it will not be a story of misery. Both essays inform readers of the topic and state the thesis. The introduction may also open with a definition of the process. It indicates how, why, and under what circumstances something occurs or is performed. It may include information about materials or preliminary preparations needed in performing the process. Sometimes, it mentions special requirements about the time when the process must be performed, or special conditions that must exist, such as temperature, humidity, freedom from dust, or ventilation.

The introduction is followed by an *overall picture* of the process, a list of the main steps that make up the process or comments necessary about the process as a whole—for example, the theory on which it is based. An effort should be made to hold the main steps to five or six, for if they are too numerous it will be extremely hard for the reader to grasp and retain an overall picture.

The main steps are then taken up one by one and each is treated as a whole process. For each division, a definition is provided if needed, and the facts about time, conditions, apparatus, personnel, and preparations are made clear. Then, if necessary, the parts of which the step consists should be listed and explained. Finally, what is really done is explained, with emphasis on the results.

Both samples end with a *conclusion*. In Sample 1, the conclusion echoes the introduction (by saying that it won't take too long to learn swimming and it's enjoyable) and gives some precautions for new swimmers. In Sample 2, the conclusion makes an observation to echo the introduction and to convey a message out of the story. There are many occasions when the explanation of the process does not need a conclusion. Where a conclusion is desirable, it might summarize the process, perhaps restating the main steps so that the reader's final impression will include the process as a whole rather than only one small part. It might evaluate the process or the results of the process. It might comment on why the process is important or indicate how it fits into some larger process of which it is a part.

Homework 1

1. Write down the activity you have described in Section One and arrange your essay with reference to the samples. Bring your first draft to class for discussion.

2. Teach a Western friend to use chopsticks.

Using Details

In the explanation of a process, as in any other writing, we need to decide how much detail is necessary. There is no reason that all parts of a process must be covered in equal detail. The main divisions of the process should be arranged in chronological order. They should be expressed in parallel form and may be numbered if numbering seems likely to be helpful, as it is almost sure to be if the number exceeds three.

Make sure that your process analysis is complete and accurate. Each main division should be based on the completion of a stage of the work rather than on some arbitrary consideration such as place or time. It would be undesirable, for example, to divide a process into work done in the field and work done in the laboratory. Even if the work done in the field comprised one specific task and the work done in the laboratory comprised another, the reader will see a better picture of the process when we identify the task rather than merely the place where it was done.

Sample 3

The 5 Stages to Learning Chinese

Vocabulary

"It's Greek to me"[1] Stage (No Study)

In this stage, Mandarin sounds like *crazy nonsense noises.* To the native English speaker, these noises are truly bizarre. The notion that these noises make up a real language akin to English is ridiculous to people in this stage. It is the natural stage to be in when you can't speak Mandarin and do not have much meaningful contact with Chinese culture. The majority of non-Chinese (especially non-Asian) people will be stuck in this stage for their whole lives. It doesn't take much to get to the next stage. One semester of Chinese classes should do it.

138

"OK, it's a language" Stage (Beginner)

At this stage, the learner has become a "learner," and has relinquished[2] the notion that Chinese cannot possibly be a real language. In this stage the learner recognizes a number of common phrases and vocabulary words, and can usually make himself understood in the most basic communication scenarios. His pronunciation, however, still has a long way to go. Tones are a complete mess, and he has not yet started to get a handle on the Chinese "r" or "y," or on the distinctions between Mandarin's "x/sh," "q/ch," and "j/zh" pairs. Many foreign teachers living in China that "can speak some Chinese" are in this stage. It takes hard work to get to the next stage. It can be accomplished through years of university study in the West, but the process is much accelerated by study in China.

"I'm speaking Chinese!" Stage (Intermediate)

Through hard work, a careful ear, and meticulous[3] self-criticism, learners can arrive in the third stage. In this stage, not only has the pronunciation of pinyin's consonants (r, y, q, j, etc.) been acquired, but tones have been brought under

1. "It's Greek to me" 天书

2. relinquish: *v.* give up; put aside

3. meticulous: *adj.* very careful

control as well. This is not to say that the speaker does not occasionally screw up[4] a consonant or get a tone wrong. But he is well on his way now.

One danger at this stage is that by the time the learner gets to this stage, his comprehension should be pretty decent as well, and because few foreigners make it to this stage, the learner can get a false picture of his "mastery" of Mandarin. Even if the learner is not overly pleased with himself, it is also easy to become complacent[5] in this stage, as basic communication is no longer a problem. At this level, what is not understood can usually be worked around or explained in Chinese.

This stage can last for a long time, as pronunciation and tonal errors are slowly reduced, fluency is increased, and vocabulary is expanded. To make it to the next stage, a lot of hard work and self-criticism is necessary, as long as prolonged, intense exposure to Chinese. Everyday exposure is not enough.

"I'm just speaking Chinese" Stage (Advanced)

In this stage, the learner is not in the least surprised by his improved communication abilities because he got there through *prolonged hard work*. Learners who make it to this level can most likely read and write as well, because of the level of dedication involved. Also, learning advanced grammar patterns and expanding vocabulary is most efficiently accomplished through extensive reading in Chinese. You know for sure you're in this stage when the only new vocabulary or grammar patterns come to you through reading or the news.

At this stage the learner should have a lot of Chinese friends, but these friends no longer feel the need to compliment the learner's Chinese because it's just become so obvious at this point. For the most part, they treat you like you're Chinese. Friends who might have once said, "you can't understand because you're not Chinese" will now reconsider that view. The learner understands almost everything that is said to him, and can express

4. screw up: *v.* make a mistake or error

5. complacent: *adj.* over self-confident

139

almost everything as well.

What's left for the learner at this point includes learning vocabulary of questionable usefulness (the names of the more famous hydrocarbons[6] in Chinese, or of Western stars' Chinese names, for example), working on expressing the most abstract concepts, and developing a sense for Chinese literature and poetry. To get to the next level requires extreme dedication (obsession?) and probably some kind of formal coaching as well. Tones have already been completely mastered, but overall sentence intonation may still require a little work to be perfectly natural.

"Pretty Much Chinese" Stage (Native-like)

At this point, the learner's Chinese pronunciation and vocabulary are probably better than half of China's. He's probably living in China, has a Chinese spouse, and has no intention of leaving China.

(http://www.sinosplice.com/learn-chinese/stages-to-learning-chinese)

6. hydrocarbon: *n.* 烃

Sample 3 informs non-native Chinese learners of the stages they will likely go through in learning Chinese. It doesn't have an introduction, probably on the assumption that anybody interested in the title already understands the importance of learning Chinese. Neither does it have a conclusion, because the writer just intends to identify the stages. Detailed tips are given to help and encourage the learners to keep learning.

Fiction writers, too, often combine process analysis with narration to portray characters and/or to reveal a theme. The following two paragraphs are taken from *Catch-22* by Joseph Heller. What's your impression of the process that the U.S. Air Force officer, Yossarian, went through in censoring letters by the soldiers?

Sample 4

Vocabulary

All the officer patients in the ward were forced to censor[1] letters written by all the enlisted-men patients, who were kept in residence in wards of their own. It was a monotonous[2] job, and Yossarian was disappointed to learn that the lives of enlisted men were only slightly more interesting than the

1. censor: *v.* delete material considered sensitive or harmful
2. monotonous: *adj.* boring

lives of officers. After the first day he had no curiosity at all. To break the monotony he invented games. Death to all modifiers[3], he declared one day, and out of every letter that passed through his hands went every adverb and every adjective. The next day he made war on articles. He reached a much higher plane of creativity the following day when he blacked out everything in the letters but a, an and the. That erected more dynamic intralinear[4] tensions, he felt, and in just about every case left a message far more universal. Soon he was proscribing[5] parts of salutations[6] and signatures and leaving the text untouched. One time he blacked out all but the salutation "Dear Mary" from a letter, and at the bottom he wrote, "I yearn for you tragically. A. T. Tappman, Chaplain[7], U.S. Army." A. T. Tappman was the group chaplain's name.

When he had exhausted all possibilities in the letters, he began attacking the names and addresses on the envelopes, obliterating[8] whole homes and streets, annihilating[9] entire metropolises with careless flicks of his wrist as though he were God. Catch-22 required that each censored letter bear the censoring officer's name. Most letters he didn't read at all. On those he didn't read at all he wrote his own name. On those he did read he wrote, "Washington Irving[10]." When that grew monotonous he wrote, "Irving Washington." Censoring the envelopes had serious repercussions[11], produced a ripple of anxiety on some ethereal[12] military echelon[13] that floated a C.I.D.[14] man back into the ward posing as a patient. They all knew he was a C.I.D. man because he kept inquiring about an officer named Irving or Washington and because after his first day there he wouldn't censor letters. He found them too monotonous.

3. modifier: *n.* 修饰语，指下文的 adverb 和 adjective

4. intralinear: 行内（文字间）
5. proscribe: *v.* delete, remove
6. salutation: *n.* a polite greeting, expression of good will, or other sign of recognition
7. Chaplain: *n.*（随军）牧师

8. obliterate: *v.* destroy, ruin
9. annihilate: *v.* destroy, ruin

10. 19世纪美国著名作家
11. repercussions: *n.* 后果；影响
12. ethereal: *adj.* 精致的，优雅的
13. echelon: *n.*【军】梯次编队
14. C.I.D: crime investigation division

141

In the novel, "Catch-22" is a military rule, the self-contradictory circular logic that prevents anyone from avoiding combat missions. The term has become a byword for the absurdity of war and of any senseless or illogical circumstance, meaning "a no-win situation" or "a double bind" of any type. It is also a general critique of bureaucratic operation and reasoning. In these two paragraphs from the opening chapter, we learn how

Yossarian fights off boredom in a military hospital. The steps he takes in his private "war" on language foil the novel's theme of the absurd response to an absurd predicament.

The process eloquently condemns the way excessive military bureaucracy treats soldiers as nameless, faceless, inhuman, expendable tools of warfare. Yossarian treats his job as a censor to waging war on words, a feeble attempt to regain the power and humanity the bureaucratic military has removed from him. He invents new rules of language, treats undesirable word like enemies, and amuses himself without any consideration of the effects on other people. While he attempts to escape the dehumanizing bureaucracy by seizing the only power he has and exercising it over the words, he violates the sanctity of soldiers' humanity, destroying their "homes and streets," leaving them with no human connection outside the war.

Using Transitional Words or Phrases

As explanation progresses from step to step, we should keep the reader aware of the progress. When we take up a new step we should remind the reader, using the sequence marker—the phraseology and the numbers. These are words such as *first, then, after that,* etc. A sequence marker is usually placed at, or near the beginning of a sentence to make it work as a signpost for the reader to recognize relationships. Some common transitional words used in process essays are listed below:

142

One time	Transition		Another time
	TIME		
	After a few hours	Immediately following	
	Afterwards	Initially	
	At last	In the end	
	At the same time	In the future	
	Before	In the meantime	
	Before this	In the meanwhile	
	Currently	Last, Last but not least, Lastly	
	During	Later	
	Eventually	Meanwhile	
	Finally	Next, Soon after	
	First, Second, Third, etc.	Previously	
	First of all	Simultaneously	
	Formerly	Subsequently	
	Immediately before	Then	

Exercises

1. The following is a summary of the text entitled "What's in the Nice Cup of Tea." In the summary, some words are missing. Read the summary and fill in each of the blanks with a suitable word or phrase.

In producing tea, the _____ is called plucking. This means collecting "Flush" from tea plant. _____ the moisture of the leaves is reduced. In the _____, the leaves are broken up physically. _____ the tea is allowed to "ferment" in air. During fermentation, the polyphenolic flavanols in the green tea are oxidized through the catalytic action of an enzyme. _____ is called firing, in which the enzyme is deactivated by passing hot air over the leaves. _____, the dried tea is sorted into different grades. _____, the processed tea is packed and shipped.

2. Distinguish **steps** (that make up a process) from **tips** (that don't necessarily form a process) in Sample 5, find out the order of the development, underline the sequence markers and discuss with your group members how details are presented.

Sample 5

How to Do Well on a Job Interview
Glenda Davis

Ask a random selection of people for a listing of their least favorite activities, and right up there with "getting my teeth drilled" is likely to be "going to a job interview." The job interview is often regarded as a confusing, humiliating, and nerve-racking experience. First of all, you have to wait for your appointment in an outer room, often trapped there with other people applying for the same job. You sit nervously, trying not to think about the fact that only one of you may be hired. Then you are called into the interviewer's office. Faced with a complete stranger, you have to try to act both cool and friendly as you are asked all sorts of questions. Some questions are personal: "What is your greatest weakness?" Others are confusing: "Why should we hire you?" The interview probably takes about twenty minutes but seems like two hours. Finally, you go home and wait for days and even weeks. If you get the job, great. But if you don't, you're rarely given any reason why.

The job interview "game" may not be much fun, but it is a game you can win if you play it right. The name of the game is standing out of the crowd—in a positive way. If you go to the interview in a Bozo the Clown suit, you'll stand out of the crowd, all right, but not in a way that is likely to get you hired.

Here are guidelines to help you play the interview game to win:

Present yourself as a winner. Instantly, the way you dress, speak, and move gives the interviewer more information about you than you would think possible. You doubt that this is true? Consider this: A professional job recruiter, meeting a series of job applicants, was asked to signal the moment he decided not to hire each applicant. The thumbs-down decision was often made *in less than forty-five seconds—even before the applicant thought the interview had begun.*

How can you keep from becoming a victim of an instant "no" decision?

144

- *Dress appropriately.* This means business clothing: usually a suit and tie or a conservative dress or skirt suit. Don't wear casual student clothing. On the other hand, don't overdress: You're going to a job interview, not a party. If you're not sure what's considered appropriate business attire, do some spying before the interview. Walk past your prospective place of employment at lunch or quitting time and check out how the employees are dressed. Your goal is to look as though you would fit in with that group of people.

- *Pay attention to your grooming.* Untidy hair, body odor, dandruff[1], unshined shoes, a hanging hem, stains on your tie, excessive makeup or cologne[2], a sloppy job of shaving—if the interviewer notices any of these, your prospect of being hired takes probably fatal hit.

- *Look alert, poised, and friendly.* When that interviewer looks into the waiting room and calls your name, he or she is getting a first impression of your behavior. If you're slouched[3] in your chair, dozing or lost in the pages of a magazine; if you look up with an annoyed "huh?"; if you get up

1. dandruff: *n.* 头皮屑
2. cologne: *n.* 古龙水

3. slouch: *v.* stand, sit or move in a lazy way, often not quite upright

slowly and wander over with your hands in your pockets, he or she will not be favorably impressed. What will earn you points is rising promptly and walking briskly toward the interviewer. Smiling and looking directly at the person, extend your hand to shake his or hers, saying, "I'm Lesley Brown. Thank you for seeing me today."

- *Expect to make a little small talk.* This is not a waste of time; it is the interviewer's way of checking your ability to be politely sociable, and it is your opportunity to cement the good impression you've already made. The key is to follow the interviewer's lead. If he or she wants to chat about the weather for a few minutes, do so. But don't drag it out; as soon as you get a signal that it's time to talk about the job, be ready to get down to business.

Be ready for the interviewer's questions. The same questions come up again and again in many job interviews. *You should plan ahead for all these questions!* Think carefully about each question, outline your answer, and memorize each outline. Then practice reciting the answers to yourself. Only in this way are you going to be prepared. Here are common questions, what they really mean, and how to answer them:

- *"Tell me about yourself."* This question is raised to see how organized you are. The wrong way to answer it is to launch into a wandering, disjointed[4] response or—worse yet—to demand defensively, "What do you want to know" or "What do you mean?" When this question comes up, you should be prepared to give a brief summary of your life and work experience—where you grew up, where your family lives now, where you went to school, what jobs you've had, and how you happen to be here now looking for the challenge of a new job.
- *"What are your strengths and weaknesses?"* In talking about your strong points, mention traits

4. disjointed: *adj.* (of talk, writing, etc.) in which it is difficult to understand how the ideas, events, etc. follow each other and develop

145

that will serve you well in this particular job. If you are well-organized, a creative problem-solver, a good team member, or a quick learner, be ready to describe specific ways those strengths have served you in the past. Don't make the mistake of saying, "I don't have any real weaknesses." You'll come across as more believable if you admit a flaw—but make it one that an employer might actually like. For instance, admit that you are a workaholic or a perfectionist.

- *"Why should we hire you?"* Remember that it is up to you to convince the interviewer that you're the man or woman for this job. If you just sit there and hope that the interviewer will magically discern your good qualities, you are likely to be disappointed. Don't be afraid to sell yourself. Tell the recruiter that from your research you have learned that the interviewer's company is one you would like to work for, and that you believe the company's needs and your skills are a great match.

- *"Why did you leave your last job?"* This may seem like a great opportunity to cry on the interviewer's shoulder about what a jerk your last boss was or how unappreciated you were. It is not. The experts agree: Never badmouth anyone when you are asked this question. Say that you left in order to seek greater responsibilities or challenges. Be positive, not negative. No matter how justified you may feel about hating your last job or boss. If you give voice to those feelings in an interview, you're going to make the interviewer suspect that you're a whiner[5] and hard to work with.

- *"Do you have any questions?"* This is the time to stress one last time how interested you are in this particular job. Ask a question or two about specific aspects of the job, pointing out again how well your talents and the company's needs are matched. Even if you're dying to know how much the job pays and how much vacation you get, don't ask. There will be time enough to cover those questions after you've been offered the

5. whine: *v.* complain in a sad, annoying way

job. Today, your task is to demonstrate what a good employee you would be.

Send a thank-you note. Once you've gotten past the interview, there is one more chance for you to make a fine impression. As soon as you can—certainly no more than one or two days after the interview—write a note of thanks to your interviewer. In it, briefly remind him or her of when you came in and what job you applied for. As well as thanking the interviewer for seeing you, reaffirm your interest in the job and mention again why you think you are the best candidate for it. Make the note courteous, businesslike, and brief—just a paragraph or two. If the interviewer is wavering between several equally qualified candidates, such a note could tip the scales in your favor.

No amount of preparation is going to make interviewing for a job your favorite activity. But if you go in well-prepared and with a positive attitude, your potential employer can't help thinking highly of you. And the day will come when you are the one who wins the job.

Homework 2

Work in groups of three to have your first draft read and discussed for improvements.

These questions may help you:
1. Is the writing on an important or interesting process that may be helpful to the reader?
2. Does the writing present a clearly stated thesis?
3. Does the writing include an interesting beginning, strong development, and an effective ending?
4. Are the steps logically and thoroughly explained with well chosen details?
5. Is the writer well informed on the topic?
6. Is the writer really interested in writing about the topic.?
7. Do sentences and ideas flow smoothly from one to another?
8. Are there any language mistakes and format problems?

Analysis of Students' Writing

Read the following essay by a student to find out if it has the problem of unnecessary change in tense, person, voice or tone.

Student's Writing

Celebrating the Spring Festival

Have over three-thousand-year history and unique oriental culture, China has her own way to celebrate the grandest traditional festival—the Spring Festival. The celebration reflects typical Chinese conventions, customs, and culture during about twenty days. The activities such as family reunion, visiting friends, admiring lanterns delight and refresh people. It is a festival of new wishes, for the spring will be coming soon.

On the 23rd of the last lunar month, called "*xiao nian*" in Chinese, people usually make dumplings, opening the prelude of the Spring Festival. From this day on the whole nation is intoxicated with the spirit of the festival, and everywhere people busy themselves with preparations of the celebration. They go to the market and buy fruit, candy, lamb, beef, seafood and select the Spring Festival couplets. They kill pigs or sheep and freeze them for the holiday season. They make dumplings, steamed buns with sticky four jujubes, fired dough twists, which will last till the end of the festival.

On the morning of the 30th of this month, people put up the couplets on the door frames, welcoming the happiness and wealth of the coming New Year. All the family members get together on this day. At noon, there will be a most sumptuous feast for dinner. Just like in America, where turkey is a must for celebrating Thanksgiving, in China, there must be fish and meat, the former indicating food fortune, the latter predicting delicious food in the new year. In the evening people make dumplings while watching TV. At midnight, the most exciting and deafening moment comes, declaring the coming of the new year.

According to legends, fireworks are to frighten and drive evil spirits away. Family members now exchange greetings with one another, and the old give the young money as gift, hoping they will make a fortune. On the first day of the new year, people visit relatives and friends with gifts and good wishes. This will last until the fifth day when people start going back to work.

Spring Festival doesn't end completely until the 15th day of the first lunar month. This special day is called the Lantern Festival. People usually eat "*yuan xiao*," sweet balls made out of sticky rice flour, meaning safety and sweetness of family life. The whole family go out and admire the traditional lanterns at night. People in the North, especially in the city of Ha'erbin, go out and appreciate ice-lanterns, a feature of northern culture. People in the south perform dragon lantern dance and dragon-boat

148

regatta. These activities bring the festival to another climax and announce the end of the grand festival. Chinese Spring Festival is a hopeful and meaningful festival. The Chinese love it because the coming spring may bring progress both in career and family life.

Comments

The essay doesn't have the problem of unnecessary change in tense, person, voice or tone. The festival celebration is clearly divided into three stages: how people prepare for the occasion, how the New Year's Eve is celebrated, and how the festival comes to a close. Clearly, the paper is meant to offer information to people not familiar with Chinese Culture. The student writer describes the distinct activities in which people engage themselves in each stage and explains the symbolic meaning of important actions. Proper details are given so that the process is easy to understand.

Nevertheless, some details need reconsideration. For instance, pig killing in paragraph 2 no longer applies to every family. It should be specified to avoid misunderstanding. On the other hand, details like the quantity of food bought for the occasion and house cleaning may be added in the first stage. To highlight the celebration, more specific details describing the New Year's Eve and depiction of the street scene on the New Year's Day may be included, too.

There are other minor problems. Faulty parallelism occurs with the list of food in paragraph 2 " ...fruit, candy, meat, mutton, beef, seafood" are not in parallel, for mutton and beef belong to the same category of meat. Some verbs such as "go," "go out" and "begin" sound weak and boring because of repetition.

The Revised Version

Celebrating the Spring Festival

With a history of thousands of years, China has created a unique culture. The celebration of grandest traditional festival—the Spring Festival—culminates typical Chinese rituals and customs. Though different regions may display their local color, this national festival features one thing: welcoming a fresh start in the new year with family reunion over a big feast.

The twenty-third day of the last lunar month, termed *"xiao nian,"* opens the prelude of the festival. From this day, the whole nation is intoxicated in the festival spirit with every family bustling about the preparation. Shopping characterizes this stage. Chicken, meat, fish and eggs are indispensable; fresh vegetable and fruit of virtually every kind, including delicacies that are normally considered to be luxuies, find their way to shopping lists of every household, not to mention the impulse buying created by the wide range of attractive items on display. The purchase of food items in large quantities is necessary as they are supposed to last the entire festival period, which lasts about 20 days. As the New Year's Eve approaches, homemakers prepare steamed buns, fried dough twists, cakes with jujubes as well as fillings for dumplings.

To celebrate the new year, everything should put on a new look. Thorough cleaning of the house, which has been going on for some time, must be completed on the last day of the last lunar month. The final dusting rids the house of the old and new decoration follows. In addition to colored lights and ribbons, many families stick the spring festival couplets on their door frames, inviting happiness and wealth of the coming year.

At noon, family members get together, drinking and chattering heartily over a sumptuous feast. Among other delicious courses on the table, fish is a must: a homonymous token of food surplus in the coming year.

Glimmering lights add to the excitement of the New Yea's Eve. Making dumplings and letting off fire crackers are customary programs. The former activity is not reserved for the housewife only, but involves several other members of the family. Thus it takes on a special meaning of harmony within the family. It is believed the deafening firecrackers can frighten and driven away all evils. Towards midnight, all sounds are drowned by explosions of firecrackers and the sky turns gorgeously red.

Family members exchange warm whishes first thing on the New Year morning, and the elderly give the young gift-money wrapped in red paper. This occasion is so cherished that many, expecting to be the first to greet others, stay up the whole night.

Starting from the New Year's Day, many streets are crowded with folk shows. Gaily decorated dragons of impressive size coil or swing to the accompaniment of drums. Lions amaze spectators with acrobatics like standing up on hind legs and doing somersaults. Amateur performers in high spirits act out folk tales, legends and myths.

Even though the holiday is officially over on the fifth day of the first month when people return to work, the celebration does not end completely until the fifteenth day. To mark the occasion, people usually eat "*yuan xiao*," sweet balls made of sticky rice flour, meaning safety and sweetness of life. Characteristically, people admire beautifully decorated lanterns which seem to warm up the cold air. In the northern part of China, in the City of Ha'erbin, for example, people take the advantage of the cold winter by building ice and snow sculptures inlaid with lights of various colors. In the south, dragon lantern dance and dragon-boat regatta are performed. These activities bring the Festival to another climax and announce the end of the holiday season.

In conclusion, the Spring Festival in China is a period of entertainment, family reunion and a time for the manifestation of traditional folk culture. Everything gives play to the warmth and eagerness of the Chinese for the beginning of a new and hopeful spring.

Homework 3

Work in groups again to discuss how to improve the second draft of your essay and write the third draft.

Further Reading

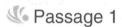 Passage 1

Bathing a Samoyed

Most pet owners take for granted the grooming of their dogs, casually hosing them down or dragging them to the tub. Most dogs eventually learn to accept baths as part of the normal cycle of dog living. Some dogs, however, not only dislike the periodic bathing that their owners inflict, they also make the bathing ritual a torment. Samoyeds, for example, have thick, tight fur that resists water and soap; in addition, their massive heads and heavy bodies, averaging about eighty pounds, create problems. Along with these natural barriers to bathing, Samoyeds readily demonstrate their disdain for the procedure by pulling away forcibly from owners who have "Now, it's time for a bath" looks in their eyes. In spite of the difficulties, bathing a Samoyed is both possible and necessary—for the dog's skin and the owner's sense of smell. First, gather all equipment. This includes a full bottle of dog shampoo, a pitcher for wetting and rinsing, a dozen towels, and an extra set of clothing for you and your helper (yes, you need a helper). With your partner's help, grab the dog and start dragging him to the bathroom. Once in, each of you needs to grab half a dog and attempt to lift him into the tub. This is no easy feat, because Samoyeds squirm constantly. Once the dog is in the bathtub, adjust the water temperature to warm but not hot (dogs can be picky). Fill your pitcher with water and begin wetting the dog while your partner holds him. Be careful around his head, watching out for his eyes and ears. He'll let you know if you get water in his eyes; be prepared for a soaking.

Completely saturate the dog's coat, and make sure you don't forget his belly just because it's underneath. Next, pour a handful of shampoo into your palm and start massaging it into the dog's hair. Scrub as hard as you like; he won't mind. In fact, he'll enjoy it very much. Wash his neck, back, tail, stomach, and legs completely. Now, fill your pitcher again and start rinsing the dog around his neck. Be prepared to refill your pitcher at least a dozen times because Samoyeds have thick hair. Continue until the dog is completely rinsed. You can tell when you're done by running your hands through the fur

151

afterwards. You'll be able to feel the soap if there's any left. Next, remove the dog from the bathtub. He will probably jump out gladly, splashing half the water in the tub all over you and the bathroom. Give your partner a towel and take one for yourself. Start at opposite ends and dry the dog. It will easily take the dozen towels you put out earlier. After about twenty minutes, stop and feel the hair. It should be dry. If you still think you could give a Samoyed a bath, here's your chance. Mine needs one. Pick her up anytime.

Passage 2

Breadmaking

The most widely used breadmaking process in the manufacture of commercial bread is the sponge and dough method. The first step of this process involves setting a mixture of flour, yeast, and water, called the "sponge," into the dough troughs. Seven hundred pounds of flour, for example, may be conveyed mechanically from the flour storage bins to the mixer. A yeast suspension is added to the flour, together with enough water to make the total water content about 460 pounds. The ingredients are then combined into the spongy mixture and placed into a dough trough where fermentation is permitted to take place. Fermentation is the second step in the sponge and dough method. The dough troughs are large, stainless steel oblong containers with rounded bottoms and are mounted on wheels, to facilitate their being rolled into the fermentation room. Here, where the temperature is held at 80 degrees F., the sponge ferments for about five hours. During this time, there is a chemical interaction of carbonates and acids, causing the sponge to rise. At the completion of the fermentation period, the sponge is ready for the next step in the method, mixing the dough. The sponge is returned to the mixer together with three hundred pounds of flour, 240 pounds of water, nonfat milk solids, and sugar. These ingredients are mixed into a dough, a process which plays an important part in determining the lightness and porousness of the ultimate loaf of bread. The fourth step is the division of the dough pieces into loaf size. The dough is conveyed mechanically to the dividing machine, which cuts the dough into pieces. From the divider, the pieces are carried to an overhead machine called a proofer, where each piece of dough remains for fifteen minutes. Here the dough is softened in preparation for the molder, which first flattens the dough pieces and then curls the dough the length of the bread pan. After the dough pieces have been panned, the pans are moved into a proof box under a constant temperature of 100 degrees F. The actual baking, of course, concludes the entire process. From the proof box, the pans go to the oven by means of traveling trays. The temperature of the oven is maintained at 450 degrees F. in order to cause the dough to rise. The speed of the trays is controlled so that the pans remain in the oven for exactly twenty-seven minutes. As the bread emerges from the oven after that time, it is dumped from the pans onto belts which convey it to the cooler. After about an hour and a half in the cooler, the bread is carried once again, this time to the slicer, where it is mechanically sliced to uniform thickness. Finally, the sliced loaf is wrapped by machine and made ready for early morning delivery to the retail stores.

The Classification Essay

Tuning-in Activities

1. **Divide the following words into groups, giving a name to each of the groups.**

brother	jump	strong	green
garden	weak	house	lawyer
healthy	soldier	forest	sing
city	village	intelligent	beautiful
biology	thoughtful	sleep	difficult

Group name:	Words:
Group name:	Words:
Group name:	Words:
Group name:	Words:

2. **Classify objects according to physical structure and characteristics.**

Materials:
- A box of assorted buttons
- An assortment of leaves

Procedure:
- Group the buttons according to any characteristics.
- What criterion do you use to group the buttons? (For example, size, color, number of holes, texture, etc.)
- Sort the plant leaves according to structure and characteristics.
- Try re-grouping them according to alternate characteristics.

Extensional Activity

Try brainstorming and classifying other groups of living things, like "domestic pets" or "animals you'd see in a wildlife park." Consider what criterion you'll use to group them.

Introduction

Human beings love to classify. We classify things according to their similarities and differences. We speak of good guys and bad guys; required courses and elective courses; comedies and tragedies; economy cars, sports cars and luxury cars.

A political science teacher may classify his/her students according to their political orientations: radicals, liberals, conservatives and reactionaries. A college student may group his/her roommates into considerate ones, messy and lazy ones, bossy ones and loners. English words are divided into nouns, verbs, adjectives, and adverbs. Apples may be classified according to size, place of origin, color, price, or quality.

Classifying is a common form of organization. Take any supermarket for instance; the first thing one might see in a supermarket is the grouping of various foods and merchandise. For example, in the produce section, fruits and vegetables are grouped according to whether they are root vegetables, vine vegetables, and leafy greens. In the fruit section you will find citrus divided into different categories: oranges, lemons, limes, and tangerines and so on. The supermarket will keep canned goods on one aisle, and frozen ones in another. Dairy and bakery goods will also be separated. And each of these can be divided into smaller units. The canned goods section is divided between canned fruits and vegetables. And they can still be divided further. One section will have canned beans, another will have potatoes, and yet another will stock okra, or tomatoes. The canned tomato section, as the others, will be organized according to brand, sizes, and prices.

While most subjects can be classified in a number of ways, the writer must classify under *one single organizing criteria/principle* that is both discriminating and non-overlapping.

Classification is one of the basic methods of exposition. It gives a clear understanding of order and relationship by a sorting-out.

Useful Expressions When Using Classification

...according to whether or not ...there is X...

X consists of... / comprises...

...according to whether there is X or not...

X may be classified

according to...
on the basis of...
depending on(upon)...

The classification is based on...

Here is a potentially useful sequence:

...may be divided...

...may be subdivided...

...may be further subdivided...

Observe Classification in Action

Consider this situation. Peter is taking a writing class, and his instructor tells him to write a paper of personal experience. Since Peter works part time in a department store as a salesperson, the instructor suggests he write about his customers. Deep in thought, Peter begins his writing.

3,042 Customers

I have been working at my job for three weeks now, and I have had three thousand and forty-two customers. The first one was a woman. She said she was only looking, and she didn't buy anything. The next person was a young man, and he also said he was a looker, and he didn't buy anything either. Then the third one was shopping for sales, and she went through the merchandise and picked out three sales items and bought them. The fourth one was looking for a specific item; I showed it to her and she bought it. The fourth, a young girl, was also a looker. The fifth one...

Of course, if Peter were to write that way, he would produce a very long and very boring paper. With the help of the instructor, Peter tries to group his customers.

Sorting Them Out

I've had several kinds of customers at my job at May Company. Specifically, I can divide most of them into three classes: the looking shoppers, the sales shoppers, and the special-item shoppers. The largest class is the *looking shoppers*. One can see them wandering around all over the store as if they were lost or maybe out for exercises. They stop for discoveries here and there, but they don't want to be bothered by salespersons. They're pretty harmless, except sometimes they bump into each other. And quite infrequently they buy something. The next class, the *sales shoppers*, are the ones who have read the advertisements. They may even be carrying an advertisement with them, matching pictures and numbers with items. If a salesperson can help them get to the merchandise before someone else does, they're grateful; otherwise, get out of their way. They are single-minded and ruthless. Beware of verbal assaults and vicious bodily contact at the sales tables. The last group is my favorite. It is the *special-item shoppers*. They know what they want, but they would like good quality and a good price. They are usually friendly, and they are appreciative of good service. On a given day, one person may move from one group to another, and when the person does, his or her behavior changes.

After serving more than three thousand customers, I can identify and classify them almost immediately.

The difference between the two efforts is remarkable. The first considers thousands of persons and discusses some of them without producing any discernible order or meaning. The second classifies the persons according to *a single principle* (why they come to the store), and the reader can follow the logical arrangement and the meaning of the presentation. The writing may be informative to the general reader and instructive to intern salespersons, serving two purposes at the same time.

Purposes of Classification

We classify **to inform** or **to persuade**. When we classify different kinds of computers, we inform readers, making more knowledgeable about computers. When Peter classifies shoppers into three classes, he might intend to persuade intern salespersons to offer help for the special-item shoppers, not to bother the looking shoppers, and to provide only one particular help for the sales shoppers. At the same time, Peter informs readers salespeople like special-item shoppers the most.

Exercise

Find out the classification principles and purposes of the sample essays.

Sample 1

Ancient Chinese Architecture

Chinese architecture, which features emphasis on the horizontal and symmetry, is ofen classified by structure into *ting* (pavilions), *tai* (terraces), *lou* (multistorey buildings), *ge* (two-storey pavilions), *xie* (pavilions or houses on terraces), *ta* (Chinese pagodas), *xuan* (verandas with windows) and *wu* (rooms along roofed corridors).

Chinese pavilions are covered structures without surrounding walls. While often found within temples, pavilions are not exclusively religious structures. Many Chinese parks and gardens feature pavilions to provide shade and a place to rest. *Liangting*, the wayside (cooling) pavilion, provides weary wayfarers with a place for rest. The "stele pavilion" gives a roof to a stone tablet to protect the engraved record of an important event. Pavilions also stand by bridges or over water-wells. Pavilions, built normally either of wood or stone or bamboo, are often classified according to their shape when viewed from above. Round, square, hexagonal and octagonal pavilions are common, while more unusual designs also exist such as the *Nanhai* Pavilion located at the Temple of Heaven in Beijing, which consists of two round pavilions joined together.

A terrace is an outdoor, occupiable extension of a building above ground level. As an ancient Chinese architectural structure, the *tai*, generally built of earth and stone and surfaced with brick, was a very much elevated terrace with a flat top. The *tai* could be built to serve different practical purposes. It could just be a place for people to have a full view of a long distance at leisure. It could be used as an observatory, as for instance the one near Jianguomen in Beijing. It could also be used militarily, like the beacon towers along the Great Wall, to transmit urgent information with smoke by day and fire by night.

A *lou* refers to any building of two or more storeys with a horizontal main ridge. Ancient buildings with more than one storey were meant for a variety of uses. The smaller two-storeyed buildings of private homes generally have the owner's study or bedrooms and upstairs. The more magnificent ones built in parks or at scenic spots were belvederes from which to enjoy the distant scenery. In this case, it is sometimes translated as a "tower." Ancient cities had bell and drum towers (*zhonglou* and *gulou*), usually palatial buildings with four-sloped, double-caved, glazed roofs, all-around verandas and coloured and carved *dougong* brackets supporting the overhanging eaves. They housed a big bell or a drum which were used to announce time, and the local officials would open the city gates at the toll of the bell early in the morning and close them with the strike of the drum in the evening.

Similar to the *lou*, the Chinese *ge* has a door and windows only on the front side with the other three sides being solid walls. *Ge* is usually enclosed by wooden balustrades or decorated with boards all around. *Ge* can sit above water, in the forest, in the temple or at the peak. The whole beautiful scenery of the far distant can be seen clearly and easily from the storied pavilion. *Ge* was also used in ancient times for the storage of important articles and documents. *Wenyuange* in the Forbidden City of Beijing for instance, was in effect the imperial library.

…

All these exquisite architectures in the ingenious structure are the momentous components of the ancient Chinese culture, which are not only the fine arts for appreciation and enjoyment but also the vivid historical records of China.

(http://www.visitourchina.com/guide/ancient_chinese_architecture.htm)

Sample 2

African American Music

Tiffany Turner

Three popular types of music that were originated by African Americans are jazz, rhythm and blues, and soul. Although individual performances have different styles, each type of music has its own distinctive sounds that appeal to a wide variety of listeners.

Jazz is a "laid back" type of music that you can relax to. After a long day of work and school, I like to come home and relax with the rhythmic beats of jazz. There are many different styles of jazz that you can listen to, and jazz players like to create their own spontaneous[1] rhythms and melodies[2]. Jazz started to appear around 1900,

based mainly on African American folk music and West African rhythms. Early jazz innovators who helped to establish jazz as a distinct type of music include Louis Armstrong, Duke Ellington, and Dizzy Gillespie.

Rhythm and blues is a special freestyle type of music. In order to listen to rhythm and blues, you have to be in a rhythm and blues mood. With this music you pour your broken heart and soul into. Many people sing the blues when they break up with their boyfriend or lose their job because it is a very expressive type of music. The blues style of singing was originally developed in the late nineteenth century and came from African American slave songs about life's hardships. In the 1940s and 1950s, performers like

1. spontaneous: *adj.* 自发的；本能的
2. melody: *n.* 旋律；曲调

158

Ray Charles and Fats Domino helped to popularize rhythm and blues.

Soul is the up-beat[3] dance music. It is easy to sing and dance to. The coordinated tones, rhythms, and syncopated[4] beats create this modern music sound. Lyrics make up a big part of soul songs. The lyrics tell the story instead of music. Soul music is what is on the radio. It began in the 1950s as a combination of rhythm and blues and gospel[5] music. Early soul artists include Otis Redding and Stevie Wonder.

Jazz, rhythm and blues, and soul each offer us something different to suit our different moods. These three types of music have been historically popular, and all originated with African Americans.

3. up-beat: *adj.* 乐观的；欢乐的

4. syncopate *v.* 切分

5. gospel: *n.* 福音；喜讯

159

Sample 3

The Ways of Meeting Oppression
Martin Luther King, Jr., PhD

Oppressed people deal with their oppression in three characteristic ways. One way is acquiescence[1]: the oppressed resign themselves to their doom. They tacitly[2] adjust themselves to oppression, and thereby become conditioned to it. In every movement toward freedom some of the oppressed prefer to remain oppressed. Almost 2800 years ago Moses[3] set out to lead the children of Israel from the slavery of Egypt to the freedom of the promised land. He soon discovered that slaves do not always welcome their deliverers. They become accustomed to being slaves. They would rather bear those ills they have, as Shakespeare pointed out, than flee to others that they know not of. They prefer the "fleshpots[4] of Egypt" to the ordeals[5] of emancipation[6].

There is such a thing as the freedom of exhaustion. Some people are so worn down by the

1. acquiescence: *n.* 默认，默许

2. tacitly: *adv.* 缄默地

3. Moses: 摩西。这里讲的是《圣经·旧约》《出埃及记》的故事。

4. fleshpots: *n.* 奢侈的生活
5. ordeal: *n.* 折磨
6. emancipation: *n.* 解放

Unit Seven

yoke[7] of oppression that they give up. A few years ago in the slum areas of Atlanta, a Negro guitarist used to sing almost daily: "Been down so long that don't bother me." This is the type of negative freedom and resignation[8] that often engulfs[9] the life of the oppressed.

But this is not the way out. To accept passively an unjust system is to cooperate with that system; thereby the oppressed become as evil as the oppressor. Non-cooperation with evil is as much a moral obligation as is cooperation with good. The oppressed must never allow the conscience of the oppressor to slumber[10]. Religion reminds every man that he is his brother's keeper. To accept injustice

or segregation[11] passively is to say to the oppressor that his actions are morally right. It is a way of allowing his conscience to fall asleep. At this moment the oppressed fails to be his brother's keeper. So acquiescence—while often the easier way—is not the moral way. It is the way of the coward. The Negro cannot win the respect of his oppressor by acquiescing; he merely increases the oppressor's arrogance and contempt. Acquiescence is interrupted as proof of the Negro's inferiority. The Negro cannot win the respect of the white people of the South or the peoples of the world if he is willing to sell the future of his children for his personal and immediate comfort and safety.

A second way that oppressed people sometimes deal with oppression is to resort to physical violence and corroding[12] hatred. Violence often brings about momentary[13] results. Nations have frequently won their independence in battle. But in spite of temporary victories, violence never brings permanent peace. It solves no social problem; it merely creates new and more complicated ones.

Violence as a way of achieving racial justice is both impractical and immoral. It is impractical because

7. yoke: *n.* 束缚；支配

8. resignation: *n.* 顺从，屈从
9. engulf: *v.* 吞没；席卷

10. slumber: *v.* 睡眠

11. segregation: *n.* 隔离

12. corrode: *v.* 腐蚀，侵蚀
13. momentary: *adj.* 暂时的

160

it is a descending spiral[14] ending in destruction for all. The old law of an eye for an eye leaves everybody blind. It is immoral because it seeks to humiliate the opponent rather than win his understanding; it seeks to annihilate[15] rather than to convert[16]. Violence is immoral because it thrives on hatred rather than love. It destroys community and makes brotherhood impossible. It leaves society in monologue rather than dialogue. Violence ends by defeating itself. It creates bitterness in the survivors and brutality in the destroyers. A voice echoes through time saying to every potential Peter, "Put up your sword."[17] History is cluttered with the wreckage of nations that failed to follow this command.

If the American Negroes and other victims of oppression succumb[18] to the temptation of using violence in the struggle of freedom, future generations will be the recipients of a desolate night of bitterness, and our chief legacy to them will be an endless resign of meaningless chaos. Violence is not the way.

The third way open to oppressed people in their quest for freedom is the way to nonviolent resistance. Like the synthesis in Hegelian[19] philosophy, the principle of nonviolent resistance seeks to reconcile[20] the truths of two opposites—the acquiescence and violence—while avoiding the extremes and immoralities of both. The nonviolent resister agrees with the person who acquiesces that one should not be physically aggressive toward his opponent; but he balances the equation by agreeing with the person of violence that evil must be resisted. He avoids the non-resistance of the former and the violent resistance of the latter. With nonviolent resistance, no individual or group need submit to any wrong, nor need anyone resort to violence in order to right a wrong.

It seems to me that this is the method that must guide the actions of the Negro in the present crisis in race relations. Through nonviolent resistance the Negro will be able to rise to the noble height of opposing the unjust system while

14. spiral: *adj.* 螺旋的

15. annihilate: *v.* 歼灭, 消灭
16. convert: *v.* 转变, 改变

17. "Put up your sword." 耶稣被捕后彼得拔剑反抗, 耶稣命其收剑, 并说出剑者必毙于剑。 Matthew 26:52
18. succumb: *v.* 屈服, 屈从

161

19. Hegelian: *adj.* 黑格尔学派的
20. reconcile: *v.* 调解, 调和

loving the perpetrators[21] of the system. The Negro must work passionately and unrelentingly[22] for full stature as a citizen, but he must not use inferior methods to gain it. He must never come to terms with falsehood, malice[23], hate, or destruction.

Nonviolent resistance makes it possible for the Negro to remain in the South and struggle for his rights. The Negro's problem will not be solved by running away. He cannot listen to the glib suggestion of those who would urge him to migrate en masse[24] to other sections of the country. By grasping his great opportunity in the South he can make a lasting contribution to the moral strength of the nation and set a sublime example of courage for generations yet unborn.

By nonviolent resistance, the Negro can also enlist all men of good will in his struggle for equality. The problem is not a purely racial one, with Negroes set against whites. In the end, it is not a struggle between people at all, but a tension between justice and injustice. Nonviolent resistance is not aimed against oppressors but against oppression. Under its banner consciences, not racial groups, are enlisted.

21. perpetrator *n.* 作恶者，犯罪者
22. unrelentingly *adv.* 不屈不挠地
23. malice *n.* 恶意，怨恨
24. en masse 一起，全体

Finding Topic for Classification

Since virtually any subject can be organized into classes, whatever interests you will probably work. And when you classify, you should use at least three categories; otherwise, you would be skirting comparison and contrast. Here are some general subject areas you might consider classifying. Keep in mind that you need to be focused.

teachers	vacations
jobs	restaurants
department stores	music
students	athletes
weddings	lies
cars	movie goers
books	TV programs
sports fans	psychological diseases
families	schools
waiters	lovers
doctors	friends

ways to acquire knowledge	ways to manipulate others
ways to bring joy to others	ways to make money
ways to get a person to say yes	ways to lose weight

⒣omework 1

Do freewriting on the topic you have chosen. Jot down your classification of a subject and your division of the subject into groups. Then list words and phrases in relation to those answers. Write sentence after sentence, spontaneously and without stop.

ⓦriting Strategies

Establish the writing purpose.

Most subjects can be classified in many different ways. How to classify a subject depends on your purpose because you classify information in order to make a point. The purpose of a classification essay can be to inform or to persuade. In Sample 2, Turner writes about the three popular forms of African American music without showing preference to any one of them. Therefore, his writing purpose is to inform. While in Sample 2, King classifies the different types of responses to oppression (acquiescence, violence and nonviolence), argues that nonviolence is a better response than the other two, and concludes that nonviolent resistance is the best way for African Americans to fight against oppression. Hence, his writing purpose is to persuade.

Apply a principle that fits the purpose.

By the principle of classification, we mean the distinguishing features used to determine membership in its types, kinds, or groups. To be meaningful, a classification must group elements according to some principles, which provide the logic for the classification.

The principle on which the division of the classes is based must fit the purpose (to inform or to persuade). Peter wants to inform the reader (purpose) about the different types of customers according to their motives (principle). Therefore, the purpose and the principle are quite similar. If he wanted to persuade the reader, say, not to work in department stores because of the stress related to dealing with customers, he might have used the idea of stress-provoking customers as a principle and classified certain unsavory customers as thieves, manipulators, and bullies. Those three classes would be discussed according to their capacity for producing stress on the salespersons.

163

Create categories.

We create categories (classes) by organizing elements according to a common principle and put subjects of common features into a category. For instance,

Subject	Principles	Categories
Crimes	Seriousness of the crimes	1. Misdemeanors
		2. Felonies
	Type of injury to victims	1. Death
		2. Physical injury
		3. Financial injury
		4. Emotional injury

The chart below shows the common feature that ties together each category of trees.

Three Ways of Classifying Trees	
Principles	Categories
Methods of Reproduction	● Cone-bearing trees
	● Seed-bearing trees
	● Spore-bearing trees
Usefulness	● Shade trees
	● Trees for windbreaks
	● Ornamental trees
Source of Food	● Trees that bear edible nuts
	● Trees that bear edible fruits
	● Trees that have edible sap

Avoid overlapping.

The "trick" to a good classification is to create clear categories that do not overlap. If the categories of certain items are already contained within another entry, the classification will become illogical.

While sorting the customers out, Peter might have come up with four categories: (1) looking, (2) sales hunting, (3) special purchasing, and (4) being informed. Although a certain number of customers are informed in various ways, item number 4 is out of place because it is not based on the principle of intention. In his groups there would be a problem of overlapping because numbers of the other groups could also be informed.

Under the principle of usefulness, if trees were classified as shade trees, trees for windbreaks, ornamental trees, and tall trees, the problem of overlapping again would arise because the first three categories may also contain tall trees.

Another example:
You could divide your classmates into intelligent and good-looking. However, perhaps some of your classmates are both intelligent and good-looking. That means those two groups overlap. Therefore, it is a bad classification.

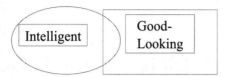

There is another reason for this classification to be bad. The types of groups should be consistent. You could use people's appearance as the principle for classification to have categories such as good-looking and ugly or intelligence as the principle to have categories of intelligent and stupid, but you cannot mix two priniciples together.

However, even with good-looking and ugly, we have a problem. Do you really think that all of your classmates fit into those categories? Probably not. There are probably plenty of average looking students in your class. It is very important that your groups include everyone in your class. Classifications have to include all the possible classes to completely cover that topic.

Good-looking	Average	Ugly

However, since anything can be classified this way, it makes little sense to do this classification.

Exercise

Are the sets of categories overlapping? Underline the parts that are overlapping.

Subject	Principle	Categories
Example:		
community college students	**intentions**	**vocational academic transfer specialty needs <u>hardworking</u>**
1. airline flights	passenger seating	first class business coach
2. schools	ownership	private religious public

3. sentences	structure	simple compound imperative complex compound-complex
4. country singers	clothing trademark	hat overalls expensive decorative costume
5. faces	shape	round square oval beautiful broad long

Complete the categories for items 6—10. Keep in mind that you should avoid overlapping.

6. waitresses	style of serving	
7. classmates		good students good fellows good organizers
8. sports		rack and field events swimming
9. walkers	mannerisms	
10. hotels		

Have you decided on a good topic to write about?

While writing a classification essay, do not produce colorless, flat, boring, and monotonous classes. Topics with two extremes and a middle position are almost always dull. Consider some of the bad ideas: good students, bad students and average students; fast runners, slow runners, and average runners, intelligent thinkers, unintelligent thinkers, and average thinkers.

When you write classifications, try to look at subjects in new and attractive ways. For instances, if you want to discuss bosses based on the principle of management styles, you can group them as dictators, cunning manipulators, buddies, and democrats, which is much better than grouping them as good bosses, bad bosses, and average bosses, or old bosses, young bosses, and middle-aged bosses.

Writing a Classification Essay

Write a thesis statement.

A thesis statement for a classification essay should do one or more of the following:

1. State the subject and the categories of classification.
2. Present the principle that is the basis of the classification.
3. Explain why the classification is important.
4. Identify relationships between categories.

Here is the basic statement for the thesis:

subject   **principle of classification**

Bosses maintain control mainly through the use of one of these management styles:

categories

dictator, cunning manipulator, buddy, and democrat.

In the thesis statement, you mention that *there are (number) types of (something) according to their (properties)*. In the developmental paragraphs, you need to define each type you mentioned in the thesis. You may also need to show the similarities and/or differences of these types. Give examples to enable better understanding.

Develop the content.

After writing the thesis statement that decides the controlling principle, you need to discuss each of the categories, which provide structure and sequence. In the developmental paragraphs, it is useful to devote one paragraph to each category.

You need to:

1. identify the group,
2. describe or define the category, the general characteristics of the members in particular,
3. give examples,
4. distinguish this category from other categories.

Consider how this outline provides a skeletal structure for the thesis on the management styles of bosses.

    I. The dictator

      A. uses fear

      B. issues command

167

II. The cunning manipulator
   A. is devious
   B. turns people against each other
III. The buddy
   A. wants to be friends
   B. loses respect
IV. The democrat
   A. treats others with respect
   B. works with consensus

Organizing the Classification Essay

The Opening Paragraph

The purpose of an introduction is to have the reader's attention and present the main idea of the essay. Put forward the thesis statement that indicates the principle of classification. For instance:

1. Men generally choose one of three types of hairstyles to reflect something about their attitude or outlook on life: conservative, contemporary, or extreme.
2. Clarity, cut, and size are three characteristics used to classify diamonds.
3. The study troops found in all college libraries fall into three categories: the industrious soldiers, the crammer cadets, and the just-for-show officers.

The Body Paragraphs

If you listed your categories in your thesis statement, then you have already organized the body of your paragraph. Your first paragraph after the introduction will be about the first category you mentioned. Your second paragraph, or section, will be about the second category you mention, and that pattern continues until you run out of categories.

The important thing to remember with paragraphs is that once you write your topic sentence, nothing should go into that paragraph which does not connect to the topic sentence.

Include details and examples that show what the items in each category have in common.

The Concluding Paragraph

Every conclusion should re-state the main ideas of the essay. Here are some tips.

● **Review the categories:**
   i.e. Jazz, rhythm and blues, and soul each offer us something different to suit our different moods. These three types of music have been historically popular, and all originated with African Americans.

● **Probe into the significance of the classification:**

i.e. Understanding whether your leaning style is visual, auditory, kinesthetic, or some combination of these styles can help you find ways to learn more effectively.

● **Make appropriate comment:**

i.e. The world would be a completely different place without tools because we can hardly construct things like buildings and vehicles merely with our hands.

The following is the part of a larger paper on off-beat hobbyists. The writer creates her categories to classify comic book collectors. She begins with a standard opening for classification pieces by clearly announcing the categories she slips her collectors into. Study how she organizes the classification essay.

Sample 4

Other fascinating off-beat hobbyists are comic book collectors. These collectors, whether sixteen or sixty, at first glance seem to be a bushy-haired, disheveled, absentminded, and disorganized lot. But after close examination you'll find their habits put them into one of the four major groups: the Antiquarians, Mercenaries, Idolators, and Compulsive Completers. You'll be able to find all these types rummaging through pile after pile of unsorted, secondhand comics in magazine marts scattered from New York to Los Angeles.

The opening sentence includes a transition from the preceding paragraph and announces the subject of "comic book collectors."

These sentences supply background and a general description of collectors while establishing four categories.

The Antiquarians cares only for age value; subject matter is of no concern. He's looking for a 1933 *Funnies on Parade* from the days when men were men and comics were comics. To the Mercenary, value is all-important. Certain numbers and titles ring a bell in his cash-register brain and start him furtively checking through a half dozen price sheets. A pristine first edition of *Action Comics* (value: $4000) would suit him just fine. The Idolator couldn't care less about age or value. He's looking for favorites: a *Sheena*, a *Flash Gordon*, or another *Incredible Hulk*. Hiding in a corner, reading those he can't afford to buy, he'll be the last one out of the mart at night and the first one back in the morning. The most frustrated collector is the Compulsive Completer. He'll examine and reject thousands of comics in his search for a badly

In this paragraph the writer presents the four kinds of collectors along with supporting details. Notice how she introduces each type by using her label in the first sentence of each section.

needed *Felix the Cat* to complete a year's set or the one *Howdy Doody* missing from his collection.

But no matter what the reason for collecting, these hobbyists share a common trait: they love the thrill of the hunt.

(From *One to One: Resources for Conference-Centered Writing* by Charles W. Dawe and Edward A. Dorna, 2nd edition. Boston: Little Brown and Company, 1984. pp.106—108.)

She closes the piece by identifying a common trait — all love the thrill of the hunt.

Exercises

Look at the scrambled five paragraphs of an essay and put them into logical order, thus forming a classification essay.

1. Just what goes into "having fun"? For many people, "fun" involves getting out of the house, seeing other people, having something interesting to look at, and enjoying a choice of activities, all at a reasonable price. Going out to dinner or to the movies may satisfy some of those desires, but often not all. But an attractive alternative does exist in the form of the free-admission shopping mall. Teenagers, couples on dates, and the nuclear family can all be observed having a good time at the mall.

2. Sure, some people visit the mall in a brief, business way, just to pick up a specific purchase or two. But many more are shopping for inexpensive recreations. The teenagers, the dating couples, and the nuclear families all find cheap entertainment at the mall.

3. Couples find fun of another sort at shopping malls. The young lovers are easy to spot because they walk hand in hand, stopping to sneak a quick kiss after every few steps. They first pause at a jewelry store window so that they can gaze at diamond engagement rings and gold wedding bands. Then, they wander into future departments in the large mall stores. Finally, they drift away, their arms wrapped around each other's waist.

4. Teenagers are drawn to the mall to pass time with pals and to see and be seen by other teens. The guys saunter by in sneakers. T-shirts, and blue jeans, complete with a package of cigarettes sticking out of a pocket. The girls stumble along in high heeled shoes and daring tank tops, with a hairbush tucked snugly in the rear pocket of their tight-fitting designer jeans. Traveling in a gang that resembles a wolf pack, the teenagers make the shopping mall their obviously made decision to attract all this teenage activity. The kids' raised voices, obscenities can be heard from as far as half a mall away. They come to "pick up chicks," to "meet guys," and just to "hang out."

5. Mom, Dad, little Jenny, and Fred, Jr., visit the mall on Friday and Saturday evenings for inexpensive recreation. Hearing the music of the antique carousel housed there, Jenny begs to ride her favorite pony with its shining golden mane. Shouting "I'm starving!" Fred, Jr., drags the family toward the food court, where he detects the

seductive odor of pizza. Mom walks through a fabric store, running her hand over the soft velvets and slippery silks. Meanwhile, Dad has wandered into an electronics store and is admiring the sound system he'd love to buy someday. The mall provides something special for every member of the family.

Logical order:

Working with Simple and Complex Forms

The outline shown for the categories of bosses is typical for most paragraphs and essays, but more complicated arrangements exist, especially in published sources. Two main patterns prevail: the simple and the complex. A subject that is presented with one principle of classification is called *simple*. Here is an example presented in the standard category-by-category arrangement.

Sample 5

Though at times there was considerable social mobility, *medieval society* conventionally consisted of three classes: the <u>nobles</u>, the <u>peasants</u>, and the <u>clergy</u>. Each of these groups had its own task to perform. Since the vassals usually gave military service to their lord in return for their fiefs, the nobles were primarily fighters, belonging to an honored society distinct from the peasant people— freemen, villains, and serfs. In an age of physical violence, society obviously would accord first place to the man with the sword rather than to the man with the hoe. The peasants were the workers; attached to the manors, they produced the crops and did all the menial labor. The Church drew on both the noble and the peasant classes for the clergy. Although the higher churchmen held land as vassals under the feudal system, the clergy formed a class which was considered separate from the nobility and peasantry.

Subject: medieval society

Categories: nobles, peasants, and clergy

Principle: task

The classifications that are based on one principle and then sub-grouped by another related principle are called complex. This is a typical example.

Sample 6

There are two principal types of glaciers: the continental and the valley. The continental glaciers are great sheets of ice, called ice caps that cover parts of the continent. The earth has two continental glaciers at present: one spreads over most of Greenland and one covers all of Antarctica save for a small window of rock and the peaks of several ranges. The Greenland ice sheet is over 10,000 ft. thick in the central part and covers an area of about 650,000 sq. miles. The Antarctic sheet has been sounded, in one place at least, to a depth of 14,000 ft., and it spreads over an area of 5, 5000,000 sq. miles. This is larger than conterminous United States in the proportion of 5 1/2: 3. It is calculated to store 7 million cu. Miles of ice, which if melted would raise the ocean level 250 ft.

Valley glaciers are ice streams that originate in the high snow fields of mountain ranges and flow down valleys to warmer climates, where they melt. Some break up into icebergs and eventually melt in the ocean. In certain places the valley glaciers flow down the mountain valleys to adjacent plains and there spread out as lobate feet. These feet are called expanded-foot glaciers. Generally the sprawling feet of several valley glaciers coalesce to form one major sheet, and this is called a piedmont glacier.

Subject: glaciers
Main categories: continental and valley

Main category I: continental glaciers

Main category II: valley glaciers

Subcategory A: conventional

Subcategory B: expanded-foot

Subcategory C: piedmont

172

Note that the valley glacier is subdivided into:

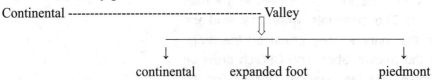

As you can see, glaciers are of two types based on their location (with implications for size): (1) the continental glacier, such as the huge one in the Antarctica, and (2) the valley glacier. The valley glacier can be subdivided into the conventional valley glacier, flowing straight; the expanded-foot glacier, which spreads out; and the piedmont glacier, which is made up of several expanded-foot glaciers. This is the way this information could be organized in a simple outline:

    I. Continental glacier

II. Valley glacier

    A. Conventional

    B. Expanded-foot

    C. Piedmont

This outline on glaciers could be cut down to the "valley glacier" part and develop into a paragraph or an essay. Moving in the other direction, we can say that almost all classifications can be part of a higher level of classification. For example, glaciers are one type of earth-altering process, together with earthquakes, volcanoes, and wind erosion.

Most papers of classification will be simple (based on one principle) in concept, informative in purpose, and category by category in organization.

Exercise

Read the following classification carefully and answer the questions below .

Sample 7

The writer discusses three kinds of book owners, but only one kind that truly owns books. If you have a collection of books, where would you be placed in this three-group classification?

Vocabulary

Kinds of Book Owners

Mortimer J. Adler

There are three kinds of book owners. The first has all the standard sets and best-sellers—unread, untouched. (This deluded individual owns woodpulp[1] and ink, not books.) The second has a great many books—a few of them read through, most of them dipped into, but all of them as clean and shiny as the day they were bought. (This person would probably like to make books his own, but is restrained by a false respect for their physical appearance.) The third has a few books or many—every one of them dog-eared[2] and dilapidated[3], shaken and loosened by continual use, marked and scribbled in from front to back. (This man owns books.)

1. woodpulp *n.* 木浆

2. dog-eared *adj.* 折角的，翻旧了的

3. dilapidate *v.* 使损坏

Questions

1. Circle the subject (what is being classified) the first time it appears in the piece of writing.

Unit Seven

2. What is the principle of the classification (on what basis is the classifying being done)?

   _____

3. Underline the categories the first time each appears.

   _____

4. State the topic sentence or thesis (the writer's exact words or your own phrasing).

   _____

5. Translate the basic parts of the classification into a brief topic outline.

   _____

   _____

6. Is the pattern of arrangement simple or complex?

   _____

7. Is the main purpose to inform or to persuade?

   _____

Homework 2

Write the first draft of your classification essay.

Writer's Checklist

Apply the following ideas to your writing as you work with a classification. Later, as a peer editor, apply the same ideas to the material you evaluate.

1. Clearly define your subject (what you are classifying) and consider your purpose (to inform or to persuade).
2. Develop meaningful categories that do not overlap. Classify your material on the basis of one principle. Don't mix principles.
3. Divide you subject into at least three categories.
4. Consider whether you need subcategories. If you do, clearly distinguish the different levels.
5. Write a good introductory paragraph with a thesis statement, get the body with main discussion well organized (give a topic sentence to each category and provide the support and sequence), and produce a logical concluding paragraph.
6. Keep your reader interested and avoid an unimaginative pattern, such as "good-average-bad" and "fast-medium-slow."

Analysis of Students' Writing

Student's Freewriting

College Stress

We often talk about stress. Yes, college students today suffer a lot of stress. We have so many courses each day, and there are some we don't

---

like at all. Before exam, we must work very hard, even the whole night. Parents told us to study hard, teachers told us to study hard, This make us tired. But can you find a good job even if you get good scores. Maybe not. Competition is so intense in society. This is a thing we're afraid of. It is too difficult to get a good job after graduation. There are many other stress, students compete for scholarship, for good chances, also economic stress, love stress, etc. We must face the stress and solve the problems. Maybe more of them. Someone say stress is not a bad thing. Perhaps. Stress can force us to work harder.

Comments

In the free writing, the student wrote whatever occurred to her without considering essay structure and worrying about grammar. Two of her classmates read her freewriting and suggested that she classify the college stress into three or four groups, covering the major stresses. After studying her classmates' response, she decided to better structure the essay, dividing college stress into academic, parental, and social stress.

Student's First Draft

College Stress

In today's society stress exists everywhere, and it certainly exists in college. We can see many students work very hard, because parents and teachers tell to do so, and we have to study hard to get a good job in the future. Generally speaking, nowadays college students suffer from great pressure.

Our county has begun to enroll more and more college students. Then the student must compete with each other in order to make themselves more qualified. To achieve their goal, the students have to study harder and harder to get good scores. This competition makes them really tired.

China is a country where parents always have a high expectation for there children. They hope their children will be successful in the future. So the parents always try their best to give the children better conditions for study. Under the pressure given by their parents, the students can do nothing but study hard because they don't want their parents to be unhappy. Stress from parents also makes them suffer.

Our society gives the young students great stress. In order to find a good job in the future, they have to make themselves more qualified. Competition is fierce, so the students can only make more effort to meet the standard the society set. Otherwise they can not be successful.

These are the three kinds of stress college students suffer. But we don't need to worry too much. We'd better adapt to the competition and make us as qualified as we can in college.

Comments

This draft is obviously better organized with an introduction, three body paragraphs discussing different stresses respectively, and a conclusion. We can see the clear categorization, namely the stress from the classmates, stress from parents, and stress from the larger society.

However, this draft is still far from satisfactory in that the student failed to give a clear thesis statement in the introduction, which can discourage the reader from further reading. Besides, it is not coherent for lack of an effective topic sentence for each body paragraph and good transitions between sentences. And although the subject is reasonably categorized, further consideration should be given regarding how to phrase the three kinds of stresses and place them in logical order. More supporting details need to be given for each point. What's more, other weaknesses like lack of sentence variety, monotonous choice of words, inappropriate shift of pronouns, and grammatical errors also undermine this classification.

Student's Third Draft

176

College Stress

As the saying goes, "Stress is the momentum of success." Obviously, stress exists everywhere and in college there is no exception. Generally speaking, stress on college students come from three major sources, employers, classmates and parents.

Stress from employers mainly rests on the fact that employers have set higher standards of qualification for undergraduates. A diploma and some certificates are no longer sufficient to convince employers about a college graduate's competence and potential for development. They prefer and demand graduates with not only good academic records, but also leadership and work experience. Naturally, they loom as a major source of pressure for college students. This is more true against the background that in recent years the number of graduates has been on the rise at a higher rate than the number of jobs, creating an employers' market. Accordingly, the undergraduates can do nothing but study harder and engage themselves in more experience, which inevitably increases their stress.

Competition among classmates also contributes to college stress. Current college students in China, mostly the only child of their family, have neither experience of living on their own nor living so closely with peers. Many of them had been well catered at home and flattered at school. In the new circumstance of college, they compete for academic distinction or family association, talent or pocket, sociability or affordability, affection or affectation, employment or enjoyment. When everybody strives to excel in some way, tension grows, adding to the college stress.

Stress from parents, blatant or latent, also accounts for college stress. The Chinese culture shapes parents' mind for high expectations over their children. They hope their children can do better than they can and be more successful in the future. For this, they spare no efforts to assist and facilitate their children's success. All of these will influence the children profoundly and press them to work harder and harder. But sometimes haste makes waste. Their children may not do as well as they are expected to in college, which automatically makes them stressed out.

Clearly, our potential employers and our parents are driving us ahead and our peers are already ahead. If we don't want to collapse under the pressure, we shall take it, adapt ourselves to it, channel it off one way or another, and enjoy our college life.

Comments

This is a good piece of classification from the perspectives of text organization, content, and language. The student gave a clear thesis statement in the introduction, logically ordered the three categories (beginning with the most important idea and proceeding to the least) with a good topic sentence for each body paragraph, more supporting sentences, and effective transitional signals to make the sentences and paragraphs coherent. In addition, she improved the language by using more formal words and different sentence structures. In general, this classification essay is unified and coherent, thus making the writer's idea more convincing.

Homework 3

Ask two classmates to comment on your first draft. Improve the text organization of your first draft, apply the writing strategies accordingly, and avoid logical mistakes.

Further Reading

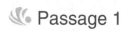 Passage 1

China Train Types

Chinese trains are divided according to their speed into various classes, identified with different letters and numbers. Passenger trains are numbered by a capital Chinese phonetic letter followed by numerals. The letters refer to different classes of trains:

• G—High-Speed Electric Multiple Units (EMU) Train, *Gaotie* (高铁) in Chinese
This is the fastest EMU train running for long distance in China, the top speed of which could reach 350km/h. Currently, the G-train could finish the 1,068-kilometers Wuhan-Guangzhou High-Speed Railway in 3 hours, the 301-kilometers Shanghai-Nanjing High-Speed Railway in 73 minutes and the 458-kilometers Zhengzhou-Xi'an High-Speed Railway in

2 hours.

- C—Intercity EMU Train, *Chengji Lie Che* (城际列车) in Chinese

This is also the fastest EMU train in China, but runs for short travel distance between two nearby cities, such as the 120-kilomter's Beijing-Tianjin Intercity Railway.

- D—Electric Multiple Units (EMU) Train, *Dongche* (动车) in Chinese

These trains are also called *Hexiehao* (和谐号, Harmony) or bullet trains in China. The designed top speed is 250km/h. These trains have been widely used for serving fast and frequent transport between main cities, such as Beijing-Shanghai, Shanghai-Suzhou and Shenzhen-Guangzhou.

- Z—Direct Express Train, *Zhida* (直达) in Chinese

The top speed of Z-trains is 160km/h, which is the most efficient transport for long-distance travel except of the EMU trains. Generally, Z-trains are none-stop on the way, but some of them have several stops. On the other hand, some Z-trains are equipped with only soft-sleepers and soft-seats.

- T—Express Train, *Tekuai* (特快) in Chinese

The T-trains have limited stops on the routes, mainly in major cities. The highest speed is 140km/h. Almost every T-series of train is equipped with soft-sleeper, soft-seat, hard-sleeper and hard-seat.

- K—Fast Train, *Kuaiche* (快车) in Chinese

The top speed of K-trains is 120km/h, having more stops than the T-trains. The K-series of trains is equipped with air-conditioning and the four classes of train berths.

- Accommodation Fast Train—*Pukuai* (普快) in Chinese

These trains' numbers are identified with four digits. Its highest speed is 120km/h but runs slower than the K-train as a result of more stops on the way. Currently, a few of Accommodation Fast Trains are not equipped with air-conditioning.

- Accommodation Train—*Puke* (普客) in Chinese

With 100km/h's highest speed, this should be the slowest train, having as many stops as possible. The trains are also numbered with four digits. Most of the trains don't have air-conditioning at all.

- Commuter Train—*Tongqinche* (通勤车) in Chinese

These trains are specially taken by railway staffs, so they are not opened to public passengers.

- L—Temporary Train, *Linke* (临客) in Chinese

This series of L-trains is in operation only during the peak travel time, such as Chinese Spring Festival and the National Holiday. These trains will not be listed in the official fixed train schedule. It is not advised to take L-trains if you have other options as they are routinely subject to delays.

- Y—Tourist Train, *Lvyoulieche* (旅游列车) in Chinese

Y-trains are for the convenience of tourists and their destinations are the popular sights. For example, there are EMU Y-trains departing from Beijing North Railway Station to suburban Yanqing County, which is a transfer station to Badaling Great Wall.

(http://www.travelchinaguide.com/china-trains/types.htm)

What do you think of the classification? Is it easy to tell? Do you have a better idea?

 Passage 2

Shades and Character

Michelle Watson

Anyone who has spent time with or around children will notice that each one has a special personality all of their own. Children, like adults, have different traits that make up their personalities. Experts have researched this phenomenon in detail and classified children into different categories, named "flexible," "fearful," and "feisty."

The first personality type is called flexible. This is the most common of the three types. About 40 percent of all children fall into the flexible or easy group. These children usually handle feelings of anger and disappointment by reacting mildly upset. This does not mean that they do not feel mad or disappointed. They just choose to react mildly. These actions mean the flexible child is easy to take care of and be around. They usually adapt to new situations and activities quickly and are generally cheerful. They are subtle in their need for attention. Rather than yelling and demanding it, they will slowly and politely let their caregiver know about the need. If they do not get the attention right away, they seldom make a fuss. They patiently wait, but they still make it known that they need the attention. These children also are easygoing, so routines like feeding and napping are regular.

Flexible children may be referred to as "good as gold" because of their cheerful attitudes. Since these are well-behaved children, the caregiver needs to make sure the child is getting the attention they need. The caregiver should "check in with the flexible child from time to time." By checking in with the child regularly, the caregiver will be more knowledgeable about when the child needs attention and when they do not.

The next temperament is the fearful type. These are the more quiet and shy children. This makes up about 15 percent of children. They adapt slowly to new environments and take longer than flexible children when warming up to things. When presented with a new environment, fearful children often cling to something or someone familiar. Whether it be the main caregiver or a material object such as a blanket, the fearful children will cling to it until they feel comfortable with new situation. This can result in a deep attachment of the child to a particular caregiver or object. Fearful children may also withdraw when pushed into a new situation too quickly. They may also withdraw when other children are jumping into a new project or situation they are not comfortable with. These children may tend to play alone than with a group.

In dealing with fearful children, caregivers find they need more attention than flexible children. A good technique for helping these children is having "a sequence of being with, talking to, stepping back, remaining available, and moving on." The caregiver can also help the fearful child by giving them "extra soothing combined with an inch-by-inch fostering of independence and assertiveness." One of the most effective techniques is just taking it slow and helping the child become more comfortable with the

179

surroundings.

The third temperament type is called the feisty. About 10 percent of children fall into this category. The feisty children express their opinions in a very intense way. Whether they are happy or mad, everyone around them will know how they feel. These children remain active most of the time, and this causes them to be very aggressive. Feisty children often have the tendency to have a "negative persistence" and will go "on and on nagging, whining and negotiating" if there is something they particularly want. Unlike flexible children, feisty children are irregular in their napping and feeding times, but they don't adapt well to their changes in their routines. They also tend to be very sensitive to their surrounding environment. As a result, they may have strong reactions to their surroundings.

When dealing with feisty children, the caregiver should know strategies that receive positive results when different situations arise. One way to calm them is the "redirection technique." This method helps when the child is reacting very negatively to a situation. To properly implement the redirection technique, begin by recognizing and empathizing with the feelings of the feisty child and placing firm limits on any unacceptable behavior. This response lets the child know that both his/her desire for the toy and feelings of anger when denied the toy are acceptable to the caregiver. At the same time, the caregiver should clearly communicate to the child that expressing anger through hurtful or disruptive behavior is not acceptable. The child will probably need time to experience his or her emotions and settle down. Then offer an alternative toy or activity that may interest the child, who is then given time to consider the new choice and to accept or reject it.

Caregivers should consider that these children generally do not have regular feeding and napping times. The caregiver should be flexible when working with these children, and try to conform more to the child. If there is going to be a change in a child's routine, the caregiver has an easier time with the child if the child has been warned of the change.

Generally speaking, children can be divided into these three groups, but caregivers must not forget that each child is an individual. Children may have the traits of all three of the personality groups, but they are categorized into the one they are most like. Whatever their temperament, children need to be treated according to their individual needs. When the needs are met appropriately, the child will be happier, and those around the children will feel better also.

Question for Consideration
Who do you think is the targeted reader of the writing?

Passage 3

Three Types of People to Fire Immediately
G. Michael Maddock and Raphael Louis Vitón

We (your authors) teach our children to work hard and never, ever give up. We teach them to be grateful, to be full of wonder, to expect good things to happen, and to search for literal and figurative treasure on every beach, in every room, and in every person.

But some day, when the treasure hunt is over, we'll also teach them to fire people.

Why? After working with the most inventive people in the world for two decades, we've discovered the value of a certain item in the leadership toolbox: the pink slip.

Show of hands: How many of you out there in Innovationland have gotten the "what took you so long?" question from your staff when you finally said goodbye to a teammate who was seemingly always part of problems instead of solutions?

We imagine a whole bunch of hands. (Yep, ours went up, too.)

These people—and we're going to talk about three specific types in a minute—passive-aggressively block innovation from happening and will suck the energy out of any organization.

When confronted with any of the following three people—and you have found it impossible to change their ways, say goodbye.

1. The Victims

"Can you believe what they want us to do now? And of course we have no time to do it. I don't get paid enough for this. The boss is clueless."

Victims are people who see problems as occasions for persecution rather than challenges to overcome. We all play the role of victim occasionally, but for some, it has turned into a way of life. These people feel persecuted by humans, processes, and inanimate objects with equal ease—they almost seem to enjoy it. They are often angry, usually annoyed, and almost always complaining. Just when you think everything is humming along perfectly, they find something, anything, to complain about. At Halloween parties, they're Eeyore, the gloomy, pessimistic donkey from the *Winnie the Pooh* stories—regardless of the costume they choose.

Victims aren't looking for opportunities; they are looking for problems. Victims can't innovate.

So if you want an innovative team, you simply can't include victims. Fire the victims. (Note to the HR department: Victims are also the most likely to feel the company has maliciously terminated them regardless of cause. They will often go looking for someone—anyone—who will agree that you have treated them unjustly. Lawyers are often left to play this role. So have your documentation in order before you let victims go, because chances are you will hear from their attorneys.)

2. The Nonbelievers

"Why should we work so hard on this? Even if we come up with a good idea, the boss will probably kill it. If she doesn't, the market will. I've seen this a hundred times before."

We love the Henry Ford quote: "If you think you can or think you cannot, you are correct." The difference between the winning team that makes industry-changing innovation happen and the losing one that comes up short is a lack of willpower. Said differently, the winners really believed they could do it, while the losers doubted it was possible.

181

In our experience, we've found the link between believing and succeeding incredibly powerful and real. Great leaders understand this. They find and promote believers within their organizations. They also understand the cancerous effect that nonbelievers have on a team and will cut them out of the organization quickly and without regret.

If you are a leader who says your mission is to innovate, but you have a staff that houses nonbelievers, you are either a lousy leader or in denial. Which is it? You deserve the staff you get. Terminate the nonbelievers.

3. The Know-It-Alls

"You people obviously don't understand the business we are in. The regulations will not allow an idea like this, and our stakeholders won't embrace it. Don't even get me started on our IT infrastructure's inability to support it. And then there is the problem of ..."

The best innovators are learners, not knowers. The same can be said about innovative cultures; they are learning cultures. The leaders who have built these cultures, either through intuition or experience, know that in order to discover, they must eagerly seek out things they don't understand and jump right into the deep end of the pool. They must fail fearlessly and quickly and then learn and share their lessons with the team. When they behave this way, they empower others around them to follow suit—and presto, a culture of discovery is born and nurtured.

In school, the one who knows the most gets the best grades, goes to the best college, and gets the best salary. On the job, the person who can figure things out the quickest is often celebrated. And unfortunately, it is often this smartest, most-seasoned employee who eventually becomes expert in using his or her knowledge to explain why things are impossible rather than possible.

This employee should be challenged, retrained, and compensated for failing forward. But if this person's habits are too deeply ingrained to change, you must let him or her go. Otherwise, this individual will unwittingly keep your team from seeing opportunity right under your nose. The folks at Blockbuster didn't see Netflix's ascendancy. The encyclopedia companies didn't see Google coming. But the problem of expert blindness existed well before the Internet.

Two of our favorites from rinkworks.com: "This 'telephone' has too many shortcomings to be seriously considered as a means of communication. The device is inherently of no value to us." —Western Union internal memo, 1876.

And "The wireless music box has no imaginable commercial value. Who would pay for a message sent to nobody in particular?" —David Sarnoff's associates in response to his urgings for investment in the radio in the 1920s.

At one point in his career, Thomas A. Edison had dozens of inventors working for him at the same time. He charged each with the task of failing forward and sharing the learning from each discovery. All of them needed to believe that they were part of something big. You want the same sort of people.

You don't want the victims, nonbelievers, or know-it-alls. It is up to you to make sure they take their anti-innovative outlooks elsewhere.

(From *Bloomberg BusinessWeek*, November 08, 2011
http://www.businessweek.com/management/three-types-of-people-to-fire-immediately-11082011.html)

Question for Consideration
What's the message you've learned from the writing?

Unit 8

The Cause and Effect Essay

Tuning-in Activities

Activity 1

Look at the following pictures and discuss whether a cause and effect relationship exists in each. If yes, list the possible reasons to form a reasonable link. Otherwise, discuss what is wrong with its cause and effect relationship.

1. panacea—academic excellence

2. Internet news—bed time

3. laugh—intelligence

4. haircut—uncle's life

5. good diet and exercise—health

6. driver talking on the mobile—accident

 Activity 2

What are the possible reasons for some students to

    (1) be addicted to the mobile phone,

    (2) be engaged in campus clubs,

    (3) live off campus out of their own will,

    (4) be obsessed with a game,

    (5) cheat in exams,

    ...

What are the effects of those activities?

Introduction

When we explain why an event happened or what could possibly happen because of the event, we are talking in terms of cause and effect (also written as cause-and-effect, cause-effect or cause/effect and known as causal analysis). When we regard B as taking place in consequence of the action of A, then we take A to be the cause of B, and B the effect of A. In other words, cause and effect is the relationship in which an action or event produces a certain response in the form of another action or event, or in which an action or event results from another action or event. We encounter matters of causes and effects every day. A student ate something unpleasant (cause), and he had indigestion (effect) as a result. Another student threw a dinner party for her friends after she won a scholarship. The Jade Emperor has fooled Monkey King, so he creates havoc in Heaven. Hamlet mops at court with grief because his father died and his uncle has married his seemingly virtuous mother. A series of powerful earthquakes struck north-east Japan on March 11, 2011, triggering a tsunami to hit Miyagi and Fukushima prefectures, damage dozens of coastal communities and sweep part of Sendai airport. In the latter case, we see a causal chain where one cause creates an effect and that effect turns into a cause and creates other effects.

$\Rightarrow$ **Underwater earthquakes** $\Rightarrow$ Tsunami $\Rightarrow$ Coastal destruction

The cause and effect analysis is a common method of organizing and discussing ideas in our efforts to understand human behavior and natural phenomena. We need the understanding to inform, to speculate and to better control over events and over ourselves. Such an understanding may enable us to make sense of our experiences and to alter our environment or our behavior by producing or preventing the occurrence of some of them and hence lead safer, healthier and happier lives. An understanding of reasons for earthquakes (mostly because underground blocks of rock or plates suddenly break along a fault and release tremendous energy to create seismic waves that shake the ground), for example, may help governments and planning agencies to try to identify the faults and to take measures in civil engineering, emergency preparedness, architectural design, etc.

185

Although one-cause-to-one-effect situations are possible in real life, both human behavior and natural phenomena are complicated and intertwined, often overlapping and making it difficult to establish a cause and effect relationship. Frequently we'll find that a cause and effect relationship might be multi-faceted rather than one-dimensional: a single cause generates many effects or that one effect is the result of multiple unrelated causes. Take tsunami for example, in addition to underwater earthquakes, volcanic eruptions and other underwater explosions (including detonations of underwater nuclear devices), landslides, glacier calvings, meteorite impacts and other disturbances above or below water all have the potential to be the cause. At the same time, although the impact of tsunamis is limited to coastal areas, their destructive power can be enormous and they can affect entire ocean basins. When multiple causes create one effect or one cause creates multiple effects, the causality branches off like a tree. Take, for example, why situation turned favorable to George Washington at the battle in Valley Forge.

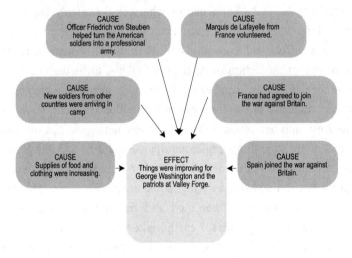

Exercises

1. Why do people go for sports? What are your personal reasons for doing sports? Read Sample 1 and find out the causes for American people to take up the tedious jogging as a sport.

Sample 1

Vocabulary

Fear of Death

Carll Tucker

I hate jogging. Every dawn, as I thud[1] around New York City's Central Park reservoir, I am reminded of how much I hate it. It's so tedious. Some claim jogging is thought conducive[2]; others insist the scenery relieves the monotony[3]. For me, the pace is wrong for contemplation[4] of either ideas or vistas. While jogging, all I can think about is

1. thud: *v.* walk/run with heavy steps
2. conducive: *adj.* likely to produce
3. monotony: *n.* 单调,枯燥
4. contemplation: *n.* 沉思,思考

jogging—or nothing. One advantage of jogging around a reservoir is that there's no dry-shortcut home.

From the listless looks of some fellow trotters[5], I gather I am not alone in my unenthusiasm: Bill-paying, it seems, would be about as diverting[6]. Nonetheless, we continue to jog; more, we continue to choose to jog. From a practically infinite array of opportunities, we select one that we don't enjoy and can't wait to have done with. Why?

For any trend, there are as many reasons as there are participants. This person runs to lower his blood pressure. That person runs to escape the telephone or a cranky[7] spouse or a filthy household. Another person runs to avoid doing anything else, to dodge[8] a decision about how to lead his life or a realization that his life is leading nowhere. Each of us has his carrot and stick[9]. In my case, the stick is my slackening[10] physical condition, which keeps me from beating opponents at tennis whom I overwhelmed two years ago. My carrot is to win.

Beyond these disparate[11] reasons, however, lies a deeper cause. It is no accident that now personal fitness and health have suddenly become a popular obsession[12]. True, modern man likes to feel good, but that hardly distinguishes him from his predecessors.

With zany myopia[13], economists like to claim that the deeper cause of everything is economic. Delightfully, there seems no marketplace explanation for jogging. True, jogging is cheap, but then not jogging is cheaper. And the scant and skimpy[14] equipment which jogging demands must make it a marketer's least favored form of recreation.

Some scout-masterish[15] philosophers argue that the appeal of jogging and other body-maintenance[16] programs is the discipline they afford. We live in a world in which individuals have fewer and fewer obligations. The working week has shrunk. Weekend worship is less compulsory. Technology gives us more free time. Satisfactorily filling free time requires imagination and effort. Freedom is a wild

5. trotter: *n.* 小跑者

6. diverting: *adj.* entertaining

7. cranky: *adj.* bad-tempered

8. dodge: *v.* avoid

9. carrot and stick: incentives and threats 【引申】威逼利诱

10. slacken: *v.* 松弛

11. disparate: *adj.* entirely different

12. obsession: *n.* 占据心思的事

13. zany myopia: foolish shortsightedness

14. scant and skimpy: little, insufficient

15. scout-master: *n.* 童子军领队

16. maintenance: *n.* 维护, 保持

187

and risky river; it can drown the person who does not know how to swim across it. The more obligations one takes on, the more time one occupies, the less threat freedom poses. Jogging can become an instant obligation. For a portion of his day, the jogger is not his own man; he is obedient to a regimen[17] he has accepted.

Theologists[18] may take the argument one step further. It is our modern irreligion, our lack of confidence in any hereafter, that makes us anxious to stretch our mortal stay as long as possible. We run, as the saying goes, for our lives, hounded[19] by the suspicion that there are the only lives we are likely to enjoy.

All of these theorists seem to me more or less right. As the growth of cults[20] and charismatic[21] religions and the resurgence of enthusiasm for the military draft suggest, we do crave commitment. And who can doubt, watching so many middle-aged and older persons torturing themselves in the name of fitness, that we are unreconciled to death, more so perhaps than any generation in modern memory?

But I have a hunch[22] there's a further explanation of our obsession with exercise. I suspect that what motivates us even more than a fear of death is a fear of dearth[23]. Our era is the first to anticipate the eventual depletion[24] of all natural resources. We see wilderness shrinking; rivers losing their capacity to sustain life; the air, even the stratosphere[25], being loaded with potentially deadly junk. We see the irreplaceable being squandered[26], and in the depths of our consciousness we are fearful that we are creating an uninhabitable world. We feel more or less helpless and yet, at the same time, desirous to protect what resources we can. We recycle soda bottles and restore old buildings and protect our nearest natural resource—our physical health—in the almost superstitious hope that such small gestures will help save an earth that we are blighting[27]. Jogging becomes a sort of penance[28] for our sins

188

17. regimen: *n.* 养生法
18. theologist: *n.* 神学家

19. hound: *v.* bother, harass

20. cult: *n.* 崇拜
21. charismatic: *adj.* emphasizing the divine gifts

22. hunch: *n.* 基于直觉的想法

23. dearth: *n.* 稀少，匮乏
24. depletion: *n.* 消耗，耗尽

25. stratosphere: *n.* 平流层，同温层
26. squander: *v.* waste

27. blight: *v.* spoil, mar
28. penance: *n.* 自我惩罚

of gluttony[29], greed, and waste. Like a hairshirt[30] or a bed of nails, the more one hates it, the more virtuous it makes one feel.

That's why we jog. Why I jog is to win at tennis.

Note:

The essay was originally published in a column entitled "The Back Door" in the *Saturday Review*, where Carll Tucker worked as editor from 1978 to 1981.

(http://schoolsites.schoolworld.com/schools/heltenham/webpages/rwilman/files/tucker-fear%20of%20dearth.pdf)

29. gluttony: *n.* 贪吃
30. hairshirt: *n.* shirt made of rough cloth with animal hair worn next to the skin as a self-punishment

Questions for Consideration

(1) What are the various reasons, according to the author, for people to jog?

(2) What does the author believe to be the reason for people to jog?

(3) How is the thesis developed? Is the essay well structured?

(4) Do you find the author's argument convincing? What makes it so?

(5) Is the essay interesting? What makes it so?

189

2. What are the effects of the earthquake and tsunami in north-east Japan in 2011? Read Sample 2 and fill the diagram with reference, but not limited, to the essay.

Sample 2

Vocabulary

Impact of Japan's Earthquake on Economy

Kimberly Amadeo

Radiation[1] from the Fukushima nuclear reactors[2] is still leaking into the Pacific Ocean, raising levels to 4,000 times the legal limit. It could take months to stop the leak. Radiation has shown up in local milk and vegetables, and briefly appeared in Tokyo's drinking water.

Japan's nuclear industry supplied a third of the country's electricity. In total, 11 of Japan's 50 nuclear reactors shut down following the earthquake. The capacity to produce electricity has been reduced by as much as 40% for now, and could remain at less than 80% of pre-quake levels for a long time.

1. radiation: *n.* 放射
2. reactor: *n.* 原子炉；核反应堆

Japan's economy was dealt a devastating[3] blow by the 9-magnitude earthquake and tsunami that pummeled[4] the country on March 11. An estimated 28,000 are dead or missing, and at least 500,000 are displaced. Many of the people in the area are elderly, and cold weather and disrupted transportation routes made rescue efforts difficult. Now, radiation contamination has been added to their concerns.

3. devastate: *v.* destroy

4. pummel: *v.* strike, hit

The World Bank estimates that Japan's disaster will cost between $100-$235 billion, and take five years to rebuild. Japan may sell U.S. Treasuries to pay for rebuilding. This would lower the value of the dollar, increasing the cost of imports to the U.S.

Although the Bank of Japan is providing market liquidity[5] to ensure the stability of financial markets, the long-term impact will be negative to the country's struggling economy. Rebuilding will lift the economy a bit, but it will be outweighed[6] by the probable increase to the national debt— already twice as big as Japan's annual economic output. It may cut Japan's credit rating, increasing the country's cost to service its debt.①

5. liquidity: *n.* 流动性

6. outweigh: *v.* exceed in value

The quake and tsunami damaged or closed down key ports, and some airports shut briefly. This has disrupted the global supply chain of semiconductor equipment and materials. Japan manufactures 20% of the world's semiconductor products, including NAND flash, an indispensable[7] electronic part of Apple's iPad. Japan also supplies the wings, landing gears and other major parts of Boeing's 787 Dreamliner.

7. indispensable: *adj.* absolutely necessary

Automakers Toyota, Nissan, Honda, Mitsubishi and Suzuki temporarily suspended[8] production. Nissan may move one production line to the U.S. A total of 22 plants, including Sony, were shut in the area.

8. suspend: *v.* stop for a period of time

Japan's economy had just started to recover from a 20-year deflationary[9] period and recession. It rebounded[10] strongly in 2010, when GDP increased by a robust[11] 3%—the fastest growth in 20 years. It fell off briefly during the last quarter of 2010, but

9. deflationary: *adj.* 通货紧缩的

10. rebound: *v.* 反弹

11. robust: *adj.* powerful, vigorous

190

was expected to pick up again with stronger exports to fast-growing neighbors in Asia. The earthquake adds to Japan's economic challenges of government debt, rising commodity prices and a shrinking labor pool.

(http://useconomy.about.com/od/criticalssues/a/Japan-Earthquake.htm)

Note:

① Japan's national debt will rise significantly as the government borrows to finance reconstruction. This may raise interest rates in Japan and further complicate recovery efforts or, in the worst case, trigger a sovereign debt crisis and loss of confidence in Japanese government bonds.

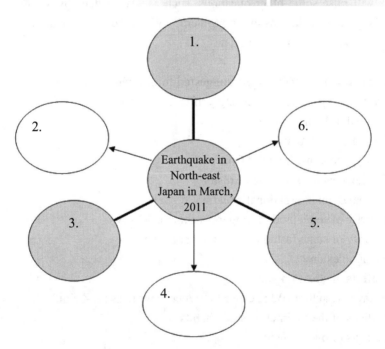

Immediate and Ultimate Causes/Effects

Causes and effects often occur at a distance in time from the situation. To explain fully the causes and effects, we often need to seek not only immediate causes and effects but also ultimate causes and effects. Immediate causes and effects are the ones we encounter first, and they are direct, superficial, and easy to recognize. Ultimate causes and effects are the basic, underlying, and less obvious factors that help to explain the more apparent ones, and perhaps it involves something in the past or faraway.

The two types of causes are usually related to each other. That is, a direct cause could not have brought about an effect unless certain indirect causes or conditions existed. For example, the immediate cause of a disastrous warehouse fire could be faulty electrical wiring, but this might be traced even further to poor management. The written analysis might logically stop at any point, of course, depending entirely on its purpose. In an analysis of the effects of a tsunami, for example, it's not necessary to trace the causes for the earthquake.

Finding a Topic for Cause and Effect Analysis

To write a cause and effect essay, we need to choose a manageable subject that yields information helpful or interesting to a specific group of people. If we want to analyze the causes of a subject, we always ask some questions, such as "Why does the event happen?" or "What does the subject result from?" If we are interested in the effects of a subject, we will raise some other questions, such as "What does the event lead to?" or "What are the possible solutions to the problem?" When we think about the questions and answer them, we can find what we aim at.

192

Discuss the causes and effects of the suggested topics below.
- an event or experience that strongly affected your life
- a personal or family problem
- effects of overpopulation
- causes of economic boom in China
- a historical event as a cause or result
- a national or an international situation
- popularity of some modern singers or other celebrity
- popularity of some fashion, a book, a game, etc.
- cheating in exams
- the effects of stress on you
- your favorite author, What caused him/her to write as he/she did?
- the effects of the Internet on study habits
- the effects of overcrowding
- the effects of the computer on the quality of your writing
- the effects of the automobile on the Chinese society
  ...

Homework 1

Decide on a topic and draw a diagram for the causes or effects.

Common Logic Errors in Cause and Effect Analysis

Important and frequently used as cause and effect analysis is, it is also one of the most commonly misused concepts. Many people, including some lawyers, journalists, and even scientists, sometimes misuse it to add legitimacy to their point, not to mention students. Learning about the logic errors in cause and effect analysis may help us to avoid them.

1. Oversimplifying causes

In the absence of solid facts, figures, or evidence, some people tend to generalize and substitute unsupported opinions for reasons. This problem often originates from choosing a topic that is too big for the length of the essay. So it is essential to choose a subject appropriate to the length of the essay, focus it into a limited topic, and support each main point with sufficient evidence.

2. Confusing a time relationship for a cause and effect

The key principle of establishing cause and effect is proving that an event of cause must happen before an event of effect in chronological order. This seems obvious. However, chronological order alone does not necessarily make a cause and effect relationship: an antecedent event may not be the cause of the following event and the following event may not be the effect of the antecedent event. The fact that sales of an enterprise increased following a new advertisement campaign does not prove the commercials caused improved sales. Bad publicity about competing brands, decreased interest rates, increased economic development, and a number of other factors could be responsible for boosting sales. Similarly, while a student's failure in a course can be attributed to the professor's poor teaching, irresponsibility or unpleasant personality, it may well be caused by other factors as well, such as poor learning strategy, negligence of academic work, poor health, nervousness in the exam, etc.(but not, as Huzi puts it in Picture 1, by the alleged fake panacea). Unless other factors which contribute to the student's failure are ruled out, it is arbitrary to attribute a student's failure to the professor.

* To prove a cause and effect relationship, you need to eliminate other potential causes.
* Cause and effect can be easier to ascertain if events can be repeated through research or experimentation. An advertisement agency that could demonstrate that its commercials consistently boosted sales for a variety of products could counter arguments that its effect on the sales was a coincidence.

It is, therefore, important to provide evidence that supports the argument and to entertain the possibility that, in many cases, there may be other equally valid explanations. Proximity of events in time does not necessarily imply causality. Being the last person to have been identified to see the victim does not necessarily make one a criminal.

193

3. Confusing association with causation

Some people assume cause and effect for two variables simply because they occur together. For instance, a person is taken to be guilty of the crime simply because he is in the same room with the victim when the crime occurs. Some Chinese strongly believe in the folk saying that a haircut in the lunar January results in death of their mother's brother, because such a tragedy coincidentally happened on him. This fallacy is often used to give a statistical correlation a causal interpretation. For example, in studying the effects of depression upon alcohol consumption, some researchers find that people who suffer from higher levels of depression drink more, and announce that this correlation shows that depression drives people to drink. However, depression could be the cause that makes people drink more but it is equally possible that heavy consumption of alcohol, a depressant, makes people more depressed. It is also possible that both depression and heavy consumption of alcohol are increased by a third variable, such as an increase in societal unrest. It is also possible that both variables are independent of one another, and it is mere coincidence that they are both increasing at the same time. This is the classic "chicken and egg" argument that can hardly be settled.

This, however, is not to deny all statistical evidence, but to remind us that there are other variables than a mere correlation that must be considered and not ruled out before claiming the causation. It is possible to build a strong scientific case for a specific cause with statistical evidence. The way to do this is to look at multiple independent correlations to see if they all point to the same causal relationship. With the above example of depression and drinking, an alcoholic drink manufacturer, invoking the "correlation is not causation" logical fallacy, could use the second interpretation to claim that alcohol is not a factor in depression and that the responsibility is upon society to ensure that people do not become depressed. But we can make predictions based upon the hypothesis that drinking causes depression. If this is the correct causal relationship, then duration of drinking should correlate with depression cases, quitting drinking should decrease depression cases, and drinking high alcohol spirits should produce a higher depression tendency than drinking wine, etc. If all of these correlations turn out to be true, then we can triangulate to the drinking causes depression hypothesis as a highly possible causal relationship and it is not a logical fallacy to conclude from this evidence that drinking probably causes depression.

4. Confusing necessary and sufficient causes

Causes are often distinguished into necessary and sufficient causes. A third type of causation, which requires neither necessity nor sufficiency in and of itself, but which contributes to the effect, is called a "contributory cause."

Necessary causes:

If x is a necessary cause of y, then the presence of y necessarily implies the presence of x. The presence of x, however, does not imply that y will occur. For example, one who doesn't know the English alphabet can't read English. If a person reads English, it implies that she knows the alphabet, but another person who knows the alphabet does not necessarily read English.

Sufficient causes:

If x is a sufficient cause of y, then the presence of x necessarily implies the presence of y. However, another cause z may alternatively cause y. Thus the presence of y does not imply the presence of x. For example, a dead battery is enough to keep a car from starting, but faulty spark plugs or an empty gas tank will have the same effect.

Contributory causes:

A cause may be classified as a "contributory cause," if the presumed cause precedes the effect, and altering the cause alters the effect. It does not require that all those subjects which possess the contributory cause experience the effect. It does not require that all those subjects that are free of the contributory cause be free of the effect. In other words, a contributory cause may be neither necessary nor sufficient but it must be contributory. For example, running a red light might cause an accident, though other contributory causes— pedestrians or other vehicles in the intersection—must also be present. In Picture 5, a good diet and physical exercises are both contributory to good health and therefore life, but other factors such as diseases and aging, which brings irreversible deterioration of the brain and other tissues have to be absent to keep physical life eternal.

195

Confusing necessary and sufficient causes results in a causal fallacy, which flaws an argument. For example:

Radiation causes cancer, Tom has cancer, and therefore he was exposed to radiation.

Exposure to radiation is a sufficient condition to cause cancer: if it is true (i.e. Tom has been exposed to radiation) then Tom will get cancer. The flaw in the argument is that exposure to radiation is not a necessary condition to cause cancer, which can result from many other causes. Similarly, a necessary cause must be there for an effect to happen, but one necessary condition alone does not provide sufficient cause for the occurrence of the event.

Exercises

1. Analyze the following examples.

1) Who said food keeps us alive? Tom died a few days ago and he was not short of good food.

2) I don't know why the professor doesn't like me: I turned in all her written assignments on time.

3) Why don't you want to spend your life with me? I love you, and am I not good to you?

4) The dean told me that to graduate I need to have earned 165 credits. Well, I've got that, but she said I won't be able to graduate this semester. How misleading!

5) The job description said that they were looking for a girl majoring in English. I'm female and I major in English, so I can't understand why they did not employ me!

2. Is the cause and effect relationship sound in Sample 3?

Sample 3

Vocabulary

Back to the Land: Why China's "Happy Farmer" Took Off

Isaac Stone Fish

China's hottest Internet craze right now is all about...farming. Since the Web game Happy Farmer was introduced in 2008, maybe 80 million people, or roughly 20 percent of China's Internet population, have started playing it or one of its many clones[1], according to some estimates. Every day, and sometimes several times a day, millions log in to accumulate[2] as many points as possible by doing such seemingly mundane[3] tasks as clicking on a screen to watch radishes grow on their own small plot of land, and to water, fertilize, weed, and harvest these virtual[4] gardens. As in the popular American version of the game, Farmville, some players visit other virtual farms and offer to help out; others sneak around the countryside and try to steal vegetables.

The game's success reflects a deep and growing nostalgia for China's traditional agrarian[5] way of life. Over the last 30 years, 225 million Chinese peasants have flooded the cities in search of better jobs and a higher standard of living. The result has been massive economic growth and the building of skyscrapers and infrastructure[6] at a blistering[7] pace. Cities spring out of nowhere, and social networking games like Happy Farmer have become a tangible[8] reminder of the sense of community that many migrants believe has been lost. Such is the isolation among China's urban population that in 2008 MTV did an Asia-wide study and discovered that China was the only country in the region where people claimed to have more friends online than off. Recently, state-run media interviewed a man who tends his virtual garden during the week

1. clone: *n.* 克隆；翻版
2. accumulate: *v.* gather or collect
3. mundane: *adj.* earthly

4. virtual: *adj.* 虚拟的

5. agrarian: *adj.* agricultural

6. infrastructure: *n.* 基础设施
7. blister: *v.* swell
8. tangible: *adj.* concrete

196

and his real-life garden during the weekend. "It's a way to experience life," he said.

The game also taps into[9] concerns among many members of the urban middle class that economic growth has far outpaced the country's environmental standards. Poor air and food quality are both major concerns, and Happy Farmer reflects a wistfulness for a rural China that at least in the romantic image does not suffer from such problems. Then there are the lingering effects of the Cultural Revolution, during which millions of educated urban youths were sent to farming villages. Despite the hardships, many of those who grew up in and survived that era, and lived through China's transition from central planned economy to "socialism with Chinese characteristics," still occasionally pine for[10] what they perceive to be a much simpler time. Some of their city-dwelling children, now adults with kids of their own, also romanticize this period, when rural peasants were considered the most prestigious class because they embodied the idea of egalitarianism.

An increasingly popular tourist trend called "Farm Family Fun" meets this need for a taste of the rural, but allows today's city slickers to do it without getting their hands dirty. It involves groups of city folk driving to farmhouses, eating food cooked in the peasant style (and supposedly without pesticides), and fishing from ponds with prestocked fish. But the Happy Farmer game takes that faux[11]-agrarian lifestyle to a new level. Its success is changing the way some city dwellers behave in real life. Urbanites have started leasing[12] farmland and are building vegetable plots across South China, where urban residents volunteer and tend their sections of the garden. The farms often go by the name of "Happy Farmer," and Chinese media refer to this phenomenon as the "real-life version" of the game.

In another twist on virtual farming, some have even set up video cameras so they can monitor their real gardens from home. In tropical Hainan

9. tap into: establish a connection with

10. pine for: long for or grieve for

11. faux: *adj.* false, man-made

12. lease: *v.* rent

197

Island, a shop has begun selling miniature[13] farms—little boxes of dirt with seeds for beans to give people their own "happy farm." In Nanjing, an entrepreneur opened up a "Happy Farmer" restaurant, complete with computers where people can play the game while eating. The menu offers a "stolen vegetable of the day" option, which is served as a free appetizer.

13. miniature: *n.* 微缩

There are no statistics on the size of the game's spillover effect. But one thing is clear: China's peasants are migrating to the cities in search of a better life—while a growing urban middle class is looking back toward its roots.

(From *The Daily Beast Newsweek*, Apr 8, 2010)

Questions for Consideration

1. Are nostalgia, wistfulness for a rural China and romanticized version of egalitarianism sufficient causes for popularity of the "Happy Farmer" game? Were there similar games that were less popular? Is the game design or/and marketing a necessary cause for its popularity?

2. What's the focus of the essay, causes for the popularity, effects of the popularity or just the popularity of the game?

3. Who is the targeted reader? Does the concern for the audience have any impact on the focus of the essay?

Developing a Cause and Effect Analysis

The Introduction

In the opening section, we usually make the thesis statement, explain whether we will focus on causes, effects, or both, and state the basic causes or effects (the major points to be discussed) and the order in which they will be presented. The thesis should clearly state the focus of the essay. Using the words "cause and/or effect" in the thesis may help alert the reader to the focus of the essay. For example, in a 2010 CNN Opinion essay entitled "Why does the U.S. need China?" Li Daokui begins directly:

> The United States needs China for two simple reasons: China can make a difference in the world after the financial crisis, and more importantly China's fundamental interests are aligned with the United States.

Another essay entitled "Why Do We Live in Three Dimensions?" by Amy Shira Teitel published in December, 2011 thus begins:

> Day to day life has made us all comfortable with 3 dimensions; we constantly

interact with objects that have height, width, and depth. But why our universe has three spatial dimensions has been a problem for physicists, especially since the 3-dimensional universe isn't easily explained within superstring theory or Big Bang cosmology. Recently, three researchers have come up with an explanation.

In a short essay of around 300 words, the introductory paragraph may well include nothing more than the thesis statement: "Headaches have a variety of different causes, including stress, various physical problems, and certain food or drinks."

The Body

Supporting details should be relevant to the thesis and reasonably arranged. Three common orders to organize a cause and effect essay are the progressive order, the chronological order and the categorical order:

☆ Progressive order: Details are arranged from the least to the most important or vice versa.

☆ Chronological order: Details are arranged in the order in which the events occurred.

☆ Categorical order: Details are arranged by dividing the topic into parts or categories.

Pattern One: Progressive Order

Some causes and effects may be more important than others. For instance, if some causes of divorce are primary (perhaps unfaithfulness and physical abuse) and others are secondary (such as annoying habits and laziness), a paper about divorce could be organized from secondary to primary in order to emphasize the most important causes. Other progressive orders include: from the most familiar to the least familiar and from the easiest to understand to the most difficult. Sample 4 is written in the progressive order, the same as Sample 1.

Sample 4

Vocabulary

Why Do Most Mothers Cradle Their Babies in the Left Arm?

By Desmond Morris

One of the strangest features of motherhood is that the vast majority of mothers prefer to cradle their babies in the left arm. Why should this be? The obvious explanation is that the majority of mothers are right-handed and they wish to keep their right hand free. Unfortunately, this explanation cannot apply, because left-handed mothers also favor their left arm for holding their babies. The precise figures are 83 percent for right-handed mothers and 78 percent for left-handed mothers.

The most likely explanation is that the mother's heart is on the left side and, by holding the baby in her left arm, she is unconsciously bringing her infant closer to the sound of the heartbeat. This is the sound which the baby heard when it was inside the mother's womb and which is therefore associated with peace, comfort, and security.

Tests were carried out in nurseries where some babies were played the recorded sound of a human heartbeat, and, sure enough, those babies were lulled[1] off to sleep twice as quickly as the others. We also know that the sound of the mother's heart is quite audible inside the womb and that the unborn baby has well-developed hearing. The constant dull thud[2] of the heart beating so close to the fetus[3], second by second, must become the single most intrusive message from the outside world that a fetus can experience. So it is little wonder that traces of this imprinting[4] appear later on, in babyhood.

It is interesting that fathers show less of this left-side bias than mothers, suggesting that the human female is better programmed than her partner for carrying a baby. Alternatively, she may be more sensitive to the mood of her baby and may unconsciously adjust her holding behavior to make her baby feel more secure.

Some new observations on our closest animal relatives, the chimpanzees[5] and gorillas[6], have revealed that they too show a strong bias for holding their babies on the left side. The precise figures were 84 percent for chimpanzees and 82 percent for gorillas, remarkably close to the human percentages. Significantly, these apes do not show the strong right-handedness of the human species when using implements[7], which confirms the fact that left-holding has nothing to do with having a dominant right hand.

Recently a possible additional value in cradling babies on the left side had been suggested. It has been pointed out that, because the two sides of the brain are concerned with different aspects of behavior, it

200

1. lull: *v.* make sb. quiet, soothe sb.

2. thud: *n.* 沉闷的声响
3. fetus: *n.* 胎儿，胚胎

4. imprinting: *n.* 印迹

5. chimpanzee: *n.* 黑猩猩;
6. gorilla: *n.* 大猩猩

7. implement: *n.* 工具

is possible that the mother, in cradling the baby to her left, is showing the baby her "best side." It is claimed that emotions are expressed more strongly on the left side of the human face and that she therefore gives the baby a better chance to read her emotional mood changes as it gazes up at her. Furthermore, the mother's left eye and ear are more tuned in to emotional changes in her baby than her right eye and ear would be. So in addition to the baby's seeing the more expressive part of its mother, there is the further advantage that the mother herself is more sensitive to the left-held baby. This may sound far-fetched[8], but just possibly, it could provide a slight extra benefit for those mothers displaying the strange one-sided bias when cradling their infants.

8. far-fetched: *adj.* trained; exaggerated

How does the bias occur? Do the mothers have an instinctive preference for it, or do they learn it by trial and error, unconsciously adjusting the position of their babies until the babies are calmer? The surprising answer is that it seems to be the baby and not the mother who controls the bias. Observations of newborn infants when they were only a few hours old revealed that they come into the world with a preprogrammed tendency to turn their head to the right. If the newborn's head is gently held in a dead central position and then released, it naturally swings to the right far more often than to the left. This happens in nearly 70 percent of babies. It means that when the mother goes to feed her infant, she finds its head more likely to turn that way, and this may well influence her decision concerning which side is best for it. If it prefers turning its head to the right, it will, of course, feel more at ease when it is held in the crook[9] of her left arm. This will bring mother and baby more "face to face." This may be part of the explanation, because the holding bias is 80 percent and not 70 percent, but it adds a further intriguing chapter to the story.

9. crook: *n.* 弯曲处

201

Questions for Consideration

1. What is the thesis of the essay? If it is stated directly, locate the relevant sentence. If it is implied, state the thesis in your own words.

2. Which statement would best serve as a topic sentence for paragraph 3?

   A. An unborn baby hears well and must be constantly aware of its mother's heartbeat.

   B. Babies who listened to recordings of a human heartbeat went to sleep more quickly than those who did not.

   C. Experiences that a baby has while in the womb can have surprising effects later on.

   D. Two pieces of evidence support the idea that babies are soothed by the sound of their mothers' heartbeat.

3. Which statement best describes the introductory paragraph?

   A. It begins with a broad, general statement that narrows to a thesis.

   B. It explains the importance of understanding why mothers tend to hold their babies with the left arm.

   C. It tells a brief story about mothers and their tendency to hold their babies on their left side.

   D. It asks a question, and then surprises the reader by indicating that the obvious answer is incorrect.

4. Which statement best describes the concluding paragraph?

   A. It ends with a summary of the research on mothers and babies.

   B. It ends with a final piece of evidence and the suggestion that there is still more to learn.

   C. It ends with a series of questions about why mothers and babies interact with one another as they do.

   D. It ends with the result of a survey on how many mothers tend to have the holding bias.

Pattern Two: Chronological Order

When causes or effects occur one after another, we can follow the natural order in our analysis, bearing in mind that two events or conditions can be associated in time without being related as cause and effect. Sample 5 is developed in chronological order.

Sample 5

Vocabulary

The 1973 Oil Crisis

The 1973 oil crisis began because of the Yom Kippur War[1] being fought between Israel and Syria and Egypt at that time. Syria and Egypt, which were members of OPEC (Organization of Petroleum Exporting Countries), convinced the Arab members of this organization to cut the supply of petroleum

1. Yom Kippur War: 赎罪日战争

to nations that supported Israel. This embargo[2] immediately affected the United States, Canada, and many of their allies in Western Europe.

While cutting back the much needed supply of petroleum to the Western world, the Arab oil powers also increased the price of oil all over the world. This sharp increase had dramatic inflationary effects on economies around the world. The United States and the Netherlands, both strong supporters of Israel, were especially targeted by this embargo and experienced immediate economic effects.

The most immediate effect of the embargo was that the price of oil by the barrel quadrupled[3]. The Arab politicians and other elites that controlled the oil suddenly became very wealthy. Many of these suddenly rich oil countries invested their newfound wealth in weapons that increased tension in the Middle East even more.

This oil shock resulted in chaos in western societies. As the retail price of gasoline by the gallon skyrocketed[4], shares on the New York Stock Exchange lost $97 billion in value in the course of six weeks. The supply of Arab oil into the US dropped from 1.2 million barrels a day to just 19,000 barrels a day. The United States suffered its worst fuel shortage since the Second World War. The US government took several measures to soften the impact of the crisis on both the public and private sector.

In order to control the long lines for gasoline at gas stations and the overcharging that resulted, the US government initiated[5] a number of measures. One measure was to limit the price of "old oil," which was already discovered, while leaving the pricing of "new oil" open, in order to encourage exploration.

Another measure was that drivers of vehicles with odd numbered license plate were only allowed to purchase gas for their cars on the odd numbered days of the month. In turn, drivers of cars with even numbered license plates were only allowed to purchase their gas on the even numbered days of the month.

2. embargo: *n.* prohibition

3. quadruple: *v.* multiply by four

4. skyrocket: *v.* increase rapidly

5. initiate: *v.* begin

203

The US government also began to encourage its citizens to reduce their use of gasoline and generally to conserve energy whenever possible. In order to implement this, the national speed limit was dropped to 55 miles per hour. Daylight savings time was also imposed[6] to decrease the need for lighting. A One popular conservation campaign used the slogan, "Don't Be Fuelish" to encourage people to cut down on their use of energy.

6. impose: *v.* force

B By March of 1974, the Yom Kippur War was over, and all of the Arab OPEC countries, with the exception of Libya, ended their embargo against US. C The supply of oil rose, and prices stabilized, but a series of recessions had already been triggered[7] and plagued many western countries throughout the 1980s. D

7. trigger: *v.* cause

Questions for Consideration
1. What caused the oil crisis in the United States?
2. What action was taken in the United States to conserve energy during the oil crisis?
3. In which of the four gray squares marked A, B, C and D will the following sentence best fit?
   Nevertheless, the impact of the oil crisis set in motion far-reaching effects.
4. Draw a diagram for the effects of the Yom Kippur War as described in the essay.

Pattern Three: Categorical Order

We can group together the various factors of causes and effects in particular categories and arrange them accordingly. For example, women's liberation plays a very important role in women's world. We can group the effects of women's liberation politically, financially, socially, and psychologically. Politically, women have gained the right to vote. Financially, women have gained economic independence. Socially, women are considered equal to men. Psychologically, women are more encouraged and confident than ever. Of course, we can also group its effects into personal, social and political categories. Sample 6 falls into categorical order.

Sample 6

Vocabulary

Urban Heat Islands
Cities are usually warmer than their surrounding suburban and rural areas, often by as much as ten degrees Fahrenheit or six degrees Celsius. Scientists attribute this to the urban heat island

effects, by which several characteristics of urban areas combine to elevate artificially the surrounding temperature.

The main cause of urban heat islands is architectural; the high buildings in city centers expose numerous surfaces that reflect and absorb sunlight. The reflected light hits other buildings and cannot escape into the surrounding air. The absorbed light, mostly by the dark materials covering the outside of buildings, heats up the buildings themselves. These materials, such as concrete and asphalt[1], have greater thermal conductivity and reflective ability than do materials used in rural or suburban construction. This tendency of heat to be trapped between and near buildings is called the canyon[2] effect. Another impact of tall buildings is that they block the wind, which normally blows hot air away and cools the remaining air.

Also contributing to this heat retention[3] is the absence of evapotranspiration[4], the loss of water by evaporation from the ground and from the leaves of plants. This phenomenon is weakened in urban locales due to the lack of vegetation and standing water, both of which have cooling effects.

People also play a role in creating urban heat islands. The population density in cities translates into more human heat-generating processes and technology, such as automobiles, buses, and trains, air conditioning units, and factory production. All of these activities result in air pollution, which leads to the greenhouse effect, in which hot air on the ground cannot escape through the air above it because of polluting particles in the atmosphere.

The influence of the heat island effect seems to be greater at night. The ground and other surfaces lose heat at night by a process of radiation into the air above. But in cities, this upward radiation is blocked by the tall buildings, tending to hold the heat at the level where people live and where temperatures are measured.

Because almost half of the world's population

1. asphalt: *n.* 沥青

2. canyon: *n.* 峡谷

205

3. retention: *n.* storage
4. evapotranspiration: *n.* 蒸发

lives in urban areas, the urban heat island effect can influence the lives of more than three billion people. Thus it is closely studied by demographers[5] and meteorologists[6]. Thousands die in heat waves every year, and urban heat islands increase the severity and duration of those waves. Nighttime on urban heat islands provides no relief since urban nights do not enjoy the same cool-down that occurs in areas outside the cities.

Another harmful consequence of urban heat islands is that more energy is needed to power air conditioning and refrigeration. One study concluded that the heat island effect costs the city of Los Angeles about $100 million per year in increased energy consumption. Local weather conditions can also be affected, for example, by altered wind patterns, more clouds and fog, greater pollution, more lightening and more rain.

One strategy for lessening the impact of heat island effects is to use construction materials in houses, pavements, and highways that reflect, not absorb, the sunlight. Another method is to cultivate more vegetation like many city dwellers do on the roofs of their apartment buildings and offices.

Some controversy exists over whether urban heat islands contribute to global warming. One school of thought stresses that no evidence has been found that the effect is any more than a local one, as the long-term upward trend in temperatures is about the same in both urban and non-urban areas. This view gained support from a 2004 study comparing a city's temperatures on calm nights with those on windy nights. No difference was found in temperatures even though the urban-heat island theory would predict that windy nights should be cooler because the wind should blow the hot air away from the city. The conclusion of the study was that global temperatures have risen as much on windy nights as on calm nights, showing that overall global warming is not caused by urban development. Those with an opposing view tend to

5. demographer: n. 人口统计学家
6. meteorologist: n. 气象学家

206

be those who are skeptical of the reality of global warming. They contend that urban heat islands account for nearly all of the warming recorded by land-based instruments. But there have been no scientific studies substantiating[7] this minority way.

7. substantiate: *v.* prove

Questions for Consideration

1. What are the causes for urban heat islands?
2. According to paragraph 2, what are the effects of tall buildings? According to paragraph 3, why is evaporation less in urban areas? According to paragraph 5, why is the heat island effect greater at night?
3. In the conclusion, why does controversy exist that global warming is not caused by urban development?
4. Is the relationship between global warming and urban development one of causation or association? How can it be proved?
5. Summarize the passage.

The Conclusion

In the conclusion part, we summarize the analysis presented in the body paragraphs, if the causes or effects are many and complex, propose a way to tackle the problem or give some expectations, or restate the thesis to emphasize its importance. "Why We Live in Three Dimensions" ends as follows:

In short, the 3 dimensional space that we live in can result from the 9 original spatial dimensions string theory predicts.

This result is only part of the solution to the space-time dimensionality puzzle, but it strongly supports the validity of superstring theory. It's possible, though, that this new method of analyzing superstring theory with supercomputers will lead to its application towards solving other cosmological questions.

In an analysis of the "failure" of the Chinese Xinhai Revolution of 1911, Prachi Mital concludes:

Undoubtedly the revolution of 1911 failed to achieve its purpose but it did not mean that the revolution was altogether insignificant.

The end of Manchu dynasty and the establishment of republic were two important achievements of the revolution. It also gave a new life and speed to the stagnant politics of China.

Transitional Words

Transitional words play a very important part in the cause and effect analysis to connect paragraphs, sentences, and clauses. Learn to use these words and phrases in your essay.

Group 1: Adverbs and prepositional phrases of cause and effect

on this account	on account of	for this purpose	for this reason
by reason of	because of	due to	owing to
thanks to	as a result	consequently	as a consequence
in consequence of	thus	therefore	hence accordingly

Group 2: Conjunctions of cause and effect

because	since	inasmuch as	in that	for
now that	so	so that	so... that	

Group 3: Verbs and verbal phrases of cause and effect

result from	attribute to	ascribe to	account for
result in	lead to	induce	bring about
conduce	contribute to	give rise to	

Go back to **Sample 1** to learn how the writer transits his ideas.

Homework 2

Develop your cause and effect diagram into an essay. Ask two of your classmates to read and comment on your first draft. Revise the draft with consideration of organization patterns and sound reasoning.

Tips for Writing Cause and Effect Essays

1. Remember your purpose. Decide if you are writing to inform or persuade.
2. Support the analysis by more than mere assertions: offer evidence, define terms, offer facts and statistics, or provide examples or careful observations that support your ideas.
3. Consider all possibly relevant factors before attributing causes.
4. Never mistake the fact that something happens with or after another occurrence as evidence of a causal relationship.
5. Be careful not to omit any links in the chain of causes or effects unless you are certain that the readers for whom the writing is intended will automatically make the right connections themselves—and this is frequently a dangerous assumption. To unwisely

omit one or more of the links might leave the reader with only a vague, or even erroneous, impression of the causal connection, possibly invalidating all that follows and thus making the entire writing ineffective.

6. Be honest and objective. The writer who brings his old prejudices to the task of causal analysis, or who fails to see the probability of multiple causes or effects, is almost certain to distort his analysis or to make it so superficial.

7. Qualify or limit your statements about cause and effect. Unless there is clear evidence that one event is related to another, qualify your statements with phrases such as "It appears that the cause was" or "It seems likely" or "The evidence may indicate" or "Available evidence suggests."

Analysis of Students' Writing

One Student's First Draft

Why Are Young People Willing to Live with Their Parents

With time flying we are sophomores. Two years later, we will graduate from our university. More and more students are beginning to ponder where we should live after graduation.

People hold different views about this question. Some people are of the opinion that they will live alone, while others point out that they will live with parents. People say that every coin has its two sides. As far as I am concerned, the latter opinion holds more weight.

For one thing, we just graduate from university and lacking working experience would be an obstacle preventing us from earn much money. Living with parents can save money which is used to rent a house, so we can use that money to buy something useful to us, such as books, clothes and so on.

For another, we can live easier with parents because they can do a lot of things for us. When we return from work, they can cook dinner for us. When we get a cold, they can buy medicine for us. Even if when we get a baby, they can look after it for us. All these things can make us live better and easier.

Last but not least, parents hope we can live with them. With the rapid development of society and economy, we are all only children. Our parents hope we can spend more time on them. Only in this way can they not feel lonely.

To sum up, living with parents is better than living alone after graduating from university. It is not only convenient for us but also delightful for our parents. So why don't we do it this way?

209

Comments

The writing is fluent with few grammar mistakes. However, disordered organization makes it hard to read. The passage has six paragraphs. The first two paragraphs are introduction; the third, fourth and fifth paragraphs are main body with reasons to support the central idea; the sixth paragraph is conclusion.

1. The first two paragraphs should be combined into one. The first paragraph introduces relevance of the topic to the writer and the second is about the writer's opinion. Both of them serve as the introduction to the thesis "Young people want to live with their parents." It is not necessary to divide them into two paragraphs. As it is, the essay now seems to have two beginnings.

2. The third paragraph gives the first reason to illustrate one benefit to live with parents, to save money, but the argument is hardly developed.

3. The fifth paragraph gives the third reason—parents hope so, from the perspective of the parents. We don't know whether young people will think the same way. This argument then is not a logic reason to support the central idea of the passage.

On the other hand, some students argue that young people should live independently, away from their parents. Here is an example.

Another Student's Third Draft

Why Do Young People Want to Live Independently

Whether we should live with our parents or not is a question. In the traditional Chinese family, it was considered a blessing for four generations to live under one roof. In contemporary times, however, I, along with many other young people, hold that we should live independently, away from our parents.

To begin with, it is much more likely for parents and young people to have conflicts living together. People of different generations always hold different understanding of many things. When we young people get up late in the morning, for example, our parents will conclude that we are idle. Chances are that we just need some rest after staying up until 2:00 or 3:00am. For another example, our parents sometimes take something necessary we buy as extravagance, judging of course with the standard of thirty years ago. Such little things in daily life create squabbles in the family. If we don't comply with parents, they are heart-broken; if we place filial piety as priority, we'll sacrifice our own sense of value, not to mention our feelings.

What's more, living together with our parents works against our sense of responsibility. We're legally adults at eighteen but remain children at twenty five or thirty five in parents' eyes. It's universally known that Chinese parents spoil their "little emperors" and make every effort to cater for our needs. We'll then be indulged in accepting everything made ready for us, with hardly any chance even to do housework. Of course, we won't need to budget our monthly or annual spending. Instead, we gradually learn to complain that one thing or another is not done to our satisfaction. When we live away from our parents, on the other hand, we may do many things ourselves and grow in the process.

On our own, we enjoy independence and freedom, have fewer conflicts with our parents and learn to budget our time and money. We will certainly have a more difficult time away from our parents' protecting wings, but we will as certainly assume responsibility sooner. How can we young people develop more fully—and fulfill our filial duty more effectively, than live independently and convince our parents of our abilities?

Comments

This essay, with its idiomatic English, neat structure and good reasoning, will probably get a high score in the TEM-4 test, as most of the topics in recent years can be developed with the cause and effect approach. It would be better if there were a third paragraph on the disadvantage of living with parents.

211

Note: For the TEM-4 test, students need not worry about the "scientific" or statistic part of cause and effect analyses. It's not the primary concern of the examiners to find scientific evidence in your composition written within a limited period of time and without access to any reference. If you happen to have a figure in your mind, all the better, it may give you credit. However, don't fabricate statistics.

Homework 3

Discuss the comments with your peers, and if necessary, your professor, and revise your essay accordingly.

Further Reading

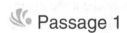 Passage 1

Our Oceans Are under a Great Threat
Mubarak Al-Khaili

Water covers three fourths of our planet. It's the main source of life for all creatures, and without it there would be no life. Most of it is available in the oceans, which contain millions of marine plants and animals. There are about a billion people all over the world depending on fish as a primary source for protein. Oceans also affect directly the earth's temperature and keep it in balance. Oceans are also considered as one of the primary oxygen sources, in view of the fact that, the microscopic plants that live on the ocean's surface take out carbon dioxide and produce oxygen. Another important point that has to be mentioned is that there are many nations like the Arabian Gulf countries, which use the ocean water to produce drinking water because the water table has been depleted. However, there are a lot of dangerous threats to our oceans, one of which is ocean pollution. There are many sources for this pollution, and it has both direct and indirect effects on people, plants, and animals which depend on the ocean for their survival.

One important source of ocean pollution, 23%, comes from boating, dumped wastes and offshore oil production. It is caused by exhaust and oil, which is thrown into the ocean from boats, and it is caused also by the garbage (all kinds) that is thrown away by humans. It's very destructive for the wildlife and it's awfully hard to get rid of it. For example in the 1994 cleanup by the Center for Marine Conservation, volunteers took out from three thousand different beaches about 5.6 million pieces of waste.

Air pollution causes 33% of ocean pollution. Air pollution includes waste from cars, factories, and combustion emissions, ash and airborne pesticides. All of them are harmful for the marine plants and the fish. As a result, the sea plants and microscopic plants become weak and they can't turn out the oxygen for us and for the marine animals. Also this makes a defect in the ecological circle of the ocean's organisms.

The most serious cause of the ocean pollution is runoff from land. It constitutes 44% of all the ocean pollution and this runoff includes many things. One of them is the chemical fertilizer that we use on the farms to make the plants grow well. Others are the trash, sewage, and chemicals that spill on the land. Hill said, "rainwater washes over roads, construction sites, animals lots and industrial areas, it picks up oil, salt, grease, pesticides and other pollutants." These things cause a horrifying ecological chain reaction, and when it reaches the bottom of the ocean it creates a huge number of "algae and phytoplankton"[1] and when these living things die, and decompose, the oxygen decreases in the water which leaves behind a great numbers of dead fish. Moreover, some of the fish, which are still alive, become poisoned and cause diseases for the people and other animals when they eat them. Also, people can get diseases from swimming in the polluted ocean. They could get hepatitis A, E. coli, cholera, gastroenteritis, and the giardia[2], which causes injury or sometimes death. As Kelli McGee of American Oceans Campaign said, "People get sick when they go to beaches, and the real problem is that some states don't even monitor their water."

The population on the coast of the US in 1990 was 80 million and this number will increase to 127 million by the year 2010. This report makes me worry about the oceans because I expect this increase of the population in the coastal area will make an increase in pollution too. As we know, the oceans are one of the biggest sources of life and we get a lot of benefits from it. We have already suffered from these effects of ocean pollution, so how about the next generation and the one after that? We have to think about them and about the future of our oceans. As the research shows, we should protect our environment from this source of pollution and all the people, nations and governments must cooperate to reach these goals.

(http://lclark.edu/~krauss/advwrf99/causeeffect/ mubarakcause)

① algae: 海藻；phytoplankton: 浮游植物
② hepatitis: 肝炎；E. coli: 大肠杆菌；cholera: 霍乱；gastroenteritis: 肠胃炎；giardia: 贾第鞭毛虫病

Questions for Consideration

1. How does the author arrange the causes for ocean pollution?
2. Which cause is the most important one? Why does the author place it where it is?
3. Why does the author talk about the importance of the ocean in the introduction?
4. How does the author echo the introduction in the conclusion?

Passage 2

Why Medical School Should Be Free

Peter B. Bach and Robert Kocher

Doctors are among the most richly rewarded professionals in the country. The Bureau of Labor Statistics reports that of the 15 highest-paid professions in the United States, all but two are in medicine or dentistry.

Why, then, are we proposing to make medical school free?

Huge medical school debts — doctors now graduate owing more than $155,000 on average, and 86 percent have some debt — are why so many doctors shun primary care in favor of highly paid specialties, where there are incentives to give expensive treatments and order expensive tests, an important driver of rising health care costs.

Fixing our health care system will be impossible without a larger pool of competent primary care doctors who can make sure specialists work together in the treatment of their patients—not in isolation, as they often do today—and keep track of patients as they move among settings like private residences, hospitals and nursing homes. Moreover, our population is growing and aging; the American Academy of Family Physicians has estimated a shortfall of 40,000 primary care doctors by 2020. Given the years it takes to train a doctor, we need to start now.

Making medical school free would relieve doctors of the burden of student debt and gradually shift the work force away from specialties and toward primary care. It would also attract college graduates who are discouraged from going to medical school by the costly tuition.

We estimate that we can make medical school free for roughly $2.5 billion per year—about one-thousandth of what we spend on health care in the United States each year. What's more, we can offset most if not all of the cost of medical school without the government's help by charging doctors for specialty training.

Under today's system, all medical students have to pay for their training, whether they plan to become pediatricians or neurosurgeons. They are then paid salaries during the crucial years of internship and residency that turn them into competent doctors. If they decide to extend their years of training to become specialists, they receive a stipend during those years, too.

213

But under our plan, medical school tuition, which averages $38,000 per year, would be waived. Doctors choosing training in primary care, whether they plan to go on later to specialize or not, would continue to receive the stipends they receive today. But those who want to get specialty training would have to forgo much or all of their stipends, $50,000 on average. Because there are nearly as many doctors enrolled in specialty training in the United States (about 66,000) as there are students in United States medical schools (about 67,000), the forgone stipends would cover all the tuition costs.

While this may seem like a lot to ask of future specialists, these same doctors will have paid nothing for medical school and, through their specialty training, would be virtually assured highly lucrative jobs. Today's specialists earn a median of $325,000 per year by one estimate, 70 percent more than the $190,000 that a primary care doctor makes. (Although a large shift away from specialty training may weaken the ability of our plan to remain self-financed, the benefits would make any needed tuition subsidies well worth it.)

Our proposal is not the first to attempt to shift doctors toward primary care, but it's the most ambitious. The National Health Service Corps helps doctors repay their loans in exchange for a commitment to work in an underserved area, but few doctors sign up. The National Institutes of Health offers a similar program to promote work in research and public health, but this creates more researchers, not more practitioners.

Many states have loan forgiveness programs for doctors entering primary care. The health care reform law contains incentive programs that will include bonuses for primary care doctors who treat Medicare patients, and help finance a small increase in primary care training positions.

Our proposal is certain to raise objections. Because some hospitals that provide training to specialists are not associated with medical schools, we will need a system to redistribute the specialty training fees and medical school subsidies. Several entities that have not collaborated before, including the organizations that license specialty training programs and medical school associations, would have to work together to manage this. For the plan to work, it will also be critical that medical schools do not start raising tuitions just because people other than their students are footing the bill.

Our plan would not directly address the chronic wage gap between primary care providers and specialists. But efforts to equalize incomes have been stymied for decades by specialists, who have kept payment rates for procedures higher than those for primary care services. When Medicare has stepped in, most of the increases given to primary care have been diluted by byzantine budgetary rules that cap total spending.

Nothing in our plan would diminish the quality of medical school education. If anything, free tuition would increase the quality of the applicants. Neither would our approach quash the creativity of medical schools in developing curriculums. Medical students would still be required to pass the various licensing examinations and complete patient care rotations as they are today.

Critics might object to providing free medical education when students have to pay for most other types of advanced training. But the process of training doctors is unlike any other, and much of the costs are already borne by others. Hospitals that house medical residents and specialist trainees receive payments from the taxpayer, through Medicare. Patients give of their time and of their bodies in our nation's teaching hospitals so that doctors in training can become skilled practitioners.

We need a better way of paying for medical training, to address the looming shortage of primary care doctors and to better match the costs of specialty training to the income it delivers. Taking the counterintuitive step of making medical education free, while charging those doctors who want to gain specialty training, is a straightforward way of achieving both goals.

(From *Now York Times*, May 28, 2011)

Questions for Consideration

1. Are the writers primarily tracing some causes or making a proposal?
2. Is there a cause and effect relationship in the proposal? If there is, what is it?
3. How likely would the proposal work?

🌼 Passage 3

The 31 Major Causes of Failure

Life's greatest tragedy consists of men and women who earnestly try, and fail. The tragedy lies in the overwhelmingly large majority of people who fail, as compared with the few who succeed.

I have had the privilege of analyzing several thousand men and women, 98 percent of whom were classed as "failures."

My analysis proved that there are thirteen major principles through which people accumulate fortunes, and there are thirty-one major reasons for failure. The thirty-one causes of failure are listed below. As you go through the list, measure yourself point by point. It will help you to discover how many of these causes of failure stand between you and your success.

(1) **Unfavourable hereditary background.** There is little, if anything, that can be done for people who are born with a deficiency in brain-power. This is the only one of the thirty-one causes of failure that may not be easily corrected by any individual.

(2) **Lack of a well-defined purpose in life.** There is no hope of success for the person who does not have a central purpose or definite goal at which to aim. Ninety-eight out of every hundred of those who I have analyzed had no such aim. Perhaps this was the major cause of their failure.

(3) **Lack of ambition to aim above mediocrity.** I can offer no hope for those who are so indifferent that they do not want to get ahead in life, and are not willing to pay the price.

(4) **Insufficient education.** This is a handicap that may be overcome with comparative ease. Experience has proven that the best-educated people are often those who are self-made or self-educated. It takes more than a college degree to make you a person of education. Any person who is educated has learned to get whatever they want in life without violating the rights of others. Education consists not so much of knowledge, but

of knowledge effectively and persistently applied. You are paid not merely for what you know, but for what you do with what you know.

(5) **Lack of self-discipline.** Discipline comes through self-control. This means that you must control all negative qualities. Before you can control conditions, you must first control yourself. Self-mastery is the hardest job you will ever tackle. If you do not conquer yourself, you will be conquered by yourself. By stepping in front of a mirror, you may see both your best friend and your greatest enemy.

(6) **Ill health.** No person may enjoy outstanding success without good health. Many of the causes of ill health are subject to mastery and control. These, in the main, are:
- Overeating of foods not conducive to health,
- Wrong habits of thought, or negative thinking,
- Wrong use of, and overindulgence in, sex,
- Lack of proper physical exercise,
- An inadequate supply of fresh air, due to improper breathing.

(7) **Unfavourable environmental influences during childhood.** "As the twig is bent, so shall the tree grow." Most people who have criminal tendencies acquire them as a result of bad environment and improper associates during their childhood or youth.

(8) **Procrastination.** This is one of the most common causes of failure. Procrastination stands within the shadow of every human being, waiting its opportunity to spoil your chances of success. Most of us go through life as failures because we are waiting for "the time to be right" to start doing something worthwhile. Do not wait. The time will never be just right. Start where you stand, work with whatever tools you have at your command, and you will acquire better tools as you go along.

(9) **Lack of persistence.** Most of us are good "starters" but poor "finishers" of everything we begin. People are prone to give up at the first signs of defeat. There is no substitute for persistence. The person who makes persistence his or her watchword discovers that "failure" finally becomes tired and makes its departure. Failure cannot cope with persistence.

(10) **Negative personality.** There is no hope of success for the person who repels people through a negative personality. Success comes through the application of power, and power is attained through the cooperative efforts of other people. A negative personality will not induce cooperation.

(11) **Lack of control of sexual urges.** Sexual energy is the most powerful of all the stimuli that move people into action. Because it is the most powerful of the emotions, if controlled it can be converted into other creative channels.

(12) **Uncontrolled desire for "something for nothing."** The gambling instinct drives millions of people to failure. Evidence of this may be found in the Wall Street stock market crash of 1929, during which millions of people tried to make money by gambling on stock margins.

(13) **Lack of a well-defined power of decision.** Those who succeed reach decisions promptly and change them very slowly. Those who fail reach decisions very slowly and change them frequently, and quickly. Indecision and procrastination are twins. Kill off this

pair before they completely tie you to the treadmill of failure.

(14) **One or more of the six basic fears** (fear of poverty, criticism, ill health, loss of love, old age, and death). These must be mastered before you can market your services effectively.

(15) **Wrong selection of a mate in marriage.** This is a most common cause of failure. The relationship of marriage brings people intimately into contact. Unless this relationship is harmonious, failure is likely to follow. Moreover, it will be a form of failure that destroys ambition.

(16) **Over-caution.** The person who takes no chances generally has to take whatever is left when others are through choosing. Over-caution is as bad as under-caution. Both are extremes to be guarded against. Life itself is filled with the element of chance.

(17) **Wrong selection of associates in business.** This is another common cause of failure in business. You should use great care in selecting the people you will work with and the people you will work for. We emulate those with whom we associate most closely.

(18) **Superstition and prejudice.** Superstition is a form of fear. It is also a sign of ignorance. Successful people keep open minds and are afraid of nothing.

(19) **Wrong selection of a vocation.** You cannot have outstanding success in work that you do not like. The most essential step in the marketing of personal services is that of selecting an occupation into which you can throw yourself wholeheartedly. Although money or circumstances may require you to do something you don't like for a time, no one can stop you from developing plans to make your goal in life a reality.

(20) **Lack of concentration of effort.** The jack-of-all-trades seldom is good at any. Concentrate all of your efforts on one definite chief aim.

(21) **The habit of indiscriminate spending.** You cannot succeed if you are eternally in fear of poverty. Form the habit of systematic saving by putting aside a definite percentage of your income every month. Money in the bank gives you a very safe foundation of courage when bargaining for the sale of personal services. Without money, you must take what you are offered and be glad to get it.

(22) **Lack of enthusiasm.** Without enthusiasm you cannot be convincing. Moreover, enthusiasm is contagious, and the person who has it (under control) is generally welcome in any group of people.

(23) **Intolerance.** The person with a closed mind on any subject seldom gets ahead. Intolerance means that you have stopped acquiring knowledge. The most damaging forms of intolerance are those connected with religious, racial, and political differences of opinion.

(24) **Intemperance.** The most damaging forms of intemperance are connected with overeating, alcohol, drugs, and sexual activities. Overindulgence in any of these can be fatal to success.

(25) **Inability to cooperate with others.** More people lose their positions, and their big opportunities in life, because of this fault than for all other reasons combined. It is a fault that no well-informed businessperson or leader will tolerate.

(26) **Possession of power that was not acquired through self-effort.** Power in the hands of one who did not acquire it gradually is often fatal to success. Quick riches are more dangerous than poverty.

(27) **Intentional dishonesty.** There is no substitute for honesty. You may be temporarily dishonest, because of circumstances over which you have no control, without permanent damage. But there is no hope for you if you are dishonest by choice. Sooner or later your deeds will catch up with you, and you will pay by loss of reputation and perhaps even loss of liberty.

(28) **Egotism and vanity.** These qualities serve as red lights that warn others to keep away. They are fatal to success.

(29) **Guessing instead of thinking.** Most people are too indifferent or lazy to acquire facts with which to think accurately. They prefer to act on "opinions" created by guesswork or snap judgments.

(30) **Lack of capital.** This is a common cause of failure among those who start out in business for the first time. You must have a sufficient reserve of capital to absorb the shock of your mistakes and to carry you over until you have established a reputation.

(31) **Got another one?** Name any particular cause of failure from which you have suffered that has not been included in the foregoing list.

In these thirty-one major causes of failure is found a description of the tragedy of life, which obtains for practically every person who tries and fails. It will be helpful if you can induce someone who knows you well to go over this list with you, and help to analyze you by the thirty-one causes of failure. It may be beneficial if you try this alone. Most people cannot see themselves as others see them. You may be one who cannot.

(From *Think and Grow Rich* by Napoleon Hill)

Note:

Think and Grow Rich, first published in 1937, is a motivational personal development and self-help book written by Napoleon Hill. While the title implies that this book deals only with how to get rich, the author explains that the philosophy taught in the book can be used to help people succeed in all lines of work. The book was the result of more than twenty years of research based on Hill's close association with a large number of individuals who achieved great wealth during their lifetimes. *Business Week Magazine's Best-Seller* List ranked it as the sixth best-selling paperback business book 70 years after it was first published.

Questions for Consideration

1. The thirty-one causes of failure are just listed without much explanation. Pick up a few and try to establish causality between the causes and failure.
2. Are any of the causes holding you back? Create a rating scale and rate yourself to find those areas where a little effort will make a huge improvement.

The Definition Essay

Tuning-in Activities

Activity 1

Choose a proper name to fill in the blank so that a complete definition explains the picture on the left.

a volcano	a mound	a ridge	a sand dune
Chinese calligraphy		jealousy	a spanner
a hammer	a zipper	a mall	a band
a lace	a swan	the dragon	a peacock
a calculator	a mobile phone	the Internet	a printer

1. _____ is a long, scaled legendary creature with four legs and a head similar to that of a lion in Chinese mythology and folklore, symbolizing good luck, success, strength and power, particularly the controlling power over water and rainfall.

2. _____ is an art of brush and ink that uses Chinese characters to communicate the spiritual world of the artist.

3. _____ is a global system of interconnected computer networks that use the standard Internet protocol suite (TCP/IP) to serve billions of users worldwide.

4. _____ is a mountain or hill with an opening through which lava, cinders, gases, etc. come up from below the earth's surface.

5. _____ is one or more buildings forming a complex of shops representing merchandisers, with interconnecting walkways enabling visitors to easily walk from unit to unit, along with a parking area — a modern, indoor version of the traditional marketplace.

6. _____ is the negative thoughts and feelings of insecurity, fear, and anxiety over an anticipated loss of something that the person values, particularly in reference to a human connection.

Activity 2

Match the following terms with their definitions.

1. culture   a. a very large powerful tailless primate most closely related to man

2. a gorilla   b. a doctor who specializes in the treatment of mental illness

3. harmony   c. a general name for printing stamps and impressions thereof that are used in lieu of signatures in personal documents, office paperwork, contracts, art, or any item requiring acknowledgment or authorship

4. a psychiatrist   d. a clinical professional who works with patients in a variety of therapeutic contexts or an academic professional who conducts research of the mind

5. a psychologist   e. in the broad sense, is the attributes of human beings, those that distinguish man from other things in the world, including materials to satisfy man's needs, social institutions man has established, knowledge and art man has developed, and the inherited ideas, beliefs, values, and customs that constitute the shared bases of social action

6. a seal   f. a Chinese concept for peace, order, agreement, accord and congruity

Introduction

Definition is a method of making explicit the meaning of a term (word, phrase or concept) or word group or a sign or a symbol. It uses terms that are already understood or whose definitions are easily obtainable to give a clear explanation about something new, abstract, obscure, elusive or difficult to understand. The term to be defined is the **definiendum** (被定义项). A term may have many different senses or meanings. For each such specific sense, a **definiens** (定义项) is a cluster of words that defines that term.

Encyclopædia Britannica thus classifies definitions in philosophy:

> Definitions may be classified as lexical, ostensive, and stipulative. Lexical definition (词法定义) specifies the meaning of an expression by stating it in terms of other expressions whose meaning is assumed to be known (e.g., a ewe is a female sheep). Ostensive definition (实物定义, 实指定义或直观释义) specifies the meaning of an expression by pointing to examples of things to which the expression applies (e.g., green is the color of grass, limes, lily pads, and emeralds). Stipulative definition (规定性定义或约定定义) assigns a new meaning to an expression (or a meaning to a new expression); the expression defined (definiendum) may either be a new expression that is being introduced into the language for the first time, or an expression that is already current.
> (http://www.britannica.com/EBchecked/topic/155805/definition)

In logic, definitions can also be classified as intensional definition and extensional definition. An **intensional definition** (内涵定义) specifies the necessary and sufficient conditions (or the properties) that a thing must have for being a member of a specific set (集), setting out the essence of something, such as that by **genus** (属) and **differentia** (种差). An **extensional definition** (外延定义), also called a **denotative definition**, specifies the extension of a term by listing every object that is a member of a specific set.

As a major form of intensional definition, a **genus-differentia definition** (种加属差定义或本义狭义定义) is composed of two parts:
1. **a genus** (or family): An existing definition that serves as a portion of the new definition; all definitions with the same genus are considered members of that genus.
2. **the differentia:** The portion of the new definition that is not provided by the genera.

For example: *a psychiatrist*: a doctor who specializes in the treatment of mental illness. Most of the definitions in the "Tuning-in Activities" are this kind of definition.

Certain rules have traditionally been given for this particular type of definition.
1. A definition must set out the essential attributes of the thing defined.
2. Definitions should avoid circularity. To define a computer virus as "a virus that destroys or disrupts software..." would convey no information whatsoever. However, it is acceptable to define two relative terms in respect of each other. Clearly, we cannot define "antecedent" without using the term "consequent," nor conversely.
3. The definition must not be too wide or too narrow. It must be applicable to everything to which the defined term applies (i.e. not miss anything out), and to nothing else (i.e. not include any things to which the defined term would not truly apply).
4. The definition must not be obscure. The purpose of a definition is to explain the meaning of a term which may be obscure or difficult, by the use of terms that are commonly understood and whose meaning is clear.
5. A definition should not be negative where it can be positive. We should not define "wisdom" as the absence of folly, or a healthy thing as whatever is not sick unless it's absolutely unavoidable.

221

Those terms in philosophy and logic may strike you as awesome and august, but we need to be aware of them in writing the definition essay for the simple reason that in such an essay, we explain what a specific, usually abstract or ambiguous, term means. Defining key terms is essential for effective writing, argumentative and expository writing in particular. In fact, sometimes a clear definition of an obscure idea or a vague term leads to clarity in problem solving. It has been said that a problem defined is a problem half solved. To write a good definition essay, we have to refine our thinking and provide sound arguments with awareness of the logical and philosophical concepts.

On the other hand, those awesome terms should not become barriers in our writing. Many terms, complex and abstract ones in particular, don't have ONE "correct" meaning: as there are more ideas or concepts than there are words, the same word or term means different things to different people at different times or situations. Conversely, different words or phrases can be used to name the same concept. Although we strive for objective definitions, it is reasonable to define a term by providing personal commentary on what it means at a given time and/or situation. In such circumstances, we are writing a personal **extended definition**.

Extended Definition

An extended definition is the organization and development of the meaning of a term beyond the limits of the lexical definition (also called dictionary definition). Abstract words such as *freedom, success,* and *quality* are elusive. An extended definition of them helps the reader have a clear idea of what they mean or what the writer hopes the reader will accept what they mean. An extended definition could attempt to explain why the term is defined as such. It could define the term directly, giving no information other than the explanation of the term. Or, it could imply the definition of the term by telling a story that requires the reader to infer the meaning. In a definition essay, the writer is concerned with describing or explaining the terms and their interrelationships, defining not only the principal terms but also the subordinate terms, discussing fully the background of the subject, its components, and its general connotations.

Extended definitions can be purely **personal** or largely **objective**. A personal definition is useful if we wish to get the reader to see a word in a different light or if we are discussing our understanding of the term. An objective definition, on the other hand, seeks general agreement.

Exercises

1. Compare a lexical definition with a personal extended definition.

Concept	Lexical Definition	Personal Extended Definition
humor	quality of being amusing or comic	a means of handling the difficult situations, the best way to keep a small misunderstanding from becoming bigger, a good way to dissolve a hostile confrontation, and one way to save face, jobs, or even life

2. Compare the lexical definition and a personal extended definition of "ghetto."

Dictionary. com: a section of a city, especially a thickly populated slum area, inhabited predominantly by members of an ethnic or other minority group, often as a result of social or economic restrictions, pressures, or hardships

A personal extended definition:

Ghetto

Carl Stearns

I learned what ghetto meant after my first drive down Washington Street on December morning. A dozen empty buildings in one side of the street had broken windows and large black smears from a fire. I saw boarded-up doors, overturned garbage pails, and clumps of newspapers along the sidewalk. Three children without coats played with the stuffing of an abandoned couch on an empty lot. A scraggly mutt stretched out on the corner. Everything looked so old and depressing and worn out. No dictionary ever gives that idea in its definition.

An objective extended definition attempts to apply in all cases at all times. Take for example, an extract from the World Bank's definition of corruption.

The term corruption covers a broad range of human actions. To understand its effect on an economy or a political system, it helps to unbundle[1] the term by identifying specific types of activities or transactions that might fall within it. In considering its strategy the Bank sought a usable definition of corruption and then developed a taxonomy[2] of the different forms corruption could take consistent with that definition. We settled on a straightforward definition—the abuse of public office for private gain. Public office is abused for private gain when an official accepts, solicits[3], or extorts[4] a bribe. It is also abused when private agents actively offer bribes to circumvent[5] public policies and processes for competitive advantage and profit. Public office can also be abused for personal benefit even if no bribery occurs, through patronage[6] and nepotism[7], the theft of state assets, or the diversion[8] of state revenues[9]. This definition is both simple and sufficiently broad to cover most of the corruption that the Bank encounters, and it is widely used in the literature. Bribery occurs in the private sector, but bribery in the public sector, offered or extracted, should be the Bank's main concern, since the Bank lends primarily to governments and supports government policies, programs, and projects.

(The World Bank Group: How Do We Define Corruption? http://www.worldbank.org/html/extdr/corruptn/cor02.htm#define, July 31 1998)

Vocabulary:

1. unbundle: *v.* separate
2. taxonomy: *n.* 分类法
3. solicit: *v.* seek for
4. extort: *v.* take illegally by reasons of one's office
5. circumvent: *v.* bypas
6. patronage: *n.* 资助
7. nepotism: *n.* 裙带关系
8. diversion: *n.* 挪用，他用
9. revenue: *n.* 税收，收入

In this extended definition, the writer identifies some distinguishing characteristics of corruption, gives examples, provides extra information and points out what can't be included in the definition.

Purposes of the Definition Essay

The purpose of a definition essay is usually **to inform** or **to persuade**. A definition of ozone layer, for example, or a straightforward definition of *humanity* will inform the reader about the meaning of the term. Definitions of abstract words like *honesty, enthusiasm, responsibility, sympathy* can be given to persuade the reader to accept the writer's viewpoint.

The purpose will decide what details to choose in the essay. For instance, if the purpose is to give the reader a fresh look on *fear* by persuading him or her to believe that fear can be a positive emotion, the writer may choose to argue that *fear* is adaptive because it ensures survival. The writer may then give examples when we would needlessly endanger ourselves were it not for fear. However, if the purpose is to inform the reader that *fear* is a psychological state everyone experiences, then the writer may include details related to people's behaviors in such a state with an objective description of fear.

224

Sample 1

A *bohemian*[1] is a person who lives an artistic lifestyle, placing freedom of self-expression above all other desires, including wealth, social conformity and status. The term originated in France during the 19th century due to the influx[2] of gypsies[3] believed to be traveling from Czech[4] Republic's Bohemia. The term quickly became generalized, however, indicative of a lifestyle rather than a nationality. In the United States, the Beat Generation[5] of the 1950s and the hippies[6] of the '60s reflected the bohemian subculture in many ways.

Writers, artists, poets, musicians and philosophers could commonly be found leading bohemian lifestyles in 19th century Paris, France. Drugs, alcohol and a freer attitude towards sexual expression were considered part of the subculture. Often lacking money, bohemians commonly found lodging in older, run down sections of town. This

Vocabulary

1. bohemian: *n.* 波西米亚人
2. influx: *n.* 流入；涌入
3. gypsy: *n.* 吉普赛人
4. Czech: *n.* 捷克人
5. the Beat Generation: 垮掉的一代（指第二次世界大战后美国出现的一批年轻人，对社会现实不满，蔑视传统观念，在服饰和行为方面摒弃常规，追求个性自我张扬，长期浪迹于社会底层，形成独特的社会圈子和处世哲学）
6. hippie: *n.* 嬉皮士（20世纪60年代出现于美国的青年颓废派一员，反越战，对社会现实抱不满情绪，常服用引起幻觉

may have led to the perception that they were not always personally well kept. Nevertheless, the thoughtful and expressive lifestyle so free of social constraints remains a romantic notion that endures.

Today, someone who leads a non-traditional lifestyle is often called a bohemian, particularly if an overwhelming[7] need to express him or herself through the arts is present. However, opportunities now make it easier for a non-traditionalist to succeed without conforming to society or corporate[8] constraints[9]. Given talent and drive, many that consider themselves bohemians might very well end up wealthy as a result of their self-expressive arts. This has resulted in what some term the *bourgeois bohemian* or *boho:* a bohemian with money and status.

Often bohemian communities will spring up in diversely populated areas where rent is cheap and freedom of expression is high. The bohemian element might even rejuvenate a community, unintentionally driving up real estate[10] values. Some areas in the United States that are home to bohemian communities today include Venice Beach, California; Austin, Texas; Greenwich Village, New York; and the French Quarter in New Orleans. Of the many international bohemian communities, Amsterdam, Netherlands; Budapest, Hungary; and the Mile End in Montreal, Canada rate high on the extensive list.

A well-known depiction of a bohemian character in cinema comes from James Cameron's 1997 blockbuster[11], *Titanic*. In the movie, fictional character *Jack Dawson,* played by Leonardo DiCaprio, is a traveling artist. Jack finds himself on the ship after winning passage in a card game minutes before Titanic's departure on its ill-fated maiden voyage. The freewheeling bohemian meets the socially constrained *Rose DeWitt Bukater*, played by Kate Winslet. Jack's bohemian lifestyle attracts young Rose, whose life becomes radically altered as a result.

的迷幻药,信奉非暴力或神秘主义,实行群居,蓄长发,穿奇装异服)

7. overwhelming: *adj.* 势不可挡的;极强烈的

8. corporate: *adj.* 团体的;公司的

9. constraint: *n.* 约束,限制

225

10. real estate: 不动产,房地产

11. blockbuster: *n.* (喻)重磅炸弹,了不起的人或事物

Despite an arguably pragmatic[12] emphasis on money and success in our current economic era, the bohemian lifestyle remains a harbinger[13] of something mystically lacking from a corporate-fed society. Perhaps it's the dedication to an inner focus that extends past the self to those expressions of art and philosophy that are the underpinnings[14] of a foundation that unites rather than divides. Whatever the reasons, the freedom-loving bohemian with the flowing eccentric clothes, unconventional ideas, and unique self-expression continues to enrich cultures worldwide.
(http://www.wisegeek.com/what-is-a-bohemian.htm)

12. pragmatic: *adj.* 讲究实际的,重实效的
13. harbinger: *n.* 通报者；先驱；前兆
14. underpinnings: *n.* 基础,根据

Questions for Consideration

1. Is the extended definition purely personal or largely objective?
2. Is the purpose mainly to persuade or to inform?
3. By what means does the writer extend the definition?

Sample 2

Vocabulary

Bookworms Are for Real

Bookworm is the name given to the larva (wormlike early stage) of several kinds of moths or beetles that feed on the binding and paste of books. Human bookworms, unlike their worm counterparts[1], feed on the words and ideas contained in books. Human bookworms probably get their not-so-attractive name because of the one trait[2] they share with wormy bookworms—the fact they spend most of their time around books. The lowly name given to book lovers is a hint of the way they are often viewed by others.

Many people think of bookworms as passive[3], dull, even lazy—a lot like a real worm. The only reason they move is to turn a page. People who view bookworms as passive don't realize how rapidly bookworm's mind is moving and how far these "passive" folk are traveling. Through their reading, bookworms encounter other cultures, witness events, and gain insight into controversial[4] issues.

1. counterpart: *n.* a person or a thing that corresponds to another
2. trait: *n.* characteristic
3. passive: *adj.* not active
4. controversial: *adj.* causing a dispute

226

Because reading is such an individual pastime, human bookworms often seem as solitary as their worm namesakes. Unfortunately, many nonreaders assume that because bookworms spend so much time alone, they are disconnected and antisocial[5]. Many human bookworms, however, are not at all isolated, disconnected, or antisocial. Though bookworms may spend a large amount of time glued[6] to the pages of a book, they are connected to the universe in extremely responsible ways. Many bookworms use what they have learned from books to do a lot of good in the world. Some do volunteer work and others choose careers they have read about, such as medicine or teaching, which help improve people's way of life.

Like the creatures they were named for, bookworms don't seem to lead a very glamorous[7] life. Don't be too hasty to judge bookworms by their appearance, though. For one thing, bookworms are usually interested in more than one subject and therefore they are more interesting to talk with than someone who focuses on only one special interest. Spending a little time coaxing[8] a bookworm into talking instead of reading might not be so boring as you think. After all, as any bookworm could tell you: you cannot judge a book by its cover.

5. antisocial: *adj.* avoiding the company of others

6. glue: *v.* stick or join things

7. glamorous: *adj.* attractive

8. coax: *v.* persuade sb. gently or gradually

227

Questions for Consideration

1. What is the purpose of this essay?
2. What is the thesis statement? Does the author give specific information to support the central point?
3. How does the author structure this essay? Is this structure effective?

Finding the Topic

Since you are providing your personal understanding of a concept or term in a definition essay and your definition conveys what your understanding and experience have taught you about the concept or term, in thinking of possible topics for this essay, you should consider subjects that you are especially qualified to discuss, such as a topic that you know a great deal about, or a concept that you like to think about.

Tips:

1. Select a term or subject that you know well enough so that you can provide specific examples to illustrate your definition.

    a. For example, if you aren't familiar with the term *plagiarism*, don't attempt to define it in an extended essay.

    b. The subject of the essay must be **familiar** enough to you that you can readily supply specific examples.

2. Don't select a subject either too broad or too narrow to fit the parameters of your essay.

    a. For example, the word *hat* may be too narrow for you to define in an extended essay.

    b. On the other hand, the term *honor* may be too broad or general since pinning it down to a single definition is very difficult.

Exercise

Here are some concepts or terms you might consider defining. Select one that you are familiar with or one that you'd like to find more about.

integrity	modesty	trust	racism
morality	charisma	ambition	frustration
maturity	intelligence	feminism	nostalgia
conservative	vanity	self-respect	thrift
human rights	physical fitness	peace of mind	a good film

Using Definition Mapping for Ideas

Once a term has been selected for definition, the writer is to consider how to develop the content of the essay so as to give the reader a fresh look on the term. **Definition mapping** is an analysis tool to display possible definitions of an abstract term. It is used to widen potential extended definition of a term and summarize major categories. To map, write the term of a broad subject area in a box in the center and then think of ideas related to that subject and add them. Continue thinking of related ideas and joining them to the appropriate circles until you group them under some categories.

Example 1: To define the concept of love, we write "love" in the center of a piece of paper and think of ideas related to it the following way. This mapping can give us adequate inspiration to write a definition essay.

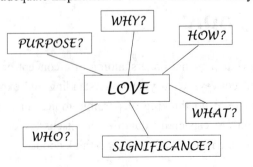

228

Example 2: If we define happiness from different aspects, we write it in the center of a piece of paper and think of ideas related to that subject.

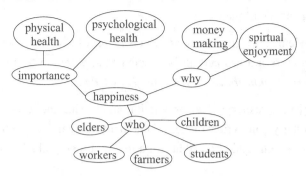

Homework 1

Decide on your favorite subject and discuss it with an extended definition. Try definition mapping and jot down answers to Who? What? Why? or How? Then list words and phrases in relation to those answers.

Structuring the Definition Essay

There is no fixed pattern to develop a definition essay. It depends on what is being defined, what the writer intends to say about it and what tone she decides to take. As the term defined is often general and broad, the approach is completely up to the writer; whether she wishes it to be serious or humorous, general or specific, to describe the term or to tell stories (anecdotes) about it, to compare or contrast it to other things, to give examples of it, to classify or identify its unique properties, to discuss causes and effects of it, or to explain its process of functioning.

The introductory paragraph, as usual, tries to get the reader's attention and states the thesis. You may begin the definition essay with a fact, statistic, or anecdote, something that catches the reader's attention and keeps her reading. You may include the traditional or dictionary definition at the beginning to provide a basis for your personal definition, although this is not encouraged as dictionary definitions sound pedantic and uninteresting; or you may open with a contradictory image to what would be your image to illustrate that definition. Then bring forth your definition (the thesis statement) with a bit of a personal touch and with an orientation for the reader to follow. See how one western writer catches attention of the reader (westerners considering coming to China) at the beginning of an extended explanation about the Chinese concept of *mianzi*.

Of all the idiosyncrasies of Chinese culture, the concept of "Face" is perhaps most difficult for Westerners to fully grasp. And because "saving face" is such a strong motivating force in China, it's also one of the most important concepts in understanding the Chinese Mind.

After arguing that love is giving, Erich Fromm, a German-American psychologist and sociologist, writes the next transitional paragraph, which is actually the thesis statement for the next seven and a half pages.

> Beyond the element of giving, the active character of love becomes evident in the fact that it always implies certain basic elements, common to all forms of love. These are *care, responsibility, respect* and *knowledge.*

The four ideas give the reader a clear orientation about what the writer is going to say in the next part. Similarly, one writer makes a statement that gambling, rather than the usual definition as sin, is an addiction that requires treatment, abstinence, and behavior modification.

Supporting paragraphs in definition essays can be structured with practically all the other approaches introduced in this textbook. The common approaches are:

Analysis: The term may be separated into different parts and those parts could be described separately. For example, if the topic is love then the many types of love could be explained individually. The writer may start with platonic love, then romantic love, unrequited love, and first love. Erich Fromm analyzes each of the four basic elements of love he puts forward.

Sample 3

That love implies *care* is most evident in a mother's love for her child. No assurance of her love would strike us as sincere if we saw her lacking in care for the infant, if she neglected to feed it, to bathe it, to give it physical comfort; and we are impressed by her love if we see her caring for the child. It is not different even with the love for animals or flowers. If a woman told us that she loved flowers, and we saw that she forgot to water them, we would not believe in her "love" for flowers. *Love is the active concern for the life and the growth of that which we love.* Where this active concern is lacking, there is no love. This element of love has been beautifully described in the book of Jonah[1]. God has told Jonah to go to Nineveh[2] to warn its inhabitants that they will be punished unless they mend their evil ways. Jonah runs away from his mission because he is afraid that the people of Nineveh will repent[3] and that God will

Vocabulary

1. Jonah: 约拿(基督教《圣经·旧约》中的先知)
2. Nineveh: 尼尼微(古代东方奴隶制国家亚述的首都,遗址在今伊拉克北部的摩苏尔附近)
3. repent: v. 悔悟;忏悔

forgive them. He is a man with a strong sense of order and law, but without love. However, in his attempt to escape, he finds himself in the belly of a whale, symbolizing the state of isolation and imprisonment which his lack of love and solidarity[4] has brought upon him. God saves him, and Jonah goes to Nineveh. He preaches to the inhabitants as God had told him, and the very thing he was afraid of happens. The men of Nineveh repent their sins, mend their ways, and God forgives them and decides not to destroy the city. Jonah is intensely angry and disappointed; he wanted "justice" to be done, not mercy. At last he finds some comfort in the shade of a tree which God had made to grow for him to protect him from the sun. But when God makes the tree wilt[5], Jonah is depressed and angrily complains to God. God answers: "Thou[6] hast[7] had pity on the gourd for the which thou hast not labored neither madest it grow; which came up in a night, and perished in a night. And should I not spare Nineveh, that great city, wherein are more than sixscore thousand people that cannot discern[8] between their right hand and their left hand; and also much cattle?" God's answer to Jonah is to be understood symbolically. God explains to Jonah that the essence of love is to "labor" for something and "to make something grow," that love and labor are inseparable. One loves that for which one labors, and one labors for that which one loves.

Care and concern imply another aspect of love; that of *responsibility*. Today responsibility is often meant to denote[9] duty, something imposed upon one from the outside. But responsibility, in its true sense, is an entirely voluntary act; it is my response to the needs, expressed or unexpressed, of another human being. To be "responsible" means to be able and ready to respond. Jonah did not feel responsible to the inhabitants of Nineveh. He, like Cain, could ask: "Am I my brother's keeper?" The Loving person responds. The life of his brother is not his brother's business alone, but his own. He feels responsible for his fellow men, as

4. solidarity: *n.* 团结一致

5. wilt: *v.* 枯萎,凋谢
6. thou: *pron.*<诗><古>汝,尔,你
7. hast: <古>have 的第二人称单数现在式(与 thou 连用)
8. discern: *v.* 看出;识别;辨明

9. denote: *v.* 表示,预示

231

he feels responsible for himself. The responsibility, in the case of the mother and her infant, refers mainly to the care for physical needs. In the love between adults it refers mainly to the psychic[10] needs of the other person.

Responsibility could easily deteriorate[11] into domination and possessiveness, were it not for a third component[12] of love, *respect*. Respect is not fear and awe; it denotes, in accordance with the root of the word (*respicere*=to look at), the ability to see a person as he is, to be aware of his unique individuality. Respect means the concern that the other person should grow and unfold as he is. Respect, thus, implies the absence of exploitation. I want the loved person to grow and unfold for his own sake, and in his own ways, and not for the purpose of serving me. If I love the other person, I feel one with him or her, but with him as he is, not as I need him to be as an object for my use. It is clear that respect is possible only if I have achieved independence; if I can stand walk without needing crutches, without having to dominate and exploit anyone else. Respect exists only on the basis of freedom: "l'amour est l'enfant de la liberté" as an old French song says; love is the child of freedom, never that of domination.

To respect a person is not possible without *knowing* him; care and responsibility would be blind if they were not guided by knowledge. Knowledge would be empty if it were not motivated by concern. There are many layers of knowledge; the knowledge which is an aspect of love is one which does not stay at the periphery[13], but penetrates to the core. It is possible only when I can transcend[14] the concern for myself and see the other person in his own terms. I may know, for instance, that a person is angry, even if he does not show it overtly; but I may know him more deeply than that; then I know that he is anxious, and worried; that he feels lonely, that he feels guilty. Then I know that his anger is only the manifestation of something deeper, and I see him

10. psychic: *adj.* 精神的, 心灵的
11. deteriorate: *v.* 恶化, 退化; 变质
12. component: *n.* 组成部分
13. periphery: *n.* 外围, 边缘
14. transcend: *v.* 超出, 超越

as anxious and embarrassed, that is, as the suffering person, rather than as the angry one.

(Erich Fromm, *The Theory of Loving*, New York: Harper & Row, pp. 26—29.)

Exercise

Compare Fromm's development of the four elements of love with a young woman's personal explanation of the different roles her boyfriend plays: a friend, a mentor, and a lover in her life. Does her writing echo Fromm's theory?

Sample 4

What Is True Love?

When thinking of the man I love, the word "boyfriend" just doesn't seem to do justice. When describing him I want to use a word that will evoke passion and tenderness; a word that shows he means more to me than such a timid title. Since we became a couple I have found a best friend, a mentor[1], and a lover. The only word that could possibly be appropriate for this shining light in my life would be "true love." Even the simple word "love" won't do. It takes a special kind of relationship to have true love.

The reason we are so deeply connected is the foundation on which we've built our relationship: friendship. We began as friends and remain friends still. It is so incredibly important to be friends with your lover. Being his friend means I'm comfortable around him. Without friendship, an infatuation[2] disguised as love can fizzle[3] and be the cause of an end. As we merge[4] our lives into one, he becomes my partner and companion. He is there to lend a shoulder just as a best friend should.

As we base our relationship on this mutual friendship, it grows because he is my mentor and my guide. When we're together it is as if our two minds become one. A friend always told me that to fall in love with someone they must present to you a challenge. He has risen and met the challenge to guide me through those times when I was in desperate[5] need. His wisdom to this day amazes

1. mentor: *n.* a teacher, instructor

2. infatuation: *n.* foolish love
3. fizzle: *v.* fail
4. merge: *v.* become one

5. desperate: *adj.* great, urgent

233

me; I treasure the countless deep conversations we've had. These beautiful conversations don't always include words. It has become easy for me to just look into his eyes and know all he is feeling.

Most importantly, he is my lover. Everyone needs to be loved, appreciated, and cared for. Because I love him I feel such a desperate need to satisfy him. Because I'm his lover, I always am most concerned with his happiness. In such a relationship, guidance and friendship mean nothing without love. This aspect of the relationship is usually glorified in romantic stories and tales. But sometimes the best part comes after they walk into the sunset. Some of our best memories don't include an expensive dinner and a moon-lit evening. It is beautiful to wake up and have him lying next to me. Even the simple moments mean the world.

So for love to be true, it must include these characteristics: friendship, guidance, and satisfaction. Fortunately for my boyfriend and me, these things come naturally. These things do not guarantee a perfect relationship, but they are the only way to come as close as you possibly can. If you are lucky enough to know your true love, cherish them, and provide these things, I truly am lucky; every day I thank God for blessing me with my very own true love.

Classification: In the definition essay, we begin with putting a term into a larger class, or set. This classification is our judgment. It informs the reader of the development of the essay and leads the reader's attitude toward accepting our judgment. For example, "pathological gambling" can either be classified as a self-indulgent sin that may incur harm to others or an addiction that needs treatment rather than punishment. Similarly, classifying a fetus as a human being has profound implications in an argument about abortion. The point is to justify the classification. Love is commonly classified as an emotion, but Erich Fromm classifies it as an "activity" in the sense that the "actor" enjoys complete inner freedom and independence, not motivated by anything else. How would you define "Brand"?

A Logo Is Not a Brand

Dan Pallotta

Lots of organizations come to our company, Advertising for Humanity, asking for "a new brand." They typically mean a new name, or icon, or a new look and feel for their existing name. Lots of people think that brand begins and ends there — that once we shine up the name they can stick it below their email signature, pop it on their website, and, voila[1], they have a new brand. Much of our work consists of disabusing[2] people of this notion.

Brand is much more than a name or a logo. Brand is everything, and everything is brand.

Brand is your strategy. If you're a consumer brand, brand is your products and the story that those products tell together. Ikea's kitchen chairs' tendency to fall apart after two years is part of the company's brand. If you're a humanitarian organization, brand is your aspirations[3] and the progress you are making toward them. Share Our Strength's audacious[4] goal to end child hunger in America in five years is its brand. The work the organization is doing to get governor after governor on board is its brand. Its seriousness is its brand. Back in 1969 NASA[5] didn't have the best logo. But man did it have a brand. It has a nicer logo now — but the brand no longer stands for anything. If you don't know where you're going or how you're going to get there, that's your brand, no matter what fancy new name you come up with.

Brand is your calls to action. If Martin Luther King had offered people free toasters to those who marched on Washington, that would have been his brand. Are your calls to action brave and inspiring or tacky? Are they consistent with some strategy that makes sense? Getting more Facebook "likes" isn't a strategy, in and of itself. If you're a humanitarian organization, the things you ask your

1. voila: *int.* 瞧,那就是(字面意义:see there)
2. disabuse: *v.* 去除……的谬误;使醒悟
3. aspiration: *n.* 志向,抱负
4. audacious: *adj.* 大胆的;敢于冒险的
5. NASA= National Aeronautic and Space Administration 美国国家航空航天局

235

constituents to do are your brand.

Brand is your customer service. If donors call your organization all excited and get caught up in a voicemail[6] tree, can't figure out who they should talk to, and leave a message for someone unsure if it's the right person, that's your brand. It says you don't really care all that much about your donors. If they come to your annual dinner and can't hear the speaker because of a lousy sound system, that's your brand. It says that you don't think it's really important whether they hear what you have to say or not. If the clerk at your checkout counter is admiring her nails and talking on her cell phone, she's your brand, whether she's wearing one of the nice new logo caps you bought or not.

Brand is the way you speak. If you build a new website and fill it with outdated copy, you don't have a new brand. If the copy is impenetrable[7] — a disease of epidemic[8] proportion in the humanitarian sector — that's your brand. If you let social service jargon[9], acronyms[10], and convoluted[11] abstractions contaminate[12] everything you say, that's your brand. If your annual report puts people to sleep, that's your brand. If it's trying to be all things to all people, that's your brand.

Message is a central part of your brand, but message alone cannot make a great brand. How many times have you encountered a product or service that didn't live up to what the copy writers told you about it? That disconnect is your brand.

Brand is the whole array of your communication tools. Brand is the quality of the sign on the door that says, "Back in 10 minutes." It's whether you use a generic[13] voicemail system with canned muzak[14]-on-hold, or whether you create your own custom program. The former says you are just like everyone else and you're fine with that; the latter says you are original. You might have a pretty sale banner that adheres to all the right visual standards, but if it's sagging[15] and hung up with duct[16] tape, that's your brand. It says you don't pay attention to the details. Can you imagine

236

6. voicemail *n.* 语音邮件

7. impenetrable *adj.* 透不过的；费解的
8. epidemic *adj.* 流行性的
9. jargon *n.* 行话
10. acronym *n.* 首字母缩拼词
11. convoluted *adj.* 错综复杂的
12. contaminate *v.* 污染，毒害

13. generic *adj.* 非特有的，普通的
14. muzak *n.* 米尤扎克(一种通过线路向餐馆、商店、工厂等用户播送录制好的背景音乐的广播系统)
15. sag *v.* 萎靡，消沉
16. duct *n.* 波道

seeing a crooked banner with duct tape in an Apple store? Never. And that's their brand. It says that the motherboard[17] in the Mac isn't hanging by a thread either.

In the digital age, user interface[18] is your brand. If your website's functionality frustrates people, it says that you don't care about them. Brand extends even to your office forms, the contracts you send out, your HR manuals. Do you rethink traditional business tools or default to convention? The choice you make says a lot about how innovative your brand is.

Brand is your people. Brand is your people and the way they represent you. Having a good team starts with good hiring and continues with strong and consistent training and development. No matter how well your employees adhere to your new brand style guide, if they couldn't care less about the job they're doing, that's your brand.

Brand is your facilities. Are the lights on, or is your team working in darkness? Is the place clean and uncluttered[19]? Does it have signage[20] that's consistent with your visual standards? Does it look and feel alive? Your home is your brand.

Brand is your logo and visuals, too. A great brand deserves a great logo and great graphic design and visuals. It can make the difference when the customer is choosing between two great brands. But these alone cannot make your brand great.

Ultimately, brand is about caring about your business at every level and in every detail, from the big things like mission and vision, to your people, your customers, and every interaction anyone is ever going to have with you, no matter how small.

Whether you know it or not, whether you have a swanky[21] logo or not, you do have a brand. The question is whether or not it's the brand you really want.

(Harvard Business Review, June 15, 2011
http://blogs.hbr.org/pallotta/2011/06/a-logo-is-not-a-brand.html)

17. motherboard *n.* 母板，主板
18. interface *n.* 界面

19. uncluttered *adj.* 整齐的，整洁的
20. signage *n.* 标记，标志

21. swanky *adj.* 时髦的，华美的

237

Exercise

Provide an argument that develops a definitional claim in the form "X is (is not) a Y."

1) Y is a controversial term with a disputed definition. For the Y term, choose a concept such as "police brutality," "courageous action," "child abuse," "creative act," "cruelty to animals," "free speech," or another, similar concept that is both familiar yet tricky to define precisely. Then the body of the argument should begin with a criteria section, which develops an extended definition of the Y term, articulating at least 3—5 criteria.

2) In the match section, argue that the X (a controversial case) does (does not) meet the criteria for Y. That is, after having established the definition of Y, <u>apply a more specific controversial case to it</u>, arguing whether the case fits or does not fit the definition. You should have at least 3—5 specific matches to the criteria articulated in the general definition.

Comparison: By comparing the subject to something else, it might make it more lucid to the reader. If the topic is Chinese concept of *mianzi*, a comparison of it with the Western idea of face or personal esteem may make the Chinese concept much clearer.

Sample 6

Western Face vs. Chinese Face

Unlike "Western face" —which is more self-oriented and individualistic—Chinese face is more other-directed and relational. In other words, it's less about your own personal pride or ego, and more about how one is viewed by others. Unlike Western face, Chinese face can also be given or earned. It can also be taken away or lost.

As a general sociological statement, Western cultures tend to focus on the individual as an independent, self-reliant being. In raising children, the focus is on helping them develop a strong sense of personal integrity and individuality (misbehavior is often blamed on lack of self-esteem).

In contrast, for some 4,000 years, Chinese culture has downplayed concept of the individual—instead emphasizing the supremacy of the family and group. It was all about bringing honor to your clan. With the emphasis on the collective, the sense of self blurred so much that it practically didn't exist. In fact, individualism was seen as immoral.

The point is that Chinese face can be communally created and owned. In her 2008 study in the Intercultural Communication Studies, "Cultural 'Faces' of Interpersonal Communication in the U.S. and China, " Yvonne Chang of the University of Texas explains:

> Deeply rooted in the Chinese concept of face are conceptualizations of a competent person in Chinese society: one who defines and puts self in relation to others and who cultivates morality so that his or her conduct

will not lose others' face. This contrasts with the American cultural definition of a person who is expected to be independent, self-reliant, and successful. The end result is that a Chinese person is expected to be relationally or communally conscious whereas an American person is expected to be self-conscious.

(http://www.china-mike.com/chinese-culture/understanding-chinese-mind/cult-of-face/)

Examples and Anecdotes: When explaining a very abstract concept, the best way to make your meaning clear is by giving examples. When defining "truth" for instance, a well placed story highlighting the truthfulness of a person may make a greater impact than a theoretical rambling on what truth could or could not mean. The more a writer can exemplify meaning by putting the term into action, the clearer will be the meaning.

Sample 7

Keep Face in China

Gregory Mavrides, PhD

The concept of "face," i.e., *mianzi,* is a very difficult one to explain in a few sentences. It is also impossible to discuss "face" without introducing the related concept of *guanxi,* i.e., "relationship" or social networking. Nevertheless, these two concepts, and how they are expressed in day-to-day life in China, are absolutely essential for foreigners to understand, prior to their arrival, if they are to avoid feeling insulted or disrespected.

A recent study conducted by the ***China Youth Daily*** found that over 93% of the 1,150 respondents surveyed admitted that face is very important to them, with 75% acknowledging that making a mistake in public was, by far, the most humiliating experience they could ever have (Shan, 2005). In other words, most Chinese will do whatever they can to avoid looking bad in public and that often manifests itself in an unwillingness to openly admit to any wrongdoing, no matter how small or insignificant the error might have been. This phenomenon goes a long way in explaining, for example, why the vast majority of Chinese students are so reluctant to voluntarily participate in class or even during less formal activities such

239

as English corners: The fear of making a mistake in front of others is just too overwhelmingly prohibitive.

According to one Asian scholar, Ting-Toomey (1988), "face" is a "trategy that protects self-respect and individual identity. Face saving activities are the rites that protect the individual's role in the *guanxi* network, preserving individual identity and social status" (p. 215). From a Chinese perspective, "lying" to either save or give face is not viewed as a lie at all when it is obvious (to them) that the intent or underlying motivation was never to deceive.

All Westerners use face-saving strategies as narcissistic[1] defenses, i.e., to protect themselves from humiliation, social embarrassment and, to some extent, personal accountability[2]: "Sorry, I was stuck in traffic," or "the check is in the mail," are two commonplace examples. Many suggest, however, that there is a significant difference between Western and Asian cultures in the intention and function of face-saving strategies. Gao and Ting-Toomey (1998) suggest that "while individualist cultures, such as western culture, use *mianzi* to place emphasis on noninclusion[3] (sic) and the creation of individual identity, collectivist cultures focus on inclusion of others and the creation of a collective identity" (p. 137).

What this means, essentially, is that face-saving strategies in the West are almost exclusively intended to protect oneself from narcissistic injury, irrespective of social context, whereas in the East, they are concomitantly[4] intended to preserve and maintain strong social relationships (in what is referred to as "face-giving"). Related, the nature of the face-saving/giving strategy employed, at the time, will vary considerably (unlike in the West) based on one's particular constructed role within the social network.

For example, imagine that a Chinese child accidentally knocks over a vase at home and breaks it. To his friends and distant acquaintances, he might simply say "I didn't do it," but to his

240

1. narcissistic: *adj.* 自恋的
2. accountability *n.* 负有责任
3. noninclusion *n.* 不包括；非内含物
4. concomitantly *adv.* 伴随地

parents, he would mostly likely alter his strategy to something like "I was feeling dizzy at the time and lost my balance. I am sorry I forgot to eat breakfast," so as not to shame them into thinking they raised a careless son. University students notoriously and deliberately "lie" all of the time when completing the teaching evaluations for their professors: "Excellent" means good; "good" means average; and "average" means poor—it's a face-giving strategy which is routinely employed by them and is well-known. (This strategy also saves them face, as it would be a significant loss of face to admit that you had a terrible professor; it might mean you were poorly educated or were unworthy of someone better.)

One of the most poignant[5] and powerful illustrations of this collectivist, inclusive face-saving/giving strategy, I have ever read, is expressed in the following example by Hammond and Glenn (1988, p. 28):

An example of this can be found in a recent Chinese colleague who was awarded a post-doctoral research fellowship in Europe. The colleague, who was studying in Taiwan at the time, passed up the prestigious fellowship. He later revealed that his father was unemployed at the time and he thought accepting the fellowship would deepen his father's shame, disrupt their relationship, and put the family relationships out of balance. "It is important," he said, "for the first son to be ready to assume the role of head of the family when the father is ready to give it up, not before."

In this case, the young Chinese scholar never directly shared his feelings with his father who would have been shocked and shamed by his position. But his father implicitly understood what his son was doing, and deeply appreciated his son's face saving choices.

...

(An excerpt from *Foreign Teachers' Guide to Teaching and Living in China*
http://www.transitionsabroad.com/listings/living/articles/
keeping_face_in_china.shtml)

5.poignant *adj.* 深刻的；尖锐的

241

Origins, Causes and Effects: Discussing the background or origin of a term is a common way for definition. Erich Fromm's definition of respect and responsibility relies on the original meaning of the words. Another writer thus traces the origin of love:

> The origin of the word is probably the most logical place to start. As with many words in the English language, love is a derivative of the Latin word "causemajoraproblemus" which means "You're miserable when you got it and miserable when you don't." The word was created to explain the biological phenomenon that existed when certain individuals came into contact with each other and either remained together or went about their lives separately. Regardless of the outcome, the relationship was usually characteristic of throat lumps, knotted stomachs, weak knees, temporary loss of language, sweaty palms, dizziness, sneezing, and occasional nausea.

Topics such as "Racism" or "Poverty" cannot be truly discussed without describing the effects that they render on the human psyche. Topics such as "Pollution" and "Global warming" lack poignancy if the results and causes are not mentioned.

Sample 8

What Is the Butterfly Effect?

The butterfly effect is a term used in Chaos Theory[1] to describe how tiny variations can affect giant systems, and complex systems, like weather patterns. The term butterfly effect was applied in Chaos Theory to suggest that the wing movements of a butterfly might have significant repercussions[2] on wind strength and movements throughout the weather systems of the world, and theoretically, could cause tornadoes halfway around the world.

What the butterfly effect seems to posit[3], is that the prediction of the behavior of any large system is virtually impossible unless one could account for all tiny factors, which might have a minute[4] effect on the system. Thus large systems like weather remain impossible to predict because there are too many unknown variables to count.

The term "butterfly effect" is attributed to Edward Norton Lorenz, a mathematician and meteorologist[5], who was one of the first proponents of Chaos Theory. Though he had been working on the theory for some ten years, with the principal question as to whether a seagulls' wing movements

Vocabulary

1. Chaos Theory 混沌理论

2. repercussion n. 影响，后果

3. posit v. 假设，设想

4. minute adj. 微小的

5. meteorologist n. 气象学家

changes the weather, he changed to the more poetic butterfly in 1973.

A speech he delivered was titled, "Does the Flap of a Butterfly's Wings in Brazil Set off a Tornado in Texas." Actually, fellow scientist, Philip Merilees created the title. Lorenz had failed to provide a title for his speech.

The concept of small variations producing the butterfly effect actually predates[6] science and finds its home in science fiction. Writers like Ray Bradbury were particularly interested in the types of problems that might occur if one traveled back in time, trailing anachronisms[7]. Could small actions taken in the past dramatically affect the future?

6. predate v. 在日期上早于

7. anachronism n. 时代错误

Fictional treatments of the butterfly effect as applies to time travel are numerous. Many cite the 2005 *Butterfly Effect* film as a good example of the possible negative changes that small behaviors in the past could have on the future, if one could time travel. Actually, a better and more critically accepted treatment of this concept is the 2000 film *Frequency*. In the film a father and son communicate over time through radio waves and attempt to change the past for the good.

In human behavior, one can certainly see how small changes could render behavior, or another complex system, extremely unpredictable. Small actions or experiences stored in the unconscious mind, could certainly affect a person's behavior in unexpected ways.

One looks at teen suicide for example, where no instance of previous depression has occurred. Loved ones are often left wondering what the many small factors were that precipitated a suicide. Further, people often agonize about the small details they did not see as possible factors for an unexpected suicide.

However, there are plenty of ways that such a behavior would be unanswerable according to the butterfly effect. Minute actions and experiences dating from childhood stored in the unconscious mind are not accessible when a person has died,

243

and they may be hard to access without hypnosis[8] or therapy[9] when a person is living.

8. hypnosis *n.* 催眠
9. therapy *n.* 疗法，治疗

Whether used in science, fiction, or social sciences, the butterfly effect remains theory. However, it does seem a reasonable explanation for the unpredictability of events. As it relates to human behavior, it does suggest that even the smallest actions may have huge consequences for good or ill.

(http://www.wisegeek.com/what-is-the-butterfly-effect.htm)

Negation: As a general rule, a definition should not be negative where it can be positive. However, some terms are so obscure that pointing out what it is not may make what it is clearer. Eric Fromm defines love as giving and argues that giving is not giving up or sacrifice.

What is giving? Simple as the answer to this question seems to be, it is actually full of ambiguities and complexities. The most widespread misunderstanding is that which assumes that giving is "giving up" something, being deprived of, sacrificing. The person whose character has not developed beyond the stage of the receptive, exploitative, or hoarding orientation, experiences the act of giving in this way. The marketing character is willing to give, but only in exchange for receiving; giving without receiving for him is being cheated. People whose main orientation is a non-productive one feel giving as an impoverishment. Most individuals of this type therefore refuse to give. Some make a virtue out of giving in the sense of a sacrifice. They feel that just because it is painful to give, one should give; the virtue of giving to them lies in the very act of acceptance of the sacrifice. For them, the norm that it is better to give than to receive means that it is better to suffer deprivation than to experience joy.

For the productive character, giving has an entirely different meaning. Giving is the highest expression of potency. In the very act of giving, I experience my strength, my wealth, my power. This experience of heightened vitality and potency fills me with joy. I experience myself as overflowing, spending, alive, hence as joyous. Giving is more joyous than receiving not because it is a deprivation, but because in the act of giving lies the expression of my aliveness.

There are many ways to explain a term. It is also possible to employ more than one of these methods of development—you may have noticed that in the sample essays. The point is the information you present in the supporting paragraphs is understandable, convincing or interesting. Hazy and uneven details and abstract ramblings will not make a good essay. Just let your wit and imagination run wild to make your essay amusing, poignant, personal and thus memorable to the reader.

Conclusion of the definition essay bears little difference from that of other approaches of development: you can review your main point, refer back to the beginning, or make a plea for action or prediction of the future. For example:

> In conclusion, hemophilia is a genetically inherited disorder which can be defined based on its causes, symptoms and treatment. This disorder is caused by a missing X chromosome or a genetic mutation. Regardless of its cause, hemophilia is characterized by bruises and bleeding. Hemophiliacs generally are treated by receiving blood transfusions and taking medication.

Homework 2

Write the first draft of definition on a topic you have selected. Then ask two of your classmates to edit and revise your first draft. According to their revision, improve the text organization of your first draft applying the writing strategies.

Writer's Checklist

Apply the following ideas to your writing as you work with an extended definition. Later, as a peer editor, apply the same ideas to the material you evaluate.

1. Does your thesis define or only describe the subject?
2. Does your introduction identify the term and its category?
3. Is your purpose, to inform or persuade, clearly stated?
4. Do you provide background information, examples, illustrations, comparisons, classifications, or causes and effects that your readers will understand?
5. Do you rely too much on a single example or description that could be misleading?
6. Are supporting details clearly linked to the thesis?
7. Do you avoid defining a word with the same word, such as inflation inflates the prices of goods and services?
8. Are there existing definitions you can use for reference or contrast?
9. Do you provide readers with a brief thesis statement they can highlight and remember? Does your conclusion summarize your thesis?
10. READ YOUR PAPER ALOUD. How does it sound? Do any sections need expansion? Are there unclear examples or narratives that should be replaced? Does your paper leave readers with a clear definition of your subject or does it just list ideas and observations?

Analysis of Students' Writing

The following is an American college student's definition of charm for the course "Research & Exposition." It is quite a successful definition essay in which special aspects are included, such as the historical background of the term, how to gain the term, the antithesis of the term, and how the term affects others. Effective strategies are employed and specific examples are given. Do you feel charmed? Read the essay carefully and find out.

Charm

"No, don't worry. You just wait right here." says Steve, being the chivalric husband that he is. " I bring the car around so you won't have to walk." He assures his pregnant wife, Mary Lou. Although it is barely drizzling outside and the car is only a few feet away, he insists on pampering her. Later, at home, after Steve safely pulls the car into the drive, he jumps from his seat to open all the necessary doors just for her. Then, he quietly occupies himself cooking lunch for the two of them while waiting eagerly for any calls in need of help.

"Steve? Could you...?" He wastes no time in rushing to Mary Lou's side and removing a box from the top shelf or taking the clean laundry out of the dryer, efficiently completing whatever task she asks of him in this instance.

Kind, considerate Steve is a delightful example of someone who possesses the quality of charm. A characteristic of an agreeable, endearing, magnetic personality, charm is particularly attractive to others and can be used to profit its beholder with both positive and negative consequences for those around him.

Historically, charm is a characteristic that has been present since the beginning of time. In the Garden of Eden, the serpent used his convincing, enchanting personality to persuade Adam and Eve to eat the forbidden fruit. Since that time, charm has not changed extremely, although it was somewhat more commonly seen throughout society in the past. Unlike today, many people used to take great concern in being proper and respectable to others. Especially important to young gentlemen courting and winning over ladies, were proper manners and chivalry. Take Prince Charming for example. These concepts were much more commonplace in the past, but today, people do not take as much pride in looking presentable and being classy. Daily sleaze seems to have taken over our society, leaving charm rather obsolete. Also, charm was once thought of merely in romantic means, whereas today, a person with a charming personality can use his appeal to get superior jobs, to be successful in doing business, or to receive a favor. Today, charm is more multifaceted.

For the most part, people who are charming are born naturally so. From birth, a charmer is blessed with this useful trait and quickly learns to use it to his benefit. In some cases, those who are not fortunate enough to simply be supplied with abundant amounts of charm can personally create their own characteristics of it. By conscientiously working to be aware of his actions and mannerisms, one can feign charming characteristics quite successfully. He needs only to attentively act in a charming manner. This ability can often be seen in presidential candidates. A person running for office works specifically to create an image of himself that appeals to voters. He wants to charm them into thinking that he is the perfect person to lead the nation, thus compelling them to vote for him. With the correct pleasant, dazzling smile and thoughtful, selfless words, any person can turn on the instant charm.

While charm is often thought of as a human characteristic, it most certainly exists outside of the human realm also. Animals especially have the potential to possess significant amounts of charm. An adorable, purring kitten rubbing against his owner's ankles emits enough charm to attain anything his feline heart could desire. In a related scenario, the golden retriever who sleeps invitingly in front of a fireplace is the essence of charm. Charm is even used when one describes an object such as a country cottage, an event such as a simple weekend trip, or even a musical piece.

Contrary to these gains, charm can also be easily lost. Just as simply as a charming attitude may be composed by acting kindly and thoughtfully toward others, charm can be lost by acting poorly. There is nothing charming about a person who is uncaring and egotistical. Even the personality of one who is born charming can change over time, causing him to lose the alluring characteristics he once possessed. Although a young person may dazzle anyone he encounters, his character may change with age and he can become dull and repulsing as an adult. It is possible for a person's persona to change in this way due to any number of reasons. A personal traumatic event or experience can leave a once pleasant person with a cold, depressed demeanor. Even stress and daily routine can cause charisma to fizzle and leave people tiring and lackluster. Charm may also become old, precariously balancing on the edge of lovability and obnoxiousness. What seems to be a gracious gesture or charismatic attitude at one point in time can quickly become mere annoyance and aggravation. Thus, just as readily as it is acquired, charm is exhausted.

Frequently, charm is a very beneficial personality quality for any person to have. A charming person has the valuable ability to manipulate any situation to his advantage. For example, a charmer may be the enchanting teenage student who never does his schoolwork and only causes disruption, but is inexplicably the teacher's pet. In another instance, the young man who leads a fairly ordinary, mediocre life still wins over multitudes of companions with his dazzling persona. Thus, a charmer can use his unique abilities in both positive and negative ways. Nearly everyone swoons over charm; everyone loves an amiable person. Consequently, such a

247

person captivates people to his benefit. In the positive aspect, charming people usually gain many friends and companions, high job positions, and general happiness. Negatively, one with charming traits uses them to his own assistance at a disadvantage to others. For instance, a flirtatious, charming young man can use his influence to allure women and use them. The world is like putty in the hand of a charming person. He can use his control to mold it into anything he likes, good or bad.

In closing, agreeable, endearing, and magnetic all describe the aspects of charm. The power of a person who possesses a charming personality may be greatly used to his benefit, but is often used at the expense of those around him in order to do so. Having existed as long as time, the concept of charm has not changed tremendously, but the effort put into a charming personality has deteriorated. The amount of charm possessed by a person is decided by he, himself. As a result, it can be gained or lost. People who do have these endearing traits gain a great deal from them in many different ways. Henri Frédéric Amiel said, "Charm is the quality in others that makes us more satisfied with ourselves." It is this truth that makes charm such a powerfully attractive, significant part of the lives of many.

(http://www.angelfire.com/oh4/meganssite/w-REdefinitionessay.html)

Homework 3

Try to improve your definition essay and write the third draft.

Further Reading

Passage 1

The Meaning of Home

John Berger

The term *home* (Old Norse *Heimer*, High German *heim*, Greek *komi*, meaning "village") has, since a long time, been taken over by two kinds of moralists, both dear to those who wield power. The notion of *home* became the keystone for a code of domestic morality, safeguarding the property (which included the women) of the family. Simultaneously the notion of *homeland* supplied a first article of faith for patriotism, persuading men to die in wars which often served no other interest except that of a minority of their ruling class. Both usages have hidden the original meaning.

Originally home meant the center of the world—not in a geographical, but in an ontological sense. Mircea Eliade has demonstrated how home was the place from which the world could be *founded*. A home was established, as he says, "at the heart of the real."

In traditional societies, everything that made sense of the world was real; the surrounding chaos existed and was threatening, but it was threatening because it was *unreal*. Without a home at the center of the real, one was not only shelterless, but also lost in nonbeing, in unreality. Without a home everything was fragmentation.

Home was the center of the world because it was the place where a vertical line crossed with a horizontal one. The vertical line was a path leading upwards to the sky and downwards to the underworld. The horizontal line represented the traffic of the world, all the possible roads leading across the earth to other places. Thus, at home, one was nearest to the gods in the sky and to the dead of the underworld. This nearness promised access to both. And at the same time, one was at the starting point and, hopefully, the returning point of all terrestrial journeys.

Passage 2

Have a Nice Day
Thomas H. Middleton

Shortly after the great Los Angeles fire disaster last year, we met Gordon Jenkins and his wife, Beverly. The Jenkinses had lived in one of the oldest and most charming houses on Broad Beach Road in Malibu. Broad Beach was one of the areas most severely affected by the fire.

Mr. Jenkins told me that when the fire leaped down the hills and started blazing across the street from their home, and the smoke billowed in, they were forced to leave. They drove to a motel and checked in for the night. Early the next morning, they went back home. Only their garage, made of cement, was intact. When they went around the garage to where their house had stood the day before, they found only ashes. They had lived in the house for over 31 years.

They went back to the motel for what I suspect was a crushingly dismal breakfast.

On their return to where they had lived, they found that the police were blocking off the street. The policeman who stopped them told them no one but residents could enter the area. Mr. Jenkins told him that he was a resident, or that at any rate he had been a resident, his house having burned to the ground the day before. The cop checked his driver's license and waved them through, calling "Have a nice day!"

They got about 200 feet down the road before the "Have a nice day" sank all the way in and their gales of laughter burst out. Surely, no other phrase could have made Gordon and Beverly laugh all the way to the ashes of their home. That mindless pleasantry brightened a dark day.

"Have a nice day" is universal these days, at least in this part of the country. It is said constantly by supermarket checkers, filling-station attendants, receptionists and just about everyone else who deals regularly with the public.

My own feeling is that it is a pleasant enough pleasantry. I grant that "Have a nice day" probably helps no more than my wife's admonition, "Don't fall down." That's what Jeannie says whenever I'm standing on a narrow ledge or a stepladder. I'd do my best not to fall down even if she didn't tell me not to. Still, it's good to know that she cares.

There is a difference between "Have a nice day" and "Don't fall down" in that the person who tells me to have a nice day may not be sincerely concerned over what kind of day I'll have, whereas if I should fall off the ladder, Jennie's day could be seriously flawed.

Years before I heard "Have a nice day," I was in the habit of telling people to have a good time, and I always meant it sincerely, for whatever good it might do. I remember long ago when I used to drive young Tom to school on those infrequent days when he'd miss the bus or the weather would be particularly foul. As I dropped him off, I always said, "Have a good time," and he always said, "Thanks," until one day, after my customary "Have a good time," he turned rather peevishly and said "Geez, I'm going to school!"

I said, "I know. Have a good time while you're learning something, or learn something while you're having a good time. They're not mutually exclusive." He brightened and said, "Hey, right! Thanks!"

I think "Have a nice day" provides one of those little indications that we do care, even if only slightly, about one another's welfare. It has taken its place for a time in the storehouse of phrases we use for civility's sake, and on at least one occasion it brought unexpected laughter in a time of heavy tragedy.

"Have a nice day!"

Passage 3

What Is Poverty?
Jo Goodwin Parker

You ask me what is poverty? Listen to me. Here I am, dirty, smelly, and with no "proper" underwear on and with the stench of my rotting teeth near you. I will tell you. Listen to me. Listen without pity. I cannot use your pity. Listen with understanding. Put yourself in my dirty, worn out, ill-fitting shoes, and hear me.

Poverty is getting up every morning from a dirt- and illness-stained mattress. The sheets have long since been used for diapers. Poverty is living in a smell that never leaves. This is a smell of urine, sour milk, and spoiling food sometimes joined with the strong smell of long-cooked onions. Onions are cheap. If you have smelled this smell, you did not know how it came. It is the smell of the outdoor privy. It is the smell of young children who cannot walk the long dark way in the night. It is the smell of the mattresses where years of "accidents" have happened. It is the smell of the milk which has gone sour because the refrigerator long has not worked, and it costs money to get it fixed. It is the smell of rotting garbage. I could bury it, but where is the shovel? Shovels cost money.

Poverty is being tired. I have always been tired. They told me at the hospital when the last baby came that I had chronic anemia caused from poor diet, a bad cause of worms, and that I needed a corrective operation. I listened politely—the poor are always polite. The poor always listen. They don't say that there is no money for iron pills, or better food, or worm medicine. The idea of an operation is frightening and costs so much that, if I had dared, I would have laughed. Who takes care of my children? Recovery from an operation takes a long time. I have three children. When I left them with "Granny" the last time I had a job, I came home to find the baby covered with fly specks, and a diaper that had not been changed since I left. When the dried diaper came off, bits of my baby's flesh came with it. My other child was playing with a sharp bit of broken glass, and my oldest was playing alone at the edge of a lake. I made twenty-two dollars a week, and a good nursery school costs twenty dollars a week for three children. I quit my job.

Poverty is dirt. You can say in your clean clothes coming from your clean house, "Anybody can be clean." Let me explain about housekeeping with no money. For breakfast I give my children grits with no oleo or cornbread without eggs and oleo. This does not use up many dishes. What dishes there are, I wash in cold water and with no soap. Even the cheapest soap has to be saved for the baby's diapers. Look at my hands, so cracked and red. Once I saved for two months to buy a jar of Vaseline for my hands and the baby's diaper rash. When I had saved enough, I went to buy it and the price had gone up two cents. The baby and I suffered on. I have to decide every day if I can bear to put my cracked sore hands into the cold water and strong soap. But you ask, why not hot water? Fuel cost money. If you have a wood fire it costs money. If you burn electricity, it costs money. Hot water is a luxury. I do not have luxuries. I know you will be surprised when I tell you how young I am. I look so much older. My back has been bent over the wash tubs every day for so long, I can not remember when I ever did anything else. Every night I wash every stitch my school age child has on and just hope her clothes will be dry by morning.

Poverty is staying up all night on cold nights to watch the fire knowing one spark on the newspaper covering the walls means your sleeping child dies in flames. In summer poverty is watching gnats and flies devour your baby's tears when he cries. The screens are torn and you pay so little rent you know they will never be fixed. Poverty means insects in your food, in your nose, in your eyes, and crawling over you when you sleep. Poverty is hoping it never rains because diapers won't dry when it rains and soon you are using newspapers. Poverty is seeing your children forever with runny noses. Paper handkerchiefs cost money and all your rags you need for other things. Even more costly are antihistamines. Poverty is cooking without food and cleaning without soap.

Poverty is asking for help. Have you ever had to ask for help, knowing your children will suffer unless you get it? Think about asking for a loan form a relative, if this is the only way you can imagine asking for help. I will tell you how it feels. You find out where the office is that you are supposed to visit. You circle that block four or five times. Thinking of your children, you go in. Everyone is very busy. Finally, someone comes out and you tell her that you need help. That never is the person you need to see. You go see another person, and after spilling the whole shame of your poverty all over the desk between you, you find that this isn't the right office after all—you must repeat the whole process, and it never is any easier at the next place.

You have asked for help, and after all it has a cost. You are again told to wait. You are told why, but you don't really hear because of the red cloud of shame and the rising cloud

251

of despair.

Poverty is remembering. It is remembering quitting school in junior high because "nice" children had been so cruel about my clothes and my smell. The attendance officer came. My mother told him I was pregnant. I wasn't, but she thought that I could get a job and help out. I had jobs off and on, but never long enough to learn anything. Mostly I remember being married. I was so young then. I am still young. For a time, we had all the things we have. There was a little house in another town, with hot water and everything. Then my husband lost his job. There was unemployment insurance for a while and what few jobs I could get. Soon, all our nice things were repossessed and we moved back here. I was pregnant then. This house didn't look so bad when we first moved in. Every week it gets worse. Nothing is ever fixed. We now had no money. There were a few odd jobs for my husband, but everything went for food then, as it does now. I don't know how we lived through three years and three babies, but we did. I'll tell you something, after the last baby I destroyed my marriage. It had been a good one, but could you keep on bringing children in this dirt? Did you ever think how much it costs for any kind of birth control? I knew my husband was leaving the day he left, but there were no goodbyes between us. I hope he has been able to climb out of this mess somewhere. He never could hope with us to drag him down.

That's when I asked for help. When I got it, you know how much it was? It was, and is seventy-eight dollars a month for the four of us; that is all I ever can get. Now you know why there is no soap, no needles and thread, no hot water, no aspirin, no worm medicine, no hand cream, no shampoo. None of these things forever and ever and ever. So that you can see clearly, I pay twenty dollars a month rent, and most of the rest goes for food. For grits and cornmeal, and rice and milk and beans. I try my best to use only the minimum electricity. If I use more, there is that much less for food.

Poverty is looking into a black future. Your children won't play with my boys. They will turn to other boys who steal to get what they want. I can already see them behind the bars of their prison instead of behind the bars of my poverty. Or they will turn to the freedom of alcohol or drugs, and find themselves enslaved. And my daughter? At best, there is for her a life like mine.

But you say to me, there are schools. Yes, there are schools. My children have no extra books, no magazines, no extra pencils, or crayons, or paper and most important of all, they do not have health. They have worms, they have infections, they have pink-eye all summer. They do not sleep well on the floor, or with me in my one bed. They do not suffer from hunger, my seventy-eight dollars keeps us alive, but they do suffer from malnutrition. Oh yes, I do remember what I was taught about health in school. It doesn't do much good. In some places there is a surplus commodities program. Not here. The country said it cost too much. There is a school lunch program. But I have two children who will already be damaged by the time they get to school.

But, you say to me, there are health clinics. Yes, there are health clinics and they are in the towns. I live out here eight miles from town. I can walk that far (even if it is sixteen miles both ways), but can my little children? My neighbor will take me when he goes; but he expects to get paid, one way or another. I bet you know my neighbor. He is that large man who spends his time at the gas station, the barbershop, and the corner store complaining about the government spending money on the immoral mothers of illegitimate children.

Poverty is an acid that drips on pride until all pride is worn away. Poverty is a chisel that chips on honor until honor is worn away. Some of you say that you would do something in my situation, and maybe you would, for the first week or the first month, but for year after year after year?

Even the poor can dream. A dream of a time when there is money. Money for the right kinds of food, for worm medicine, for iron pills, for toothbrushes, for hand cream, for a hammer and nails and a bit of screening, for shovel, for a bit of paint, for some sheeting, for needles and thread. Money to pay in money for a trip to town. And, oh, money for hot water and money for soap. A dream of when asking for help does not eat away the last bit of pride. When the office you visit is as nice as the offices of other governmental agencies, when there are enough workers to help you quickly, when workers do not quit in defeat and despair. When you have to tell your story to only one person, and that person can send you for other help and you don't have to prove your poverty over and over and over again.

I have come out of my despair to tell you this. Remember I did not come from another place or another time. Others like me are all around you. Look at us with an angry heart, anger that will help you help me. Anger that will let you tell of me. The poor are always silent. Can you be silent too?

Letters and Notes

In spite of all the convenience of advanced technology such as the mobile phone, email, wiki, micro blog, virtual communities, etc., we need to write a hard copy letter or note every now and then to communicate something to another person or a group of people. There are times when sending a real, hard copy letter in the mail is not only the proper and polite thing to do, but it is just "the" correct thing to do. As social creatures, we still need to feel in touch with other people and to be touched with tangible communication. We want to hold on to something as evidence for care and concern! We want to see or to show handwriting! As a "social observance," letter writing is subject to rules or formats to be followed. These rules are extremely important in business letters.

Business Letters

Business letters deal with official or public matters. The purpose is to get or give information, to obtain something that one wants from someone else, to persuade or to negotiate. Business letters are of many different kinds, and their level of formality varies according to the particular circumstances and the type of relationship that exists between the writer and the addressee. However, they should always be polite, specific, accurate, brief and clear. The writer may represent himself/herself or an organization. Business letters have the following major parts:

1. The heading: Where the stationery does not have a letterhead, the heading, also known as the return address, includes the writer's name, address, postal code and optionally, phone number and email address. Each line of the writer's return address starts at the same margin, and there is no punctuation at the end of them.

2. Date: Where the stationery has a letterhead, the date should be typed two to six (normally three) lines below the letterhead; where the stationery does not have a letterhead, the date should be typed below the heading.

3. Reference line: If the recipient specifically requests information, such as a job reference or invoice number, the information is typed on one or two lines, immediately below the Date. In reply to a letter, the reference is typed immediately below the Date.

4. The inside address: The name and address of the organization to which the letter is addressed. Whenever possible, the inside address should include the name of a particular employee or department within the organization. The inside address is placed at the left margin.

5. <u>The salutation</u>: Usually beginning with "Dear Mr., Mrs., Miss, or Ms.", followed by the addressee's title and last name. In case the addressee's name is not available, a general greeting like "Dear Sir or Madam, To Whom It May Concern" may be used. The salutation starts at the left margin of the page and is followed by a colon in a business letter.

6. <u>The body</u>: Detailed but brief and to the point explanation of the business. The body begins on the line following the salutation. The opening paragraph of a letter should state the purpose of the letter. The middle paragraph(s) should explain the details, beginning a new paragraph for each main point. The closing paragraph should state the course of action needed or repeat the purpose of the letter. This part is normally typed in double space. Most business letters are brief and don't run over one page.

7. <u>The complimentary close</u>: Such expressions as "Sincerely yours (formal), Sincerely (typical), Very truly yours (polite, neutral), or Cordially yours (friendly, not very formal)," are often used, followed by a comma. The closing is written on the line below the last line of the body. The first word of the closing should align with the first words of the heading.

8. <u>The signature</u>: The writer of the letter signs his/her name below the closing. Leave four blank lines for the signature before typing the writer's name.

255

A business letter usually takes the block form or the indented form. In the block form, every part of the letter begins at the left margin. A blank line is left between paragraphs. In the indented form, the heading, closing, and signature are kept at the right side of the page. Paragraphs are indented and no extra space is kept between them.

 ## The Block Format

The Indented Format

The style of the letter varies depending on who it is addressed to. Register is another important thing. The writer should always bear in mind who (s)he is talking to and how this should affect the "tone" of the letter. As with all writing, the writer should always have the audience in mind. Too formal letters may alienate many readers and too casual letters may seem insincere or less than profession.

Tips for a few types of business letters:

Letters Asking for/Giving Information

• Their style can be either formal or informal.

Introduction

Paragraph 1: Appropriate opening remarks. State the purpose of the letters. If you are responding to an advertisement, say where you saw it.

Main Body

Paragraph 2: Make a specific request for information or give the appropriate information.

Paragraph 3: Finish the letter politely (offering to send any more information required if it is a letter *giving* information).

Conclusion

Appropriate closing remarks.

Letters of Complaint

- Letters of complaint are normally written in a formal style.
- Mild or strong language can be used depending on the feelings of the writer or the seriousness of the complaint, but abusive language must never be used.

Introduction

Paragraph 1: Appropriate opening remarks. State the purpose of the letter and give enough detail for the reader to understand the correct nature of the complaint.

Main Body

Paragraph 2: Give all the detail(s) of the complaint. Make sure you include all necessary dates, times. People involved, the inconvenience you faced, etc.

Paragraph 3: State what you would like to be done about the matter. Suggest actions to be taken.

Conclusion

Use appropriate closing remarks.

Letters of Application

- A formal letter of application is written when applying for a job, a scholarship, enrolment in an educational institution for further study, etc.
- A letter of application for a job should be similar in style to the advertisement; that is, if the job advertisement is written in a less formal style, the letter could also be written in a less formal style. On the other hand, if the job advertisement is written in a formal style, the letter must be formal, too.
- Advertisements for temporary jobs (holiday or summer jobs) may be written in a less formal style. A letter of application for such a job may not include extensive reference to experience, qualifications or skills.

Introduction

Paragraph 1: Appropriate opening remarks. State the reason for writing. In applying for a job, mention the position you would like to apply for and where and when you were informed about the vacancy.

Main Body

Paragraph 2: Give details of qualifications, present / past employment, qualities and skills and any other details required or you consider relevant.

Paragraph 3: In applying for a job, express your interest and eligibility for the job and give your present / past employers' opinions of you. When applying for a scholarship, in addition to your eligibility, express how important the scholarship is to you. Use appropriate closing remarks.

Conclusion

State that you are willing to attend an interview and look forward to a favourable reply.

258

Cover Letters

If you apply for a job that requires you to submit a resume, you should include a cover letter with your resume and application. The purpose of the cover letter is to:

- introduce yourself to the employer;
- indicate which position you are applying for;
- explain why you are interested in that specific position;
- direct their attention toward information on your resume that is of particular relevance to the position.

Tips for writing cover letters:

- Modify your letter to fit the company or institution and their needs. Include any information appropriate to the job or course you are applying for.
- Show concern, interest, and pride for your profession and your skills, or your interest and qualifications for the course.
- State briefly what is enclosed. If there are several items, list them. Keep the letter simple and to the point. Tell the truth. Don't try to be overly friendly, but don't be too remote either.
- Include your telephone number or numbers where you can be contacted. When writing the letter, address the person you are sending it to, not to a title.
- Indicate any response you are expecting from the company. Ask for the next step, such as an interview or some other meeting.

Tips for writing resumes:

- Include your name, address and phone number.

- Describe your work experience, education, honors/awards and skills.
- You do not need to include every single job you have ever had. You should focus on your education and experiences that are related to the position for which you are applying.
- Tell the truth. Show that you are confident and well-educated.
- Your layout and word choice should be clear and simple.
- Avoid attempts at humor and irrelevant or unnecessary information.
- Do not mention salary on your resume.

 ## Sample Cover Letter

Andy Li

Batch 11109, School of English, Tianjin Foreign Studies University
117 Machang Road, Tianjin, 300204, China
(86) -22-2328-1111
andyli@tjfsu.edu.cn

10 March, 2012

John Janssen
Personnel Manager
ABC Company
118, East Changcheng St.
Beijing, 100369

Dear Mr. Janssen:

I was excited to see your advertisement on March 8, 2012 in *China Daily* for a summer intern. An internship with your company would be a perfect opportunity to develop my skills as a double major of English and Business at Tianjin Foreign Studies University.

My professional capabilities would make me an asset to your company. For example, my experience as intern with Arch Electronics Inc. and part-time producer at Happy. Net adequately prepares me for the promotional work at ABC this summer.

I would greatly benefit from working with knowledgeable professionals in my field of study, and working for ABC would provide such an opportunity.

I would love to be part of your team. I am available to meet with you at your earliest convenience.

Thank you for your consideration.

Sincerely,

Andy Li

Andy Li

259

Sample Resume

Andy Li

Batch 11109, School of English, Tianjin Foreign Studies University

117 Machang Road, Tianjin, 300204, China

(86) -22-2328-1111

andyli@tjfsu.edu.cn

Education:

2010—
School of English, Tianjin Foreign Studies University Tianjin, China
Study guide for Batch11109
Founder: Campus & Wudadao Tour English Service Club
Member: TFSU Volunteer Association; Tennis Club

Experience:

Summer 2012
Arch Electronics Inc.—a mobile phone & electronic dictionary company
Summer Intern   Tianjin, China
- Initiated, designed and developed 3-day sales training program targeting 10% sales increase.
- Re-evaluated potential market size and identified inconsistencies of over 5% that contributed to overall strategy realignment. New strategy expected to capture additional 15% market revenue.
- Outlined multiple internal and external communication strategies currently under consideration and expected to increase efficiency and enlarge market share.

2011—2012
Happy.Net
Part-time Producer—The Internet Zone and Marketing Analyst
- Redesigned point-of-sales ("POS") sales strategy and structure to increase sales by 7%.
- Created, produced, and co-hosted a weekly 2-hour online interview about Happy.Net.
- Established a key sponsor (Angel's Airlines) and solicited a donation of RMB 500,000.

Awards:
Scholarship of Tianjin Municipal Government, 2012.
Distinguished Volunteer for the 9th National University Games, 2012.
1st Prize Scholarship, Tianjin Foreign Studies University, 2011.

Interests:
Tennis, swimming, travelling, classical music

Avoid using adjectives and adverbs. Use powerful or unusual nouns and verbs instead. Don't make the resume too wordy. Try to use as few words as possible and still make it effective. Most resumes shouldn't be more than one page, particularly for college students, unless the person has several years of experience (10+ years) in the field.

Follow-up Letters

Tips for writing follow-up letters:

- A follow-up letter after a job interview provides an opportunity for you to further clarify anything you desire and may sway the interviewer's opinion in your favor. This letter should state how much you enjoyed the interview, how much you like the job and how much you are willing to provide additional information or references.
- Mention your reason for writing the letter. Use phrases like, "I haven't heard from you, so I thought I would contact you again to see..."
- If you are confirming an appointment, make sure you refer to the date, time, location and subject of the meeting. "I wanted to confirm our meeting time at 2:00 pm on Tuesday, November 16th for a talk about..."
- If this is a second follow-up letter, and you have not yet received a response from your original letter, include a copy of it with your new letter, or repeat the message. Emphasize the importance of his/her response.
- When writing your letter, avoid negative remarks. Do not imply that the reader is thoughtless, forgetful, or negligent. If you make the reader feel defensive, they will not be likely to respond in a positive manner.

Acceptance Letters

Tips for writing acceptance letters:

- Start your letter by simply thanking the company for the job offer. Keep the letter as brief as possible, do not go overboard with gratitude. Do not mention anything about salary. Save that for the phone call or the initial meeting.
- Unless they have already informed you, ask them when you can meet again for orientation or review. If the job is out of town, ask how soon you can relocate. You may also want to ask if they will provide any accommodations until you have the opportunity to find your own place.

(From http://www.aueb.gr/lessons and http://depts.gallaudet.edu/englishworks,etc.)

[H]omework 1

Write to the admission officer of a real university in one of the English speaking countries, tell the person about your interest of pursuing further study in a certain discipline and ask the person to send you forms of application and other documents you deem as necessary.

Personal Letters & Notes

Personal letters are those that concern the writer as an individual person rather than a social role and those that are not written to businesses. Generally speaking, personal letters can be much less formal than business letters. However, formality of personal letters varies from intimate to very formal depending on the relationship between the writer and the addressee. Whereas intimate letters do not have to follow many rules, social letters—those between people who are not intimately related or those written on formal occasions, have certain standards. Major differences between a personal letter and a business letter include:

1. A personal letter doesn't have the inside address.
2. The salutation "Dear" in a personal letter is followed by the addressee's first name, which in turn can be followed by a comma if the letter is not very formal.
3. The closing may be much less formal with such words as "Yours / Love / Best Wishes / Regards" etc.
4. The writer of a personal letter usually signs his/her first name.

Another important way of sharing appreciation, respect or information with people around us is through short notes. As short notes are passed or left directly to the addressee without going through the mail, they are usually handwritten and less formal than letters. However, the five essential parts of personal letters, date (day), salutation (greeting), body, closing (regards) and signature, are also normally indispensable in short notes.

1. The date (day) can be put at the upper right hand, or traditionally, at the end, and to the left of the signature, of a note. The day (like "Thursday"), is sufficient unless the note is an invitation for more than a week ahead, in which case the date (like "January 9" or "the ninth of January"), should be used. The year is not necessary since it can hardly be supposed to take a year for the addressee to read the note.
2. The salutation (greeting) often mentions the addressee's first name, such as "Dear Mike, Dear Aunt Sally (or Aunt Sally), Dear JellyBean (nickname), Hi, Miss Red Nose," followed by a comma, or a colon in a business note.
3. The closing (regards) of a note depends on how well the writer knows the addressee. Many use "Love," "Yours," "Warmly," "Fondly," etc.
4. The first name will be enough for the signature in personal notes.

Whatever the occasion is, notes should be clear, concise and polite. The body of notes usually begins with direct expression for the definite purpose and closes with politeness. The following are some typical types of personal letters and notes.

1. Letters and Notes of Invitation

We write a letter or note to someone for an action of some sort: to visit a place, to attend a social gathering or entertainment, to make a contribution and so on. Invitation notes range from the casual to formal occasions.

Tips for writing invitations:

- State the occasion, date, time, and place. Include addresses and a map if necessary. Mention if refreshments will be served. Include a telephone number for RSVPs [the French phrase "Répondez s'il vous plaît" ("reply, please")]. If there is a dress code, state it in the lower left-hand corner of the card.
- If you need a response, include a self-addressed, stamped reply card or envelope with your invitation.
- Do not use abbreviations and do not use contractions (don't; we'll) except for name titles, such as Mr., Mrs., etc.
- If dinner will be served, state two separate times: the time people can start arriving and the time dinner will be served.
- Make sure you send your invitations out with ample advance notice.
- If you are inviting someone to speak at a conference, your invitation should include the following information:
  * Name of the conference and the sponsoring organization;
  * Date, time place of the conference and speech;
  * Type of audience;
  * The type of speech, topic, and how long the speech should be;
  * Any accommodations that will be made, including lodging, meals, and transportation;
  * The name of the contact person along with phone numbers and addresses where the person can be contacted; and
  * Articulate your pleasure of having the person speak at the meeting.

 Expressions for Notes of Invitations

We are wondering if you could come to dine with us on Thursday, July 1st, 7:00 p.m.
We would like to invite you to my daughter's birthday party.
We are hoping that you can take part in the dance held on Friday evening, Oct. 4th, at nine o'clock.
We have the honor of inviting Mr. Tone to our reception.
I've asked a few friends to stop by after work on Monday, Aug. 12th. Can you join us?
I am looking forward to seeing you.
I request the pleasure of your company.
We hope nothing will prevent you from coming, as we are waiting for your visit.
It will be so good to see you again.
I hope you can join us.

A Sample Letter of Invitation

December 1, 2012

Carla and family:

My 21st birthday falls on December 21st and I am counting the days of happiness. I am waiting for my friends and family to gather at my home on December 21st and shower wishes on me. On this special occasion, I cordially invite you and your family to be present with me. Your presence will be most eagerly awaited. Looking forward to seeing you on that day. The details of time and venue are given below.

Yours lovingly,

Benne Dickson

11:30am to 2:00 pm
2012, Maya Avenue
Washington D.C.

A Sample Note Inviting Close Friends to Dinner and the Theater

Oct. 18th

Dear Ann,

We have four seats for Arthur Miller's <u>The Crucible</u> at Binhai Theater this Saturday, the 23rd. Will you and Paul join us here for dinner at seven sharp, and then go on with us later to the play? We'll be looking for you Saturday evening, so don't disappoint us!

Yours,
Catherine

Exercise

During the summer vacation you would like to invite your best friend to your hometown. Write a letter/note to him/her, extending your invitation and telling him/her when and where you will meet.

2. Letters and Notes of Appointments

A schedule puts a person's work and life in order, so a letter/note of appointment is necessary if we plan to visit or see some people. A letter/note of appointment should include a request and reasons, the available date, time, place, the writer's address or phone number, and appreciation for the addressee's concern. If the writer desires to change or postpone an appointment, he/she should restate the appointed time and place, make a new appointment, apologize and ask the addressee to confirm the new time and place. If the writer has to cancel an appointment, he/she repeats the appointed time and place, states the necessary reasons and apologizes.

Expressions for Notes Making an Appointment

I will be glad to meet with you in ... on ..., at ... to ...
If you are unable to make the meeting on ..., please let me know.
I will appreciate ... of your time ... to ....
I'll give you a call ... to ... if you can schedule a meeting with me.
Let me know as soon as possible if this is convenient for you.

Expressions for Notes Changing an Appointment

I am unfortunately obliged to change the date we set earlier.
Can we change our meeting on ... from ... to ...?
I'll be on a business trip and unable to meet you on ...at ...

Sample Notes of Appointment

265

Dec. 28th

Dear Lisa,

I have got two tickets to the old film <u>Gone with the Wind</u> at the new cinema near your home. Please meet me at the Children Park on Sunday afternoon, at 4. After the film, we may dine out in a restaurant. If you can't come, call me as soon as possible or leave a message in my mail box.

Yours,
Paul

Feb. 28th

Nancy,

I am sorry to tell you I have to postpone our appointment at 4 o'clock tomorrow afternoon, because I have to meet my sister at the airport at 5. Shall we discuss the matter at 4 p.m. the day after tomorrow? If it isn't convenient for you, please ring me to make another time. Thanks a lot.

Yours,
Jim

March 1st

Dear Karl,

I have to cancel the meeting we set on for Thursday, March 6th, at 10 p.m., because we have got a little trouble on the farm, so I have to go there to handle the problem. I should be back on March 10th and will call you then to set up another appointment.

Thank you for your understanding.

Sincerely yours,
Jim

Exercise

Write a note to make an appointment. You would like to discuss some problems of culture differences with your professor Mr. Green and ask him to arrange the time.

3. Letters and Notes of Request and Inquiry

A letter/note of inquiry is written to obtain information or to make a request. The note begins with a request of some sort (for action, for something, for permission) and continues with the reason or explanations for the request. The request should be direct, specific, and most of all, reasonable. An inquiry requiring clerical help, for example, should be accompanied by an offer to pay for the expenses involved.

Expressions for Letters/notes of Request/Inquiry
Acquiring Information

I would like to acquire information relative to your MA program.

Can you direct me to the appropriate agency/provide us with details about the project?

I wonder if you could give us an explanation of the bill.

Is there any chance of your giving information to me?

Would it be possible for you to send me an application form?

I am very interested in learning more about your company.

Expressing Expectation/Appreciation

We eagerly anticipate a favorable response from you.

I hope to hear from you as soon as possible.

I look forward to hearing from you soon.

Any information you may provide will be greatly appreciated.

I would appreciate your help/I would be very grateful to you if you could ...

Many thanks for any information you can send me.

A Sample Note of Request and Inquiry

> Oct. 29th
>
> Dear Parker,
>
> This morning I met Orin and he said you wished to sell your laptop. I don't know why you want to dispose it, but I'd like to buy it for my further study if possible. Will you please let me know about its present condition, specific functions and its price?
>
> I will appreciate your answer.
>
> Yours truly,
>
> Owen

4. Message Notes

Message notes are written when you leave some information to someone, such as asking someone to call, to return something or to do something for you, or telling someone that something has been scheduled, finished or canceled, or telling someone where someone else or something is, or borrowing something from someone. On these occasions, you leave a direct, brief but detailed, casual message to the person.

A sample message note introducing a vacancy to your friend:

> April 11
>
> Dear George,
>
> Yesterday I read on the notice board that our university library is looking for a part-time library assistant who can work at weekends. I know you've been looking for a part-time job, so I'm writing to tell you about the vacancy. I think you're the right person for the post, since you meet all the listed requirements. I suggest that you go for an interview.
>
> Wish you good luck.
>
> Yours truly,
>
> Tom

A sample message note giving a gift:

> Nov. 19
>
> Dear Sidney,
>
> I have got a ticket to a fashion show this Sunday, but I won't be able to attend it as I will go to Beijing on business this weekend. I am now sending the ticket to you, for you are always keen on the fashion design. I think you may like to go to see the show.
>
> Please find the ticket enclosed. Wish you would enjoy yourself.
>
> All the best,
>
> George

A sample message note asking for a call:

Dec. 20

Dear Kerry,

You have happened to be out this afternoon when I call on you. I want to borrow your <u>MLA Handbook</u> because I have been working on my thesis these days. I want to await you until you return, but your neighbor tells me you won't come back until 6, so I leave. I shall be grateful if you find time to call me as soon as possible.

Yours,
Jenny

Exercises

1. Lily, your classmate is looking for a part-time job in the coming summer vacation. You saw an advertisement for an English tutor for a schoolboy. Write her a note, telling her what the job is and strongly recommending it to her.

2. You are Mark or Sally. You have got a ticket to a concert, but you now find that you are unable to go. Write a note to your friend explaining why you are sending the enclosed ticket to him or her and tell him or her briefly how to get there.

5. Letters and Notes of Apology

Occasionally, we fail to do something, or do something so embarrassing or wrong. When this happens, the only solution is a letter/note of apology, which is the need of courtesy to avoid misunderstanding and offence. Such letters/notes will consist of a description of the issue; an apology for an action, mistake or omission; an explanation for the action, mistake or omission; a promise to rectify the situation if possible. An apology for inexcusable behavior must be accompanied by restitution or offer of restitution if damage was done. A letter/note of apology should be prompt and sincere.

Tips for writing apology letters:

- Write as soon as possible after the incident. Keep it simple and to the point. Summarize what you are apologizing for, and apologize only for the particular situation or problem. Be brief. Apologize cheerfully and sincerely.
- Explain what you will do to correct the mistake or situation. Assure the person that this will not happen again.
- Do not put blame on another person and do not blame problems on computer errors or carelessness.
- Thank the person for bringing the problem to your attention if you were unaware of the situation.

For example, in the body of an apology letter for missing an appointment, you can write:

I would like to apologize for missing our scheduled appointment last Wednesday, April 1, 2012. I also apologize for not calling in advance to cancel. I will call your office this week to reschedule a meeting with you.

Thank you for your understanding and patience.

Expressions for Notes of Apology

I feel awful about what I have done to you.
I am terribly sorry/ embarrassed/ most upset about my behavior last night.
I sincerely apologize what I have done yesterday.
Please accept my sincere apologies for my inattention/ thoughtlessness...
I can only hope you will forgive this serious lapse of good taste on my part.

Offering Reasons and Explanations for the Failure or Mistake

Sadly, I regret to say that I hurt you inattentively.
Unfortunately, I'm afraid I can't fulfill what you ask me to do.
I am not excusing my errors, but I hope you can forgive me.
The reason for this was that I misunderstood what you meant.

Making Promises to Remedy / Express Hopes for Future (improvements)

I promise that I will remedy my mistake.
I hope to (be able to) compensate/reimburse you for loss.
I will make certain/assure you that this doesn't happen again.

Sample Notes of Apology

Dec. 26th

Dear Rolf,

I am extremely sorry to tell you that I have lost the valuable book you were so kind to lend me last month. Yesterday when I came to my room, it was nowhere to be found. If I fail to find it, I will buy a new one for you.

But I am afraid it can never take the place of the old one. Old books are like old friends. Once lost, they can never be replaced. I should be to blame for this irrecoverable loss, and it is a warning to me to be more careful.

Cordially,
Reid

269

An apology for breaking an appointment

> Jan. 11th
>
> Dear Prof. Day,
>
> I must apologize for my breaking an appointment with you yesterday. My roommate Lucy and I left our residence together. But on our way to university she had an accident, so I had to take her to hospital first, forgetting to phone you.
>
> I hope you can forgive me, and I promise this won't happen again. Please phone me whether you can make a new appointment next week. I am looking forward to your call.
>
> Sincerely yours,
>
> Eileen Calvin

Exercise

You promised to help a teacher organize an evening party the next weekend. For personal reasons you will be unable to be there. You feel you are letting the teacher down, so you desire to write a note of apology to explain the situation.

270

 ## 6. Letters of Declination

Tips for writing declination letters:

- Be polite and appreciative.
- Make a clear explanation for the declination.
- Be to the point and avoid any kind of negative statements.
- Leave the reader the impression that you are declining the offer or proposal because of some genuine reason and not because of your reluctance.
- Let the reader get the feeling that you are happy with the association with them and would like to continue with the relationship in the future.
- If you have decided to accept any kind of offer elsewhere you don't need to given an explanation about who has made the offer to you.

A Sample Letter of Declination

Wei Chen
117 Machang Rd.
Tianjin, 300204

March 11, 2012

Dear Mr. Gold:

I am thrilled that I was chosen for the job of Head Engineer at Gold Architects Inc.

Unfortunately, I will not be able to accept this position, as I have already started a new job at another firm and the job is well suited with my qualifications, experiences, and future goals.

I want to thank you for giving me the honor for this very prestigious job.

I hope we may be able to work together in the future!

Best regards,

Wei Chen

Wei Chen

 ## 7. Letters and Notes of Condolence and Sympathy

In times of sadness, loss, failure or tragedy we express appropriate condolence and/or sympathy. In offering commiseration, we might also wish to offer help. Two things are required: a reference to the event or issue, and an extended or brief expression of commiseration. A letter/note of condolence or sympathy should be tactful and sincere, encouraging and optimistic.

Tips for writing condolence letters:

- A simple "I'm sorry" is sometimes the only thing that is necessary to say. Avoid being overly dramatic. Keep the letter as brief and as short as possible.
- Make sure you include the name of the person who died or mention the specific incident that caused sorrow for the person.
- If you knew the deceased, mention something positive about the person, such as a memory, a short story, or anything else that pays tribute to their life.
- Condolences can be offered through thoughts and good wishes, but avoid being too religious if you do not know the person very well.
- Offer to help in some way.
- People should be allowed to mourn in their own way and in their own time. Do not tell

the person to look at the bright side.

- Be careful with your word choice. Avoid using uncomfortable words that may indicate that the death was tragic or gruesome.
- When writing your letter, imagine yourself in the other person's place.
- Close with an expression of sympathy or affection.

The body of a condolence letter may include:

> I was saddened to hear that you lost your job at the Academia Institute. I know that you were really excited about the prospect of working there. I hope that this time does not become too difficult for you. I wish you luck in finding a new job, and in all your other pursuits.
>
> Remember I am your cousin and will do anything I can for you. Please let me know if there is anything I can do. Take care of yourself.

 ## Expressions for Letters/Notes of Sympathy

Your illness causes us considerable concern.

I am very sorry/grieved/saddened to hear that you have the great grief of losing....

The bereavement was a heavy blow to all of us.

I found myself at a loss for words of consolation.

The father's sudden death was a tragedy to his family.

No words can express my deep sorrow at the death of ....

I want to express to you my most heartfelt sympathy.

Remember me with the tender affection to your mother.

I hope that you can find some comfort in your many special memories and in the thought of the happy years you shared.

May the love of family and friends comfort and strengthen you in the days ahead.

My heart/prayers/thoughts are with you and your family.

You have all our love/the warmest thoughts.

With best wishes for your quick and complete recovery.

A sample note of sympathy to someone who has been injured in an accident:

Feb. 22nd

Dear Mrs. Stark,

I can't tell you how sorry I was to learn of your accident. We were shocked and saddened beyond words by the news. But we were grateful that your injuries were not worse.

Please let me know if there's anything I can do to help. I hope you can progress nicely and recover soon.

With every good wish for your recovery.

Sincerely yours,
Tina

Exercise

Your friend, Jane, has failed in the final exam, and is feeling very unhappy about it. Write a note of sympathy to comfort her and give her some encouragement.

8. Letters of Congratulations

We express feelings of pleasure and shared excitement when people are the recipients of life's bounties. A letter/note of congratulation begins with the occasion for congratulation and continues with reasons for congratulations and good wishes.

Tips for writing congratulations:

- Say your best wishes early in the message and again when you close. Make sure you mention the occasion that is being celebrated. Express how happy you are for the person and how you learned about the delightful news.
- Avoid going overboard on flattery.
- Be positive and pleasant.

The body of a congratulation letter may include:

> Congratulations on receiving your BA degree in English! I am sure that graduation was a sensational day for you after all the years of studying. I wish you all the success in the world! Again, congratulations on a memorable achievement.

273

Expressions for letters/notes of congratulations:

Congratulations on the milestone in your life and your great accomplishments.

I am delighted/pleased/glad to hear of your recent promotion. I congratulate you on the marvelous opportunity.

Please accept my heartiest congratulations on your winning the State Scholarship.

It's the most joyful news I have heard for a long time.

You have no idea what a thrill I got when I heard that you have got the Dance Award.

I think that you deserve the position after years of service and experience.

Congratulations and best wishes to you for your health, happiness and prosperity.

 A Sample Note of Congratulation

Oct. 1st

Dear Pearl,

My warm congratulations to you on your university scholarship. It is a reward you richly deserve for these years of splendid study. I'm delighted to hear it.

It is fine to know you have achieved the goal toward which you've been studying. I wish you great success in the future.

My heartiest congratulations!

Sincerely yours,

Neva

Exercise

Write a note of congratulations to a friend who has been enrolled in the law program of Peking University for the master's degree.

9. Letters of Appreciation and Thank-you Notes

A letter of appreciation or thank-you note is written whenever you receive a gift, or when someone renders a special service, shows kindness, congratulation or condolence, or invites you for something, or when you have been someone's guest. Everybody hopes to be appreciated and social manners require gratitude.

In a letter of appreciation, state what you appreciate and briefly explain why. Do not add other news or information not related to the appreciative gesture. The message of appreciation should stand alone. Be brief, warm and sincere.

Thank-you notes are usually very short, simple and direct; over-flowery thank-you notes may well invite the accusation of being insincere. Sincerity is the most important quality of all in a thank-you note. The very essence of sincerity is the expression of your own true feelings and sentiments.

Expressions for Letters of Appreciation and Thank-you Notes

I am very grateful to you for your...

I appreciate this opportunity of ...

For this noble effort, I thank you from the bottom of my heart.

I can't tell you how grateful I am for your wonderful and fancy present.

It was most thoughtful and generous of you to send me such a beautiful gift.

Thank you for doing so much to make my trip to Berlin interesting.

I enjoyed myself enormously in...

This is to thank you again for your wonderful hospitality and to tell you how much I enjoy seeing you again.

We are looking forward to seeing you again.

If I can in any way return the favor, please let me know.

It was a great pleasure to spend some time with you.

The body of an appreciation letter may look like this:

> I am very grateful for the numerous financial contributions you have made in support of my education. Without your help, I may never have been able to complete my studies. Your generosity and help have been an inspiration to me.
>
> Again, thank you for your encouragement and financial support.

Sample Thank-you Notes

Thanking someone for a special service or an extra effort made on your behalf

> June 10
>
> Dear Professor Baker,
>
>   I have received confirmation from the fellowship committee that my application was in order.
>
>   Thank you so much for your letter of support. I have appreciated your help and encouragement during my time at the university, so your recommendation means a great deal to me. I owe an incalculable debt of gratitude to your help.
>
> Sincerely yours,
Thomas Jones

Thanking a hostess for her hospitality

> Sept. 20
>
> Dear Joy,
>
>   Thank you so much for the wonderful weekend we spent at the beach. Your new house is delightful, welcoming and comfortable.
>
>   Please do send me your special Spanish recipe, for we really enjoyed your cooking very much. It was so nice to see you and your husband again. Again, many thanks for the lovely time.
>
> Yours,
Mary

Thanking someone for a gift

> Dec,12th
>
> Dear Mrs. Baker,
>
>   It was most kind of you and Mr. Baker to send us a handsome Christmas gift. We are simply thrilled with the book ends, for they are just what we needed for our library desk.
>
>   We hope that you and Mr. Baker will come soon and see for yourselves how beautiful the book ends look.
>
> Cordially,
Billie Arden

Unit Ten

Exercise

Write a thank-you note to a friend who has taken the trouble in another city to help you buy two books that are not available in local bookstores.

(Tips and samples for personal letters are developed by Janel Muyesseroglu, from < http://depts.gallaudet.edu/englishworks/writing/letter/writingletters.html>)

Homework 2

Write a letter of thanks to a parent or grandparent, expressing your gratitude for what the person has done for you.

商务英语写作系列丛书

这套教材体系完整,应用性强,商务内容丰富,十分贴近英语教学改革的需要和广大学生提升未来就业能力的需求,填补了我国商务英语写作领域内没有高质量商务英语写作教材的空白,并得到15所商务英语专业院校教学协作组和中国英语写作教学专业委员会相关专家的联合推荐。

本套丛书既是职场英语写作的优质教材,又是商务写作的经典教材,教材深入浅出,语言简明,可帮助学生理解、记忆和应对多种国际商务场合下的写作需求。通过本丛书的学习和训练,学生可提高写作水平,为踏入职场做好准备。本套丛书可用作全国大专院校的商务英语学生和教师的写作课教材和参考书,还可供经管类学生学习商务英语写作之用,同时也可供爱好商务英语写作的广大社会读者和各类公司企业人员提高英语写作使用。

商务沟通:以读者为中心的方法(英文版)(第6版)(上)18605–3 定价:45元
商务沟通:以读者为中心的方法(英文版)(第6版)(下)18603–9 定价:55元
Paul V. Anderson
职场英语写作(英文版)(第7版)(上)17923–9 定价:48元
职场英语写作(英文版)(第7版)(下)17922–2 定价:28元
Donald H、Cunningham, Elizabeth O. Smith, Thomas E. Pearsall
成功商务英语写作(英文版)(第九版)(上)17919–2 定价:42元
成功商务英语写作(英文版)(第九版)(下)17918–5 定价:54元
Philip C. Kolin
最新商务报告写作(英文版)(第9版)(上)17921–5 定价:36元
最新商务报告写作(英文版)(第9版)(下)17920–8 定价:48元
Daniel G. Riordan
商务沟通与写作(英文版)(第6版)(上)18347–2 定价:48元
商务沟通与写作(英文版)(第6版)(下)18346–5 定价:38元
Rebecca E. Burnett